ATMOSPHERES OF VIOLENCE

ATMOSPHERES OF VIOLENCE

STRUCTURING ANTAGONISM AND THE

TRANS/QUEER UNGOVERNABLE

ERIC A. STANLEY

DUKE UNIVERSITY PRESS *Durham and London* 2021

Designed by Amy Ruth Buchanan
Typeset in Arno Pro by Copperline Book Services
Printed and bound by CPI Group (UK) Ltd, Croydon, CR0 4YY
Library of Congress Cataloging-in-Publication Data
Names: Stanley, Eric A., author.
Title: Atmospheres of violence: structuring antagonism and the
trans/queer ungovernable / Eric A. Stanley.
Description: Durham: Duke University Press, 2021. | Includes
bibliographical references and index.
Identifiers: LCCN 2020055320 (print)
LCCN 2020055321 (ebook)
ISBN 9781478013303 (hardcover)
ISBN 9781478014218 (paperback)
ISBN 9781478021520 (ebook)
Subjects: LCSH: Transgender people—Violence against—
United States. | Gender-nonconforming people—Violence
against—United States. | African American transgender people—
Violence against—United States. | Transgender people—
Minorities—Violence against—United States. | Gender-
nonconforming people—Minorities—Violence against—
United States. | Minority transgender women—Violence
against—United States. | Transphobia—Political aspects—
United States. | Homophobia—Political aspects—United States.
BISAC: SOCIAL SCIENCE / LGBTQ Studies /
Transgender Studies | SOCIAL SCIENCE / LGBTQ Studies
General Classification: LCC HQ77.965. U6 S73 2021 (print) |
LCC HQ77.965. U6 (ebook) | DDC 306.76/80973—dc23
LC record available at https://lccn.loc.gov/2020055320
LC ebook record available at https://lccn.loc.gov/2020055

Cover art: Every Ocean Hughes, *The Piers Untitled*, 2010–20.
Courtesy of the artist.

For those lost to the world
and all who remain
as its antagonism

CONTENTS

READING WITH CARE

This book describes a number of anti-Black, ableist, racist, and anti-trans/
queer scenes of violence. This structuring violence appears as corporal attack, medical neglect, murder, suicide, and suicidal ideations. Throughout the
text I articulate why I believe the event calls for a renarration while, in other
moments, I refuse to reproduce the incident. These imperfect decisions are
guided by a radical commitment to keeping each other alive and toward ending the world that produces this unfolding archive.

Another way we might read with care is by supporting people that are
locked up with little access to materials. To this end, all author's profits from
this book will be donated to the LGBT Books to Prisoners program, a "trans-
affirming, racial justice-focused, prison abolitionist project," which provides
books to imprisoned people for free. Please join me in supporting them or
other Books to Prisoners projects. The mission statement follows.

> LGBT Books to Prisoners is a donation-funded, volunteer-run organi-
> zation based in Madison, Wisconsin, that sends books and other edu-
> cational materials, free of charge, to incarcerated LGBTQ people across
> the United States. We have been doing this for over ten years and have
> sent books to over nine thousand people in that time.
>
> LGBT Books to Prisoners
> c/o Social Justice Center Incubator
> 1202 Williamson Street, Suite 1
> Madison, WI 53703
> lgbtbookstoprisoners@gmail.com

ACKNOWLEDGMENTS

Recalcitrant to the fiction of the singular author, *Atmospheres of Violence* has been formed in collective struggle. From affinity groups and breakaway marches to nights turned mornings doing jail support—pedagogies of action are everywhere in these pages.

My family, grown between Santa Cruz and San Francisco, is the precondition of this book's completion. Their support has allowed me to stay in the terror and joy that is this project's archive and the world in which it was written. For the last many decades we have built kinship against the limits of blood. Beck, Bells, Jazzon/Joy, Kenny T, Logan, Luton, Momzo, Mr. Fibblers, Patsy, Slakes, T, Tran, thank you.

Toast, you have read most of these words and continue to shelter me when it all collapses.

Much of the thinking that eventually became this book began while I was a student in the History of Consciousness department at the University of California, Santa Cruz. Adam Reed's friendship helped me survive those first years. Many from that time remain coconspirators today, including Anika Walke, Apryl Berney, Cindy Bello, Erin Gray, Eva Hayward, Felice Blake, Greg Youmans, Jennifer Watanabe, Jeremy Tai, Kalindi Vora, Nick Mitchell, Nicole Archer, Marcos Becquer, Martha Kenny, Michelle Erai, SA Smythe, Soma de Bourbon, Trevor Sangrey, and Trung Nguyen.

Angela Y. Davis, Donna Haraway, and José Esteban Muñoz formed a constellation of mentors who, together, pulled me through a dissertation that threatened to remain undone while undoing me.

Angela has continued to be a mentor and friend for the last two decades. She exemplifies the almost impossible position of inhabiting an institution without becoming its terrible logic. I took every class she offered, many of them more than once, which is among the reasons I stayed in graduate school for so long. In between her incisive textual readings in seminar, I learned so much from her asides—the beautiful way she wove narratives of revolutionary possibility. Along with her teaching, Angela's warmth and care, her willingness to be in community and resist the hierarchy of the structure, affirm that remaining a student of the world is the only way we might transform it.

I first encountered Donna when I was a student in her undergraduate course "Science as Culture and Practices." Her wild storytelling pedagogy lured me deep into a world-building optimism that pushed against my skepticism. I was then, as I continue to be, captivated by her ability to fashion seemingly disparate histories into ways of knowing that teach us how, as she might say, to stay with the trouble. Her insistence that it's often much more important to hold something together than it is to take it apart is a lesson that I try to stay with. In addition, she ushered me through the university's logistics and patiently guided me through its aftermath.

José, although far from California, offered me protection from the often-treacherous waters of queer studies. Through the dialectics of gossip and advice, he gave form to an intellectual life that existed in the fullness of the social and not simply as its commentator. He, like many in this book, was stolen from a world that could not hold his multitudes and we are all the more lost without him here.

At the University of California, Riverside, Mariam Lam and Snowflake made a home for me in theirs. My community there also included Amalia Cabezas, Ashon Crawley, Crystal Baik, David Lloyd, Dylan Rodríguez, Donatella Galella, Emily Hue, Erica Edwards, Fred Moten, J Sebastian, Jane Ward, Jayna Brown, Jodi Kim, Keith Miyake, Laura Harris, Loubie Qutami, Maile Arvin, Melanie Yazzie, Ren-yo Hwang, Ricky Rodriguez, Sarita See, Setsu Shigematsu, Sherine Hafez, and Tammy Ho.

The Department of Gender and Women's Studies at the University of California, Berkeley, has provided forms of belonging not often associated with the academy. The staff, Althea Grannum-Cummings, Gillian Edgelow, Lauren Taylor, and Sandy Richmond, are responsible for the often-hidden labor that holds us all together. The faculty, including Barbara Barnes, Courtney Desiree Morris, Jac Asher, Laura Nelson, Leslie Salzinger, Mel Y. Chen, Minoo Moallem, Paola Bacchetta, and Trinh T. Minh-ha have built an intellectually exciting and deeply communal space rooted in practicing the feminism we teach. I'm also thankful to work with Anne Walsh, Anne-Lise Francois, Damon Young, Erin Kerrison, Juana María Rodríguez, Jovan Lewis, Judith Butler, Julia Bryan-Wilson, Karen Nakamura, Lawrence Cohen, Nadia Ellis, Rizvana Bradley, Seth Holmes, Sharad Chari, Sonia Katyal, Sunny Taylor, and Victoria Robinson.

At Duke University Press, Elizabeth Ault has been an ideal editor. Amid our unfolding catastrophe when it feels that words can offer little, her insistence on the book's necessity kept me going. Jade Brooks also provided advice when the project was in an embarrassingly premature stage. I'm indebted to the anonymous readers whose feedback helped me clarify the book's claims and whose careful insights allowed me to hold contradictions and proceed when there seemed like nowhere left to go.

Craig Willse's editorial direction helped place the floating parts of this manuscript into a much more cohesive order. I'm grateful for all of that labor and our enduring friendship.

As is evident throughout this text, my desire to wade together is definitive. My years of collaboration with Chris Vargas—our filmmaking and exhibitions, our laughter and trauma—is evidence that we are remade by each other.

I first met Tourmaline when we were organizing toward CR 10, Critical Resistance's ten-year anniversary conference. Now, many years later and through numerous collective projects, she still teaches me that our dreams of freedom are little more than nightmares if they are not fashioned through pleasure and beauty.

Among those that continue to invite me into collective thought are Alexis Pauline Gumbs, Andreana Clay, Andrew Szeto, Aren Aizura, Ash Stephens, Beth Richie, Bobby Benedicto, C. Riley Snorton, CeCe McDonald, Chandan Reddy, Che Gossett, Christina Hanhardt, Christopher J. Lee, Clio/Thatcher, Craig Calderwood, David Marriott, Dean Spade, Deeg, Demian DinéYazhi´, Elizabeth Freeman, Erica Meiners, Eva Hageman, Gayatri Gopinath, Irene Gustafson, Iván Ramos, J. Kēhaulani Kauanui, Jemma DeCristo, Jenny Kelly, Jih-Fei Cheng, Jin Haritaworn, Joanne Barker, Johanna Burton, Justin Leroy, Kadji Amin, Marshall Green, Karma Chávez, Kay, Lauren Berlant, Leon Hilton, Liat Ben-Moshe, Liz Kinnamon, Mariame Kaba, Mattilda Bernstein Sycamore, Michelle Velasquez-Potts, Miss Major, Nat Smith, Neda Atanasoski, Ralowe T. Ampu, Ronak Kapadia, Ruth Wilson Gilmore, Ryan Conrad, Ryan Tacata, Stasha Lampert, Stevie Wilson, Susan Stryker, Sunaina Maira, Tavia Nyong'o, Tory, Treva Ellison, and Yasmin Nair.

This research has benefited from a University of California President's Post-doctoral Fellowship under the mentorship of Patrick Anderson and a University of California President's Faculty Research Fellowship. I'm also grateful to the numerous audiences and friends that have offered feedback on preliminary versions of this project.

A very early version of chapter 1 was originally published as "Near Life, Queer Death: Overkill and Ontological Capture," *Social Text* 29, no. 2 (107). In a radically truncated form, chapter 3 was first published as "Anti-Trans Optics: Recognition, Opacity, and the Image of Force," *South Atlantic Quarterly* 116, no. 3 (2017): 612–20.

In the end, which is to say the end's beginning, this book is indebted to the world yet to come and to those whose love and rage are building it now.

If they attack me, I'm going to
attack them, with my bomb.
—*Marsha P. Johnson*

> But how do we pass from the atmosphere
> of violence to violence in action?
> —*Frantz Fanon*

The soft blue-black wake rhythmically
laps at the rocky shore—gravity's reminder of trans/queer endurance on the
edge of a city, at the end of the world. Marsha P. Johnson's body was pulled
from the Hudson River's brackish water on July 6, 1992, not far from the Christopher Street Piers and the neighborhood where she spent most of her life.
The piers were a sacred place for trans/queer people of color who gathered
there, building life from discarded hope and corrugated cardboard—capital's
debris refashioned so that marooned community could grow on the banks of
the island the Lenape call Manna-hata. In the years after her death, the force of
development has all but annihilated what remained of the piers, as they were
enclosed by razor wire then infilled with the bullish desolation of luxury condos and the austerity of their new owners. Gentrification's protracted accumulation has left little evidence of the generations that called the piers, for lack of
anything better, home.[1]

Marsha P. Johnson's official cause of death was suicide, but many of her
friends, including the now legendary Puerto Rican trans activist Sylvia Rivera,

believe she was murdered, perhaps by a trick that turned violent, or the police. Along with the anecdotal evidence that circulated through the gossip of the street, which suggested her ends were not her own, Sylvia said that the two had a pact to die together and that Marsha would not have left without her: "Every time I look at that damn river and I sit there and meditate on the river I feel her damn spirit telling me, 'You gotta keep fighting, girlie, cause it's not time to cross the River Jordan!'"[2] For Marsha and Sylvia, the River Jordan, the name they gave to the Hudson, was the metaphoric (non)space where they would transition, together, out of the bondage of a life circumscribed by imminent risk and into the promise of an elsewhere.

Marsha P. Johnson and Sylvia Rivera's chaotic splendor militantly unsettled the coercive gender normativity of both the dominant culture and the growing lesbian and gay activism of early 1970s New York City. In contrast to many others in the scene, Marsha and Sylvia were committed to surviving by any means necessary, which included sex work, hustling, and boosting. They lived in the underground of the economy and were always on the run from landlords, cops, and sometimes each other. Collectively they founded STAR (Street Transvestite Action Revolutionaries) in 1970 and then STAR House, first in a trailer, then in a building on 2nd Avenue, a mutual aid survival project that attempted to steady the perpetual instability of their besieged community. As Black and Brown street queens, their social worlds collided with the vengeful drive of gay respectability that rendered them, and their people, as parasitic impediments to the spoils of assimilation. That is to say, while their organizing labor was central to the emerging Gay Liberation Front (GLF) and later the Gay Activist Alliance (GAA), they were produced as resistant objects, unwilling to adhere to the lesbian and gay party line. Their struggle against the mandates of the GLF, GAA, and other activists was met with the same malignant hostility that mainstream culture served them.[3]

This antagonism was dramatized at the 1973 Christopher Street Liberation Day, when Sylvia scaled the stage and took control of the microphone from Vito Russo, which ignited a hissing thunder and faint applause. In response to the crowd's disgust, she shouted, "Y'all better quiet down!" continuing, "I've been trying to get up here all day for your gay brothers and your gay sisters in jail that write me every motherfucking week and ask for your help, and you all don't do a goddamn thing for them." Just four years after Stonewall, she was already living the painful betrayal of the movement's assimilatory agenda. Sylvia's radiant solidarity with others experiencing houselessness and incarceration was meant to implode the joyful celebration—a barricade against the good feelings that are assumed to be on the other side of struggle. "I have been thrown in jail. I have lost my job. I have lost my apartment for gay liberation and you all treat me this way? What the fuck's wrong with you all?" Her treatment by lesbian and gay activists was a mirror for the ways she was abused by the thrust of heteronormativity and its gendered directives, which, in theory, they were all fighting to radically transform. Through exhausted rage, she concluded her manifesto with a twist of condemnation and a call to action: "The people are trying to do something for all of us, and not men and women that belong to a white middle-class white club. And that's what y'all belong to! Revolution Now! Gay Power! Louder! Gay Power!"[4]

In response to these historical and ongoing forms of degradation, which include the booming whiteness and gender normativity of what consolidates under the sign LGBT history, Marsha and Sylvia have been revived as emblematic of a trans of color politic from Stonewall to the current moment. While important, this vital recovery performs a second-order displacement by solidifying their identities, which were, in practice, constantly lived in beautiful inconsistency. Imposing a more current identity on a subject of history is part of the trouble—a trouble we can never avoid—as we account for specificity and also for tendencies of reoccurrence that build beyond themselves. What I hope *Atmospheres of Violence* preserves is the spirit of Sylvia and Marsha's commitment, conscious or not, to being against the intelligibility culled by a liberal state. In other words, they were working, by way of theorizing, the messy points of contact between the ends of language and the chaos of a desiring life experienced as the force of discipline and escape. To this end, both their organized disappearance in LGBT history and their reemergence as an activist ideal extinguish their disruptive legacy—the unruly ways they refused cold abjection and calcified memorialization. Sylvia and Marsha, along with so many others, ought to be brought into the collective archive, but if their appearance does not destabilize the mode of their arrival, then we have failed to do more than accommodate difference—the neoliberalization of identity as modernity's sedimentation.[5]

In an attempt to be with the ungovernability of Marsha and Sylvia, this book refuses an ascendant narrative that situates the potentiality of trans/queerness as but an expression of a sterile identity. And while I'm deeply aware of how queer (and by extension its theorization) has been ambivalent and at times hostile toward gender nonnormativity (trans or otherwise), following the ways Marsha and Sylvia brilliantly confused an understanding of gender and sexuality as idiosyncratic, it is the phenomenology of racialized violence

FIGURE I.1. Sylvia Rivera photographed on the Hudson River dock in front of her home at the encampment where she lived. March 19, 1996. Photo by Valerie Shaff.

that brings them back into contact. Much of the violence that gets marked as homophobic is retaliation against an assumed gender transgression; relatedly, more often than not, anti-trans violence is accompanied by what might otherwise be understood as homophobic utterances. I don't mean to conflate the two at the level of identification, nor at the intensity of attack. Yet that trans women are often called "fags" during a moment of harm, and those who might otherwise identify as fags (trans or not) are brutalized, like many lesbians (trans or not), because of their *inappropriate* masculinity, calls for us to attend to how gendered and sexualized violence emerge together yet unfurl differently.[6]

My insistence that anti-trans/queer violence structures the social remains necessary as it unravels the stability of an LGBT identity outside the viscosity of context. What holds that fantasy together enables the material undoing of so many others. It was, after all, white gays and lesbians that forcefully confronted Sylvia on the stage, as it has also been (some) lesbian and gay people who have been deeply committed to destroying trans as a way of being in the world, along with the people who find life within it. This is not to suggest that trans people do not also identify as lesbian, gay, and/or bisexual (or any other a/sexuality), or that the attacks lodged by LGB people have the same structural power as their avowed hetero/gender-normative coconspirators, but here we are tasked to think of trans/queer as tendencies and not codified identities as both a theoretical intervention and a fact of history.[7]

States of Equality

We are living in a time of LGBT inclusion. This is evidenced, at least in the United States, by the legal expansion of marriage, lesbian and gay military recruitment, and the proliferation of LGBT characters in popular visual culture. Against the narrative arc of rainbow progress that proclaims that these changes mark a radical shift in the social, *Atmospheres of Violence* argues that inclusion, rather than a precondition of safety, most properly names the state's violent expansion.[8] I do this by attending to a wicked archive of murders, the ongoing HIV/AIDS pandemic, suicide notes, incarceration, police video footage, and other ephemera of attack. These scattered cases, when read together, build my claim that anti-trans/queer violence is foundational to, and not an aberration of, modernity. Related, rather than imagining the law as the mechanism through which relief from such harm might be offered, it is one of its methodologies of proliferation. Following the ungovernable, we are asked to release the fantasy of reforming these same institutions, here the law and by extension the state, that have caused and continue to cause destruction, not simply in effect but as their aim. Such abdication also recalls the interplay between the horizon, as José Muñoz might have it, and horizontalism. Here the pragmatism of the present is smashed in the name of a life we might survive. This shuttling between description and experience remains the tension that holds the possibility of transformation. To this end, I write through the pedagogies of direct action that remind us how disciplinary power's force resides in its resolute incoherence. My ambivalence, then, rises as both a procedural commitment to the dangerous task of representing violence and a defense against the counterrevolution of public policy, with its offer of salvation outside the thickness of struggle. However, this unease does not emanate from a confusion toward the kinds of worlds I hope grow and those that must be obliterated, nor from a belief that study is in contradiction to action, but from the turbulent insight gleaned from this collective planning.⁹

The time of LGBT inclusion is also a time of trans/queer death. From the phenomenological vault of nonexistence lived as quotidian withdrawal, to the gory details of gratuitous harm—the archive engulfs. Nonetheless, anti-trans/queer violence is written as an outlaw practice, a random event, and an unexpected tragedy. Dominant culture's drive to dissolve the scope and intensity of this violence is expected. Yet mainstream LGBT politics also colludes in this disappearance in exchange for recognition, however partial and contingent. Through this privatization, meaning the continued trafficking in a belief that things might be any other way while leaving the social intact, the enormity of anti-trans/queer violence is vanished.¹⁰

Thinking violence as individual acts versus epistemic force works to support the normative and normalizing structuring of public pain. This is to say, privatizing anti-trans/queer violence is a function through which the social and its trauma are whitewashed, heterosexualized, and made to appear gender-normative. This relegation of anti-trans/queer violence, which always appears in the syntax of race, casts the human—the referent for cis white mourning—as emblematic. While mainstream LGBT politics clamors for dominant power through a reproduction of the teleological narrative of progress, it also reproduces the idea that anti-trans/queer violence is an aberration of democracy—belonging only to a shadowed past, and increasingly anachronistic.¹¹

This privatization of violence also compels through the managed translation of cultures of attack into personal incidents. At the center of this privatization is the figure of the human that produces itself as the sole beneficiary of rights before the law. The human's singularity comes into relief against its ability to trade the many with the particular. In contrast, rights, the mechanism of protection from the state's discipline, are assumed to be the province of all. Yet by reading the anterior magic of the law, it is not so much, or at least not only, that humans (alone) have rights. It is the conditional enactment (granting of rights) that constitutes the human as benefactor of its own creation. This recursive logic is important as it troubles the deployment of equality under a system of law imagined and maintained, at the atomic level, as exclusion. This double lie of formal equality is necessary for the law to lay claim to, and act as arbiter of, what might be called justice. The law, then, is a systematic and systematizing process of substitution where the singular and the general are shuttled and replaced to inform a matrix of fictive justice. Consequently, for the law to read anti-trans/queer violence as a symptom of civil society, justice would demand the dismantling of its own administration.[12]

Against the law, the constitutive possibility evidenced by trans/queer generativity—its disruptive worlding—guides my own attachments. Yet this striking capacity resides within the context of a state that always seeks its managed liquidation. Or, to put it another way, while people who do identify as trans and/or queer figure largely in this text, I make no claim about identification other than that sexuality and gender, as nodes of power, are formed in and as a relationship to racialized violence. I say this in an attempt to stall a misreading that might claim I have something definitive to say about trans/queer or otherwise LGBT people. In contrast to such generalizations about identity, this is a study of the shattering power that threatens, and at times erupts into the deadly force that not only kills but makes life unlivable—an atmosphere of violence.[13]

Here, violence takes on a set of shifting definitions—it appears sometimes as the force that ends life, and at other times it is the only way life might unfold. This is to suggest that what gets called violence under a regime of racialized and gendered terror can also yield the terrain that allows for safe passage out—a leap that freedom fighters invite us to take. I focus on scenes of harm where my explicit stake is in ending those iterations in the name of a more habitable planet, yet I also resist the idea that all forms of violence are interchangeable. This line of thought renders minoritized defense as equal to the mechanisms of the settler state. Or, this equivocation produces community resistance as indistinguishable from genocide. Under such logic, which we might also call legal equality, all instances of force appear undifferentiated, while survival is castigated. Indeed, *equality* concretizes the structuring antagonism that produced it in the first place, which means subjugation becomes intensified. This is another way to tell the story of the New Jersey 4, a group of Black lesbians who were strangled and punched by a straight man in New York City's West Village. In the aftermath of the night's events, it was he who declared it "a hate crime against a straight man" and was awarded restitution, while the four women were sentenced to prison for the crime of surviving.[14]

If the privatization of anti-trans/queer violence delineates not only what constitutes injury but also what redress might approximate, then this is also one of the ways state violence is made ordinary. Further, while I'm attentive to what is more generally understood as state violence, the ways individual acts, like the audience attacking Sylvia, collect up in the name of authority also calls for an expansion of what demarcates those borders. As a material concept, the state remains important because, as Karl Marx reminds us, "It is therefore not the state that holds the atoms of civil society together, but the fact that they are atoms only in imagination in the heaven of their fancy. . . . Only political superstition still imagines today that civil life must be held together by the state, whereas in reality, on the contrary, the state is held together by civil life."[15] While this definition accounts, in part, for Marx's optimism toward the state form as a vehicle for redistribution, that optimism decomposes under the weight of difference as it is instrumentalized through racial capitalism's accumulative drive. Moreover, the parameters of "civil life" as the domain of the human in turn produce the fiction of the state that distributes it. As anarchists like Kuwasi Balagoon saw in nationalism, and Frantz Fanon discerned in his analysis of colonialism, the state is fashioned from singularities, yet the structure maintains the racialized, gendered, and classed demands that enable its appearance as an intelligible force.[16]

Further, the state relies on this theo-juridical genealogy to lay claim to its own inevitability. We are under the administration of the state because we are its subjects; we are subjects because we reside under the state's rule. Through this tautology, the state is not something external to the social but is civil society's collective projection. This relationship between those held by the state (perhaps most importantly as exclusion, or negative value) and the state form might be called, by Michel Foucault and others, normativity. Yet just as the state is able to maintain itself through adjustment and absorption, normativity too is defined not exclusively by its rigidity but through its flexibility. While this argument allows us to see how power's methodologies are strikingly incoherent, their impacts remain rather predictable. Indeed, those categories most viciously subjected to violence have persisted since the moment of settler contact and chattel slavery, yet the tools administering this cruelty are ever adapting, which is among the reasons for their endurance.[17]

Thus, I work to apprehend, as might be expected, direct attacks—the personal or group acts committed against specific people where consistency and similarity build a frequency of shared destruction that undoes the assumed singularity of their actors. Through an attention to the phenomenology of these murders, we are able to push against the narrative that argues these are *random acts* that express nothing beyond the will of their instigators. However, in tandem with these direct attacks is a paradigmatic neglect, perhaps akin to Ruth Wilson Gilmore's "organized abandonment," where rhythms of restriction that might not reveal themselves as such forcefully reduce one's capacity toward the world.[18] This includes the anti-Black distribution of HIV/AIDS, imprisonment, houselessness, and other practices that do not simply impact populations but forge such a totalizing power that they radically constrict not only life chances but life itself. This structuring antagonism offers a method for considering violence as a generalized field of knowledge that maintains this collective undoing, lived as personal tragedy, of those lost to modernity. Yet violence also remains a tactic of communal interdiction, anticolonial struggle, and trans/queer flourishing against an otherwise deadly world.[19]

On Divinity

Written in the ashes of the devastation that was the First World War and before its hyper-intensification in the second, Walter Benjamin's "Critique of Violence" remains a place to think the connections among violence, the law, and the question of justice. For Benjamin, the task is to address how one might disaggregate those spheres, or by what criteria one might conclude whether the means or ends of violence are just. Benjamin elucidates: "One might perhaps consider the surprising possibility that the law's interest in a monopoly of violence vis-à-vis individuals is not explained by the intention of preserving legal ends but, rather, by that of preserving the law itself; that violence, when not in the hands of the law, threatens it not by the ends that it may pursue but by its mere existence outside the law."[20]

For Benjamin, law produces violence while also adjudicating its own production. It thus resides as a limit mechanism outside/in the very jurisdiction it prescribes. It is impossible, then, to think of violence outside of law, because the law (either lawmaking or law preserving) is entangled with and constituted through force. This, for Benjamin, produces a feedback loop, a repetition where there seems to be no outside—mythic violence. This reading prohibits the juridical common sense that proclaims that law is aimed toward, or even capable of, ceasing violence in the name of justice. Indeed, here the law appears as the instantiation and compulsory replication of the founding violence of its own necessity.[21]

In Jacques Derrida's extended reading of Benjamin's text, he suggests that "law tends to prohibit individual violence and condemn it not because it poses a threat to this or that law but because it threatens the judicial order itself."[22] Derrida goes on: "The State is afraid of fundamental, founding violence, that is violence able to justify, to legitimate, or to transform the relation of the law, and so to present itself as having a right to law."[23] For Derrida, this founding violence is that which is able to denaturalize the law's inevitability as well as our relation to it. The state, then, is both fearful of and produced by violence, and therefore its aim is to monopolize violence so that its monopolization cannot come under suspicion.

As an example, Benjamin offers the modern police. The police under parliamentary or liberal democracy, and not monarchy, are both the limit and the sign of law as they simultaneously produce and then enforce this production. Through this structure, police become spectral, everywhere and nowhere—a phantom abstraction with deadly consequences. Derrida suggests this is because "in absolute monarchy, legislative and executive powers are united. In it violence is therefore normal, in keeping with its essence, its idea, its spirit. In democracy, on the other hand, violence is no longer according to the spirit of the police. Because of the supposed separations of powers, it is exercised illegitimately, especially when instead of enforcing the law the police make the law."[24] This leads Derrida to suggest that "democracy remains to come: engender or regenerate"[25]—*avenir*, yet-to-come. His declaration, when turned on itself, helps show that democracy might not be avenir but indeed is already here. The violence of sovereign rule is transformed in its distribution but not necessarily its impact. Perhaps reading Derrida beyond himself, democracy maintains the force of monarchical violence while concealing its own spirit. Tracing this weave of law, police, and democracy, but with radically different ends, this book argues that racialized anti-trans/queer violence is a necessary expression of the liberal state. This claim resides in a long genealogy of anticolonial feminist thought that sees the connections between settler colonialism, chattel slavery, and their legal and extralegal afterlives that form the celebration of unfreedom we call democracy.[26]

While both Benjamin and Derrida expand our vocabularies for reading violence and the law, Sylvia, Marsha, and other militants fill this analysis with the fleshiness of lived theory. That the law is the foundational excess of its own condition has always been known, yet differently articulated, by those held under its racial and gendered subjugation—fugitivity's philosophy in action. For example, organizers fighting against the impunity with which police have and continue to murder Black people as the twin of the prison's drive to capture Black flesh elucidates the ruse of justice within the system that bears its name. Or, this praxis collapses the law's image as administrator and representation of justice, when that same system was built on and sustains itself through an anti-Blackness concretized in the U.S. through chattel slavery, whose abolition has yet to come. Growing such an analysis loosens our deep attachment to the idea that the legal system's function is to end violence, while it also weakens the faith in the law as the sign of freedom's recital.

Going further, it is not that I'm arguing that the United States is a broken democracy, through which a change in leadership or a representational electorate would bring into being a more egalitarian civil society. Indeed, it is democracy in action, and not its attrition, that betrays the radical potential we so easily believe it to possess. This is not to say that the historic and ongoing obstructions of the democratic process, including racist poll taxes, felony disenfranchisement, and so on, are fictitious but that they are structured into democracy, as is a fatal belief that it could be otherwise. Given this, what we must confront, as it perpetually confronts us, is that the multiple prohibitions that reside under democracy's watch are not its inconsistencies but its central logics.

Following this abolitionist epistemology, and with an anticolonial anarchism that recognizes the state form (democratic or beyond) as the dreadful condition it has always been, I continue to ask, perhaps without the fantasy of a response: How do we dream the concept of justice through—which is to say against—the law? Or, if we know that the law is not the remedy to violence as promised, then we might look toward infrastructures of interdependency—aesthetic, organizational, and more—that attend to harm without reproducing its inevitability under a claim of its cessation. By extension, if the state, even as an experiment in democracy, is unable to offer us relief, then what forms of being together in difference might grow the world we want and need?[27]

Ma Commère

Staying with this shattering state of violence, Frantz Fanon's corpus, written during his short life, is the most consistent anchor of this book. His sustained attention to the mercilessness of colonial violence, a ferocity that not only organized life for those under its administration (and its administrators) clarifies how its completeness seized the very possibility of being for those in its grasp. Beyond the "individual question" he read in Sigmund Freud's version of psychoanalysis appears Fanon's sociogeny, a mode of analysis that understands the psychic world as always in a bounded relationship to its externalization in the physical.[28] Methodologically, a sociogenic approach prohibits us from falling back into the idea of Cartesian subjectivity and its fantasy of an internal/external split. As informed by his clinical posts as he was by his work with the Front de libération nationale (FLN) and the Armée de libération nationale (ALN) in an armed struggle for Algeria's decolonization, Fanon's theorization of racialized violence and its gendered and sexualized contours continues to animate not only this book but generations of insurgent study.[29]

Among the anxieties that returning to Fanon summon is the ethopolitical limits of thinking Fanon outside of his geopolitical and historical context. Indeed, specificity matters, and stretching his work is always a risk; however, as with most theorists of coloniality, this suspicion can also act as a kind of discipline by assuming that we, as his posthumous readers, know where he properly belongs. At the same time, white European thinkers are permitted to travel and then return to explain the entirety of the world. However, as his readers know, Fanon was working in scattered locations, and just as many registers, from his childhood in Martinique and education in Lyon, to his post in Algeria's Blida-Joinville Hospital, exile in Tunis, and his deathbed in Bethesda, Maryland. This is not to dismiss these concerns, as they must always stay with us, but to ask again: What is preserved, and what is displaced by provincializing Fanon?

Perhaps more unorthodox than thinking with Fanon beyond these geopolitical and historical confines is my insistence that his work ought to be, in that it already is, trans/queer study. While I am not the first to state this proposition, there is still much that Fanon brings to any consideration of racialized gender and/or sexuality, and that these concerns can and must be read back onto Fanon's texts. In other words, it is my hope that I've not worked through a process of application in which his analysis is overlaid onto our historic moment but rather a chaotic disruption, a rebellious training, and, in the end, an experiment in collective thought.[30]

While sexuality and its vicissitudes are everywhere in Fanon's writing the place where he most directly addresses on the level of description the existence of gender nonnormativity in both the colony and the metropole, is the following footnote from *Black Skin, White Masks*:

> Let me observe at once that I had no opportunity to establish the overt presence of homosexuality in Martinique. This must be viewed as the result of the absence of the Oedipus complex in the Antilles. The schema of homosexuality is well enough known. We should not overlook, however, the existence of what are called there "men dressed like women" or "godmothers" [*ma commère*]. Generally they wear shirts and skirts. But I am convinced that they lead normal sex lives. They can take a punch like any "he-man" and they are not impervious to the allures of women—fish and vegetable merchants. In Europe, on the other hand, I have known several Martinicans who become homosexuals, always passive. But this was by no means a neurotic homosexuality: For them it was a means to livelihood as pimping is for others.[31]

A cursory reading of the passage might place Fanon in the long tradition of homophobic/transphobic thinkers who are able to imagine the world-ending force necessary for decolonization yet are unable to envision gender beyond the binary. This may be partially true. But we might also want to approach this passage, as we do many others, as symptomatic of the colonial condition, which in the first instance maintains the fiction of gender and sexual normativity. Keguro Macharia's incisive attention to the footnote suggests, "perhaps, more simply, Fanon cannot imagine the possibility of the desiring black homosexual within the frames provided by colonial modernity."[32] Along with Macharia, who helps guide us through both the boundaries and openings in Fanon's thought, how do we read with and not in spite of this impossibility? In other words, how does an impasse become yet another door?

Curiously, Fanon also confuses "godmothers," the figurative stand-in for gender nonnormativity, who he assumes to have "normal sex lives" (meaning non-homosexual), with the more tragic figure of the homosexual. The Black queer, for Fanon, either is absent, as he is in Martinique, an effect of the lack of the Oedipal complex, or in Europe he is imagined to be exclusively male and only queer as a condition of survival, not of pleasure and/or identification. The place of Black queer women's sexuality, not unlike all women of color's sexuality, remains elusive at best. In the end, Fanon depathologizes transness (if we are willing to read godmothers as such) through his assumption of their sustained affiliation to heterosexuality—the "allures of women" and their ability to "take a punch." In short, godmothers, for Fanon, seem to be straight men in drag—a misreading that aligns with, and does not challenge, the colonial parameters of gender and sexuality.[33]

However, reading this passage within his general scheme for thinking the totality of occupation, we might also see how Fanon is working toward an argument where heterosexuality and normative genders are fashioned and reconfirmed by this same colonialism he is committed to opposing. Or, here he is also sketching the ways colonialism produces and does not simply constrict already existing categories of gender and sexuality. Again, if we attempt to work with Fanon by simple substitution, where we look for existing terms in an attempt to overlay them, then we will gain little. Yet what remains in his incompleteness, and more importantly what resides around it, continues to be vital for thinking gender as among the disciplining forces central to colonialism, a point anticolonial feminism has long made.[34]

Further, while Fanon's thoughts on nonnormative gender and homosexuality often fall out of focus, his theorization of violence fills the void. This analysis of violence is often overdetermined by its many commentators, illustrating the very relations of colonialism he studied. For example, in Hannah Arendt's infamous condemnation of his work, which was situated within her overall critique of student movements of the late 1960s, Black radicals specifically and Black people in general served as her primary target.[35] There she blended anti-Black racism with a post-left liberalism in a performance of Enlightenment rationality where, for her, Marx's resistance to emotions stands against her assumed hyper-affectivity of Blackness. Through a categorical misreading of Fanon, Arendt, along with many others, dismissed the question they are never forced to ask: "But how do we pass from the atmosphere of violence to violence in action?" I stay with it, because for Fanon, and for us, the question is not whether we engage in violence or not but an insistence that the time of violence is already here.[36]

Speaking from a jail cell on the question of violence in 1972 — a decade after Fanon's death but no doubt informed by his work — Angela Davis confirms that "because of the way this society is organized, because of the violence that exists on the surface everywhere, you have to expect that there will be such explosions, you have to expect things like that as reactions."[37] By enumerating the relentless legal and extralegal forms that she as a Black woman, and Black people in general, experience, from deadly church bombings to armed Klan attacks, Davis repositions violence's temporality: "When someone asks me about violence, I just find it incredible. Because what it means is that the person asking that question has absolutely no idea what black people have gone through, what black people have experienced in this country, since the time the first black person was kidnapped from the shores of Africa."[38]

Here Davis asks, as a Black feminist provocation: What constitutes the moment of violence — its beginning or its ends — for those living and dying under the relentless force of total war? This question reminds us that violence names the deadly atmospheres of colonialism, as well as the "reactions," or what Fanon called revolutionary violence, that might offer preservation. Thus it remains both a practice of aimed liquidation and at times the only modality through which life can and must unfold. This antagonism prohibits the wholesale rejection of violence (even as means) or a politics of nonviolence, when its time is already here. Or, put more bluntly, pacifism, as methodological sanctity, as ends without means, remains not as violence's end but, under the current order, is the gaslight the state always leaves burning.[39]

Looking Away

The specter of representation, its world-building and world-destroying power, is everywhere in these pages. Connected to this affective materiality is how representation drags with it the question of aesthetics in the multiple scenes of devastation that I'm attending to. I do not reproduce these scenes in image because of the ways they circulate as objects of pleasure that do little to confront their ongoingness. However, I do anxiously narrate a number of them in an attempt, however failed, to pay quiet attention to the specificity of not only lives but also deaths. In translating these untranslatable episodes into the written word, of retelling the horrors that consumed and continue to stalk the everyday of many more, any claim to purity must be lost. We are left to ask: How might we enter into these scenes as a praxis of care, as an exercise of solidarity, when the very possibility of ethics has already been destroyed? Pushed further, while we must forcefully resist a pornography of violence where death becomes yet another metaphor for the still living, turning away from the scene ensures its continuation. Or, as C. Riley Snorton and Jin Haritaworn ask, how do the deaths of "trans women of color circulate, and what are the corporal excesses that constitute their afterlives as raw material for the generation of respectable trans subjects?"[40]

Indeed, one of the reasons graphic images of violence, from lynching postcards to current videos of police violence against Black people, are so pervasive is because of the visual pleasure imbued in such consumption. Following this logic, my narration would also allow for such libidinal satisfaction, yet I keep returning to what is perhaps an even more overwhelming consequence—the calcification of this violence with no plan to break through. Perhaps put another way, I stay with the harm not because I want to reviolate those of us who have already survived such violations but because I want us to end the version of the social that demands this continuum. For such a strategy, we have no clear path that might be known in advance, or from the outside; all we have is the commitment, however provisional, however incomplete, to a world of images that imagines the world against differential death.

Internal to this question of representing violence is the fact that representation itself is a mechanism of extraction and reduction. Indeed, I remain ambivalent, along with Saidiya Hartman, because of the ease with which "such scenes are usually reiterated" and how "they are circulated and the consequence of this routine display of the slave's ravaged body."[41] This routine display of durational terror is also coupled with the realization that pleasure, too, is incited, not only by those who might be properly phobic, but also by a social that sighs in relief, however unconsciously, that its established order is once again confirmed. And yet these scenes will only return as a surprise to those who do not live them. This is not to trivialize the ways trauma persists, seized by an image and distributed in its reproduction, but that this violence is allowed to go unannounced is among the reasons it continues. I take my etho-methodical query alongside Fred Moten: "Is there a way to subject this unavoidable model of subjection to a radical breakdown?"[42]

Pay It No Mind

Atmospheres envelop. Held by gravity, the layers of vapor that constitute them are the conditions of breathing life but also the possibility of that life's rendition. For Fanon, *atmospheres* summon the plastic totality of colonization. Rather than an event, or an era of imperial expansion that has a beginning and an end, for him, and for us now, atmospheres describe not simply the assemblages of gendered and racialized force and their contestation but the thick hang of fog that allows us to know little else. As a methodology of molecular relationality, violence holds us to the world, an atmospheric constant whose consistency must be fundamentally disturbed if we are to survive. Thinking atmospherically, then, reminds us that there is no escape, no outside or place to hide, yet through techniques of struggle collective life might still come to be.

Atmospheres of Violence is grown through four chapters that serve as an extended meditation where scenes of direct attack and cases of paradigmatic neglect build an entangled archive of trans/queer destruction. While extending outward, the majority of the cases I attend to occur within the emergence of what might be called the time of LGBT inclusion, here inaugurated by the Stonewall uprisings of 1969 and their intensification in the last two decades of assumed legal protections. Of course, this temporality is suspect, and among the arguments I make is that the assimilatory agenda has been coterminous with radical demands, as evidenced by Sylvia's disgust at the upper-middle-class whiteness of the early 1970s. Rather than anti-trans/queer violence being remnants of the past, the ways harm is coupled with, and at times intensified through claims of equality are central to understanding how modernity is contingent upon violence's continuation. To this end, along with Fanon and many others, I insist that the liberal state, or more precisely the para-colonial democratic state, can never be anything other than an engine of brutality. This assertion, rather than a descent into nihilistic inaction, opens up our histories and futures of practicing interdependency otherwise—a post-politics for the end of the world that might just save us from the present.

Further, while the majority of the book is an attempt to put into words these forms of violence and trace their ontological echoes, I am equally committed to the ways trans/queerness has and continues to spectacularly endure, and how this persistence is marked by a generativity that finds form in artistic and organizing practices, and in quotidian acts of getting by in a world that wishes our end. To be clear, this is not to suggest that the aesthetic will save us from the aggregate hardness of the social, nor to contend that the aesthetic is not central to organizing, which includes organizing ourselves. Yet what I want to hold is the nondialectical, where resistance might not necessarily get us free, but freedom surely won't come with anything less.[43]

Chapter 1, "Near Life: Overkill and Ontological Capture," focuses on the ruthless pageantry of anti-trans/queer murders. It opens with a reading of a political funeral organized by Gay Shame, an activist collective in San Francisco. The action was in memory of Gwen Araujo, a trans Latina woman who was murdered, and Jihad Alim Akbar, a Black man who was shot to death by police in the Castro. Through an attention to the physicality and intimacy of ruthless attacks, I show how these acts are not simply about killing the individual but about ending trans/queer possibility. By reading the legal concept of overkill, the name given to forms of murder that go beyond biological death, I argue that these killings produce an ontological limit of trans/queer subjectivity. In the wake of Fanon's rereading of Hegel, I offer the concept of "near life," or a form of (non)subjectivity that resides adjacent to the fully possessed rights-bearing subject of modernity.

Chapter 2, "Necrocapital: Blood's General Strike," shifts from the hypervisual scene of murder and mutilation and toward the everyday forms of abandonment that can be tracked through the material semiotics of blood. Stretching from chattel slavery and its afterlives to the days following the Pulse shooting, where prospective blood donors were turned away because of a ban on "men who have sex with men," I trace the ways racial capitalism produces meaning and profits from HIV/AIDS. This attention to how the affective and materialist economies of blood allows for, or more precisely demands, an expanded definition of exploitation that includes cellular labor. Throughout, I chart forms of exclusion that are also productive, or what I call negative value, which troubles the idea that compensation offers remedy. Ending with ACT UP's Ashes Action, I ask what forms an anti-necrocapitalist demand might take.

Chapter 3, "Clocked: Surveillance, Opacity, and the Image of Force," opens with a reading of a closed-circuit TV scene of Duanna Johnson, a Black transgender woman who was viciously beaten by Mississippi police while in custody in 2009. Through this video, I center the question of representation's form, and not only its content, as constituted by anti-trans and anti-Black optics. Against this scene stands *Time* magazine naming 2014 as the "Transgender Tipping Point." Here I trace how the demand for positive representation, as a practice of assimilation, is offered as the primary, and perhaps exclusive, space of struggle. In contrast, through a reading of Tourmaline and Sasha Wortzel's 2018 film *Happy Birthday, Marsha!* I ask how we might build a radical trans visual regime that does not collapse into expanded surveillance and its consequences.

Chapter 4, "Death Drop: Becoming the Universe at the End of the World," offers a close reading of a 2010 note written by Seth Walsh, a gender-nonconforming thirteen-year-old. In its lucid cruelty, the note ends with the line, "Hopefully I become the universe." After writing these words Walsh took a step off a stump in their backyard and into the obliteration of self-negation—a death drop. The other case in the chapter is the incarceration and forced gender transition of Ashley Diamond, a Black trans woman who smuggled video testimonies of the abuse she endured out of her Georgia prison cell. Here, I reflect on how, for modern forms of violence, surviving, too, becomes a space of torture. The note and the videos, read with Fanon's "new man" from the final pages of *Wretched of the Earth*, helps us anticipate what "becoming the universe" means for those who live against the vestiges of Enlightenment's colonial universalism.

I end with a coda, "Becoming Ungovernable," which meditates on Miss Major's decision to change all of her identification documents as a way of marking herself as a trans person. While surveillance practices of all kinds are attempting to expand their reach, Major offers a divergent path for a trans life that is not moored to positive representation or state recognition. Along with Major, I think with the precarious double bind of trans/queer youth of color that the state has deemed "ungovernable." This legal designation can also lead toward their capture in juvenile jails, which again shows the limits and possibilities immanent in being labeled as such. It is the collectivizing of these practices that offers an alternative to democracy and its mandates of legibility. These commitments to becoming ungovernable—gender fugitives on the run from classical recognition by way of provoking an encounter with unintelligibility—illustrates the fierce strategies necessary for being, as Denise Ferreira da Silva suggests, a "nobody against the state."[44]

FIGURE 1.2. Marsha P. Johnson pickets Bellevue Hospital to protest treatment of street people and gays, ca. 1968–75. Photo by Diana Davies, Manuscripts and Archives Division, New York Public Library.

The Marsha P. Johnson quote opening this introduction comes from an interview in which she was asked about the dangers of street-based sex work (figure I.2). In response, she said she always carried her mace, or her "bomb." Going further, her will to survive necessitates a readiness to be prepared for an attack, and to respond to that violence in any way that might end it. Johnson, like many other trans women of color, was exiled to the edges of civil society—she rocked between chronic houselessness and incarceration in psychiatric facilities, while also living with HIV. Her commitment to protecting herself and "her people" again demonstrates that for those in the crucible of force, the violence/nonviolence binary crumbles. Her claim to a revolutionary form of violence is also productively spoiled by her campy reading of the austerity of early 1970s radical politics. The interviewer asks her about her bomb: "Did you ever have to use it yet?" Marsha replies, "Not yet, but I'm patient."

The River Jordan also patiently awaits. As monument to history's future, cruising and communion gather at the water—reminding us all that death is not inevitable and that pleasure, too, is our inheritance. The metaphor is also material as we work to assemble meaning in the ruins of modernity's still unfolding catastrophe and in the hope of organizing its end. In this atmosphere of violence, its incessant flow is a testament to the brutal ends Marsha P. Johnson and so many others have met. Yet the haunt of the past, like the laze of the river, reminds us that against the current of time, and of time's end, trans/queer existence, even as nonexistence, remains.

CHAPTER 1 **NEAR LIFE**

OVERKILL AND ONTOLOGICAL CAPTURE

> A feeling of inferiority?
> No, a feeling of nonexistence.
> —*Frantz Fanon*

What if it feels good to kill
or mutilate homos?
—*Anonymous*

"**Y**our whole life you think you're a heterosexual. Then you get pleasure from a homosexual. It disgusted me,"[1] Jose Merel, one of Gwen Araujo's murderers, proclaimed during his trial. While at a party, Araujo, a seventeen-year-old Latina trans woman, was confronted by Merel and three other men, Michael Magidson, Jason Cazares, and Jaron Nabors, at least two of whom she had previously had consensual sex with. The attack began when Merel's older brother's girlfriend, Nicole Brown, sexually assaulted Araujo by grabbing her with transphobic elation. Brown's violent assessment of Araujo's body publicly unsheltered the assumed heterosexuality of the two that had maintained a sexual relationship with her. Magidson then pushed Araujo to the ground and forcibly stripped her, in confirmation of his sustained ability to overpower Araujo—the reclamation of his cis heterosexuality. While a heterosexual man having sex with a trans woman does not make him "homosexual," Merel's reaction highlights the bind between forced gender and heteronormativity and the matrix of constitutive misrecognition that police their borders. After slapping Araujo a few times, Merel grabbed a skillet from the kitchen and started striking her, resulting in a head wound that began to gather as a stain where she was held captive. Fearing this evidence, Merel ordered her off the couch as Magidson repeatedly punched and kneed her. Merel began anxiously scrubbing the fabric in an attempt to disappear her existence—the DNA remains of their vicious attack. As he continued, Magidson tied her wrists and ankles, then, anticipating more blood on the carpet, he wrapped her not-yet-dead body in a blanket and moved her to the garage, where Magidson strangled her with the end of the rope.[2]

Expecting trees and the cover of night would help hide their attack, they drove a few hours away to a dense forest. Still unsure whether she was dead, Cazares hit Gwen with a shovel, dragged her into the shallow grave they had dug, and covered her with dirt, rocks, and brush—camouflaging the cruelty of their night's work. According to court testimony, on the way home Nabors said that he "couldn't believe that someone would ever do that, would be that deceitful,"[3] affirming that for them the real assailant, even after her torture and death, was Gwen. Hungry, they ended the night turned morning with a celebratory breakfast from a McDonald's drive-through and, seemingly unbothered, continued their lives.

Four days after the murder of Gwen Araujo, Jihad Alim Akbar was assassinated at the corner of 16th and Market Street in San Francisco's Castro district. The shooter was Michael Celis, an officer with the San Francisco Police Department. Akbar, a Black man in his twenties, lived in Oakland, and according to reports, grabbed two knives out of the Bagdad Café's kitchen and was waving them above his head and dancing, while muttering "fags," "homosexuals," and "white power" in almost inaudible low tones.[4]

From an undisclosed distance, Akbar is said to have "lunged" in the direction of two officers, which, according to their own reports, left them with no option but to shoot him twice in the chest, killing him. Neither Michael Celis nor his fellow officer, Joelle Felix-Zambrana, was scrutinized, beyond the mandatory overview, for their deadly use of force. What scant news coverage followed the murder reproduced the police narrative: that an *outside agitator*— a homophobic Black Muslim with a troubled past—was threatening the sovereignty of an otherwise gay safe space. In the deep shadow of the then newly intensified war on terror, and with the long history of the structuring anti-Blackness that is the Castro, which Marlon Riggs's *Tongues Untied* documented a decade before, in the final instance another Black person was shot dead by the San Francisco police.[5]

"Political Funeral for Murdered Queers Jihad Alim Akbar and Gwen Araujo," Gay Shame's poster called for an action a month after the two murders. Gay Shame is a radical trans/queer direct-action collective that began in the late 1990s in New York City in opposition to the inexhaustible exhaustion of gay pride's commercialization. The group was reconfigured in 2001 and continues as an antiauthoritarian tendency in the Bay Area. The political funeral was an attempt to recast Akbar as a murdered queer and a victim of the lethal rage that is police force, concealed by the anti-Blackness of the Castro, which colluded in his murder. Akbar's sexuality was not the primary reason they linked his killing with that of Gwen Araujo. It was Akbar's inability or unwillingness to cohere to the neurotypical ableism of the Castro, which rendered him, in the instance of state power, as a queer in *need* of sudden death. Further, Gay Shame wanted to destroy the media's fascination with Gwen's brutal killing that sought to equally distribute the blame between a "deceitful" trans woman of color and those *forced* to kill her—the enduring logic of transmisogyny.[6]

Both instances of anti-trans/queer violence, which were carried out by a small number of individuals, were subsequently folded into the drives of state power. Even after accounts otherwise, it was suggested that both transgressed in such a way that only death could reconcile. Alameda County Assistant District Attorney Chris Lamiero, who represented the prosecution against Araujo's killers, said, "I would not further ignore the reality that Gwen made some decisions in her relation with these defendants that were impossible to defend." He added, "I don't think most jurors are going to think it's OK to engage someone in sexual activity knowing they assume you have one sexual anatomy when you don't."[7] As an agent of the state theoretically sent to do justice in her name, Lamiero placed responsibility not on those who tortured, strangled, and beat her to death with the kinesthetic intimacy of their bare hands but on his projections of the epistemology of her anatomy. This line of thought also argues that their sexual desire was in spite of and not because of Gwen's trans identity. In other words, transness becomes a force so wild, so destabilizing to the order of things, it must be met with equal intensity, in this case, public death. Years after Akbar's killing, officer Michael Celis, who was found to have used justifiable force, was among a group of SFPD officers caught in a texting scandal that included messages using "fag" and proclamations of "white power." To be clear, this is not to suggest that Celis murdered Akbar because he is a homophobic white supremacist in the conversational sense (although he might be) but that he, as a proxy for police force, carried out its collective will by way of this murder. In other words, while the actions of Celis and those who murdered Araujo matter, it's in whose name they act and whose worlds they hold open that must also be of concern.[8]

Gay Shame's insistence on thinking both these iterations of racialized anti-trans/queer violence together is also the methodological commitment of this book. Araujo's tragic murder might be primarily understood to be that of intersubjective violence, the phobic eruption of a personal relationship that became unbearable, and Akbar's might function as a generic expression of the violence of the state form, once again levied against Blackness. Bringing them together, then, builds an analysis that is attentive to the scale of direct attack that is always staged within the language of the state that demands it. By tracing these edges, not only does an analysis of anti-trans/queer violence appear, but these connections allow for, or more pointedly order, a reading of normative power—modernity's common sense—where Enlightenment's dreams become our nightmares.[9]

This antagonism melds the spectacular murders of Jihad Alim Akbar and Gwen Araujo with the quotidian desires for destruction, including the sterilizing glares that rob one of the ability to sink into comfort. Besieged, the threat of harm reverberates in the fleshiness of the everyday, producing a kind of death-in-waiting lived as what Frantz Fanon called a "feeling of nonexistence." Catastrophically, this imminent danger constitutes for the trans/queer that which is the sign of vitality itself, as possibility and limit are collapsed into one.

What, then, becomes of trans/queer *life*, if it's produced through the negativity of forced death and at the threshold of obliteration? Pushed further, if trans/queer life is constituted in the social as empty of meaning beyond the anonymity of bone, what kind of violence is done to that which is never properly here?[10]

In another time and place, "*Tiens, un nègre!*"[11] ("Look, a Negro!"[12]) opened Frantz Fanon's chapter 5 of *Black Skin, White Masks*, "The Lived Experience of the Black" (*L'expérience vécue du Noir*), infamously mistranslated as "The Fact of Blackness." Fanon enters here, as he does throughout this text, against a logic of flattened substitution and toward a political commitment to non-mimetic friction—the messiness of history and that history's reemergence. After all, the racialized phenomenology of Blackness under colonization that Fanon illustrates may be productive to read against and with a continuum of anti-trans/queer racialized violence in the settler colony that is the United States. The visual's capacity to capture through the dialectics of recognition and the scopic must figure with such a reading of race, gender, and sexuality. It is argued, and rightfully so, that the instability of trans/queerness obscures it from the epidermalization that anchors the idea of race in the fields of the visual. When thinking about the difference between anti-Semitism and racism, which for Fanon was a question of the visuality of oppression, he similarly suggests, "the Jew can be unknown in his Jewishness."[13] However, here it may be useful to reread Fanon through an understanding of the visual that reminds us that Jewish people can sometimes not be unknown in their Jewishness (including Jews of color), evidenced by the endurance of anti-Semitism. Or, this is to suggest that domination always exists within and also in excess of the representational, which includes the sensorium of its arrival—the extra-diegesis of difference.[14]

Similarly, I ask why anti-trans/queer violence, more often than not, is *correctly* levied against us. In other words, the discursive aim of liberalism that subsists under the sign of equality argues that trans/queerness is indistinguishable under the social order. This misses, or more precisely disappears, in the name of its own coherence—differences it cannot endure, while also harnessing difference as its organizing principle. Against such claims, I suggest that there are moments of figuration where trans/queerness does in fact signify differently, not because of an innate ontological structure but because of the ways ontology is naturalized through one's place in the world. I'm not suggesting that there is an always locatable trans/queerness that exists outside historicity, but such a fiercely flexible semiotics might conditionally offer a way of knowing this violence that can withstand the weight of generality.[15]

Indeed, not all who might identify as either trans and/or queer experience the same relationship to violence. Such differentiation is the underside of this book as the consolidation of LGBT politics operates, perhaps most vividly, through an endless drive toward recognition before the law. As I glossed in the introduction, this demand for inclusion through the architecture of formal equality solidifies the attachment to the state as the primary, if not exclusive, method of transformation. Beyond thinking that equality is a less effective tactic in the struggle for freedom, here I understand equality as that which ensures that anything other remains unthinkable. While at times strategically necessary, organizing movements under its banner solidifies the idea that the same system that has been built and maintained through deadly inclusive exclusion is also where relief can be found.[16]

The betrayal that is LGBT equality takes form in the grim fact that the overwhelming proportion of trans/queer people who are murdered in the United States are of color; specifically, Black trans women endure the most vicious forms of quotidian and spectacular attack.[17] Similarly, Black, Brown, and/or

Indigenous trans/queer people who are surviving in spaces of hyper-control, from jails and psych prisons to public housing and ICE detention centers, along with those whose labor is criminalized, including sex workers and drug dealers, experience the intensification of this structuring violence as the predisposition to interpersonal attack. In contrast, many LGBT people in the United States who otherwise exist within white cis normativity may in their daily lives *know* very little about either systematic or personal harm. The long history and magnified present of LGBT assimilation illustrates these varying degrees of life chances available to some, that under the democratic order come at the expense of others. In contrast, I am marking *trans/queer* as the horizon where identity crumbles and vitality is worked otherwise. Here, trans/queer might be a productive placeholder to name a nonidentity where force is made to live. This is not to suggest that the negativity of trans/queerness and methodologies of annihilation define the end of our sociality or that the parameters of opposition are sedimented as such. As is cataloged throughout this text, our legacies of wild revolt—fashioning a world without vertical genealogies—insists that trans/queerness remains as generativity's future present.[18]

I stay with Fanon because he continues to offer us among the most compelling analyses of structural abjection, (non)recognition, and psychic/corporal violence that returns as symptom. "Look, a Negro!" violently freezes Fanon in a timeless place as a black object, overdetermined from without, as a signifier with no meaning of one's own making. This process does not reveal the fact of Blackness but the truth of anti-Blackness as an order of a coloniality maintained through organized disorder—the ever-changing restrictions, lived as compulsory inclusion, that allowed Fanon to be in the world only by being outside it. In a similar way, there is the habitual shouting of "faggot" and "he-she" at a Black trans woman on the street, the common practice of braided aggression that tethers, even against the target's will, gender and sexuality. In that hostile utterance, she is known from without but that naming is always a calculated misrecognition intent on solidifying the generalized cis normativity in the face of its lie. This vocal outburst, like the words of Gwen Araujo's killers, does not describe its victim but is an attempt to reconcile the stability of binary gender, which is also binary sexuality. Here, then, such phobic announcements are not the symptomatic evidence of a repressed homo- and/or transsexuality, which is still one of the primary explanations deployed. Resisting such diagnosis is important as it, once again, places these deaths as but the logical expression of trans/queerness itself.

Through an attention to the meaning of corporal violence and its affective and psychic fallout, this chapter attempts to understand how trans/queerness approximates the cutting perimeter that marks the edges of subjectivity. Here the forms of violence that are of concern are not introduced after the congealment of something that might be called identity. I am using the term *trans/queer* to precisely index the collision of difference and violence. In other words, trans/queer is being summoned to labor as the moment when race, nonnormative sexuality/genders, and force materialize at the impasse of subjectivity. Against an identity that assumes a prior unity, trans/queer disrupts this coherence and also might function as a collective of negativity, void of a subject but named as object, retroactively visible though the hope of a radical politics to come.[19]

Found and Lost

"There is a crime scene somewhere, we just haven't found it yet,"[20] stated a New York City police officer about the now-cold case of Rashawn Brazell. Rashawn Brazell, a nineteen-year-old Black gay man, went missing on the morning of February 15, 2005, from the Brooklyn apartment that he shared with his mother. Witnesses reportedly saw Brazell leave early in the morning with an unknown man who rang his doorbell and met him outside. Two days later, around 3 a.m., New York City transit workers found two "suspicious" bags alongside the tracks at the Nostrand Avenue station in Brooklyn. Upon closer inspection of the black garbage bag, which was lined with a blue garbage bag, they discovered two legs and the arm of a then-unidentified Black male. A week later, on February 23, 2005, workers at the Humboldt Street recycling plant in New York made another discovery of body parts in an identical blue bag stuffed inside another black trash bag. Among these remains was a fingerprintable hand, which confirmed the body parts were Rashawn Brazell's. According to the autopsy and coroner's report, Rashawn Brazell was kept alive for two days before he was surgically dismembered. The report also suggests that the murderer had a "working knowledge of human anatomy" as all the cuts were "clean" and on the joints. Moreover, the cuts were all first traced with a sharp object, probably a knife, using precision and care, before the heavier work of cutting through bone. The assorted wounds on the torso suggest, according to the report, that there was probably a struggle before death. However, the actual cause of death is medically and legally undetermined, as Rashawn's head is still missing.

The never-found knife that traced Rashawn Brazell's body into pieces is but one of the artifacts that assemble the afterlives of this murder. The original offense, the mutilation, torture, and disarticulation of Rashawn Brazell, is made to repeat, to reiterate, its trauma and terror as a grammatical constellation of the long histories and cultural narratives that equate Black queer sexuality with inevitable catastrophe. The reiteration of the murder serves as a monument to what *must* become of young Black queers who find pleasure in the anonymity of sex. His actual murder, along with the logic that argues that his death was of his own making, draws the inescapable circle that carved not only his body but also his history. How, then, might we read the specificity that ended the life of Rashawn Brazell dialectically with the cultural violence that rewrites his death as an inevitable end?

The case of Rashawn Brazell, like that of Gwen Araujo, is, in many horrific ways, ordinary. From the gruesome murder itself, to the ritualistic dismembering, and the aftermath of silence punctuated by sensationalistic pulses, Rashawn Brazell, like the overwhelming majority of murdered Black, Brown, and Indigenous trans/queer people in the United States, remains in the swimming generality of cold cases, murders never solved, killers never really feared, and body parts never found. Rashawn Brazell's death, even with all the shocking details, is made unremarkable by the social that demands it. This typicality is not because of Brazell's worth but should be read as an indictment of the world that produces his life in particular, and Black queerness in general, as such. The true terror is felt once we begin to read this case as so chillingly common. Such consistency places Brazell in a mass grave of anonymity, a queer burial of unmarked pain.

Case after case of mutilated trans/queer people in various states of decomposition build this terrible archive. A random name in a news report of a murdered trans woman leads to another story of unassimilable harm. In 2000, not all that far from Rashawn Brazell's house, in Queens, New York, a large green plastic tub was found with a foot, crushed bones, and a human skull belonging to nineteen-year-old Steen Keith Fenrich.[21] Fenrich's stepfather later confessed to killing his stepson and then trying to frame Steen's boyfriend because he was gay. Another question found me at the murder of "A. Fitzgerald Walker,"[22] a Black trans woman living in Fayetteville, Arkansas. According to court testimony, two men picked up Walker outside a gay bar, then all three went back to her apartment. One of the men, Yitzak Marta, later stated that once in her apartment they "discovered" that she was trans and so they left. Neighbors became suspicious because the tires on Walker's car had been slashed. Three days later the police entered her apartment to find her lifeless body and "KKK" in two-foot-high letters written in her blood.

Confronted by the horrors of these murders, I follow Saidiya Hartman, "how does one rewrite the chronicle of a death foretold and anticipated, as a collective biography of dead subjects, as a counterhistory of the human, as the practice of freedom?"[23] Here I rehearse these cases in hopes of capturing momentarily the unconfinable, the affective weight, the terror, and the pain of trans/queer life and of that life's end. What remains is a composition sketched from missing body parts that the social produced as unmissed. The question, then, of signifying loss, of rewriting violence, and of representation must be surfaced. Representing death, even only in word, tends to reproduce a pornography of violence through which the fullness of those harmed, their material lives and the force of their ends, is decomposed into tropes of speculative pain and sensational disappearance. As impossible necessity I stage my ethomethodological query by imagining how one might inhabit a space of representation so overdetermined by the rot of the world. It is not enough, however, to only write otherwise, but against accommodation we must abolish the ease with which it endures. This hope is but a stand-in, or perhaps a horizon, that foresees a subjectivity in the hold; Rashawn Brazell's mother seizes us with a similar plea: "I want who did this off the street, and I want the rest of my child."[24]

Cold Calculations

Can one recognize what is made to exist beyond recognition—the remains of a missing queer or the identity of an unnamed trans woman whose body is never claimed? How do we measure the pain of burying generations of those we love and those we never knew? Rashawn Brazell's brutal end asks these questions through its calculus of trauma. This kind of loss instructs a precarious organization, a kind of trace of that which was never there, a death that places into jeopardy the category of life itself. My aim here is not an investigation that simply confirms that which those living this proximity to death already know but to build out a vocabulary for a war of position that might collectively overwhelm the world in which it persists.

The numbers, degrees, locations, kinds, types, and frequency of attacks—the statistical evidence that is meant to prove that a violation really occurred, are the legitimizing measures that dictate the ways we are obliged to understand harm. Data are translated into policy that calls for yet another study—the loop of bureaucratic knowledge ensures we know little. Indeed, statistics as an epistemological project may be another way the enormity of anti-trans/queer violence is disappeared. The trouble with thinking only or primarily statistically about violence is both a theoretical and a material trap. Although statistical evidence is assumed to account for rates of occurrence and severity, statistics seem to have a way of ensuring that Rashawn Brazell's head is never found. Horrifically, because his head has yet to be recovered, the "actual" cause of death still cannot be officially determined. Not yet dead according to the parameters of the law but experienced as nothing other by his mother and community, Rashawn Brazell's murder has for this reason, among others, never made it into "hate violence" statistics, which confirms the law's anti-Black and anti-queer functionality.[25]

Further, the FBI, through the Criminal Justice Information Services (CJIS) division, collects the only national data of targeted violence. Their database contains categories for religious, racial, and disability "bias," and anti-homosexual (male and female), anti-bisexual, and anti-heterosexual incidents (for 2017, thirty-two "anti-homosexual" and 106 "anti-transgender" incidents were reported).[26] This report is optional for local jurisdictions, and 2017 recorded only 119 incidents based on "gender identity," consisting of infractions ranging from vandalism to murder, and only sixty-nine "victims" who experienced "multi-bias" incidents. It would seem misguided at best to suggest that the number 119 can really tell us anything about the work of anti-trans violence. Reported attacks on "out" trans/queer people like these data can, of course, only work as a swinging signifier for the incalculable referent of the actualized terror. This is not simply a numerical issue; it is a larger question of the friction between measures and effect. Not unlike the structuring lack produced by any representation that offers us, the viewer, the promise of the real, statistics can leave us with only a fragmented copy of what it might index.[27]

Reports on anti-trans/queer violence, such as those from the CJIS, reproduce in tandem the impossibility of statistical completeness along with the actual loss of those that fall outside of accounting. The excesses of the official record also constitute it—the subaltern remains of that which can never enter into representation reminds us of the arresting horror of the ever-disappearing archive. Or, put another way, the quantitative limits of what gets recorded as anti-trans/queer violence cannot begin to apprehend the numbers of bodies that are collected off cold pavement and highway underpasses, nameless flesh whose stories of cruelty never find their way into an official account beyond a few scant notes in a police report of a body of a "man in a dress" discovered.[28]

Even when a murderer is not successful and there is a survivor who could enter the act into the official record, incidents are not often reported to the

FBI or local police.[29] Abolitionists remind us that the police are still among the largest perpetrators of racist anti-trans/queer harm, from sexual assaults and street harassment to imprisonment and murder.[30] With the police or some other tentacle of the prison industrial complex, namely the FBI, as the only collection, processing, and reporting agency for such data, people's resistance should come as no surprise. This apprehension lives within the collective consciousness that the legal system is organizationally indifferent, at best, toward survivors. Those with proximity to the system know by way of living the second order violation of becoming evidence for a district attorney whose singular aim is convictions.[31]

However, even with these fragmented and disjointed accounts, missing numbers, and never-recovered body parts, anti-trans/queer violence engulfs. Story after story of dismemberment, torture, mutilation, lynching, and execution coagulate a bleeding history of what it means to exist against the gender and sexual mandates of the state. All available discourse seems unable to get at the terrible enormity of this phenomenon. How can we measure the loss of Rashawn Brazell? The grinding task of transforming memories and skin into calculated data offers us little. Even if his murder made the official number rise, what would we know then that we don't know now? Would we believe the interlocking systems that emptied his body of the possibility of life would dissolve? Or would we trust that the legal system that has spent its history imprisoning and otherwise disappearing trans/queer people of color would suddenly reverse its architecture of power? What we need, then, is not new data or a more complete set of numbers; our task, it seems, is to radically resituate the ways we conceptualize the meaning of violence as fundamental and not antagonistic to our current condition. It is only by beginning there that we might find an ending.[32]

Killing Time

"He was my son—my daughter. It didn't matter which. He was a sweet kid."[33] Trying to reconcile at once her child's murder and gender, Lauryn Paige Fuller's mother thus proclaimed to a journalist outside of an Austin, Texas, courthouse. Lauryn Paige was an eighteen-year-old trans woman who was stabbed to death. According to Dixie, Lauryn Paige's best friend, it was a "regular night" as the two were planning on turning a few tricks. After Dixie and Lauryn Paige had made a bit of cash, they decided to call it a night and return to Dixie's house, where they both lived. On the walk home Gamaliel Mireles Coria and Frank Santos picked them up in their white conversion van. "Before we got into the van the very first thing I told them was that we were transsexuals," said Dixie in an interview. After a night of driving around, partying in the van, Dixie was dropped off at her house. She pleaded for Lauryn Paige to come in with her, but she said, "Girl, let me finish him," so the van took off with Lauryn still inside. Santos was then dropped off, leaving Lauryn Paige and Coria alone. The details of the night reappear only through the autopsy report, which cataloged at least fourteen blows to Lauryn Paige's head and more than sixty knife wounds on her body. The knife wounds were so deep that they almost decapitated her—a clear sign of overkill.

Reaffirming that any identification cannot withstand the weight of its whole, in response to the reporting of her murder, not only did lesbian and gay people write in an attempt to exile Lauryn Paige, a common display of transphobia in an attempt to gain access to the punitive class via claims of similarity. However, other trans people also responded that she was "not a member of our community" and her life had "no meaning." Kim Ciara's revulsion affirms, "Many of us . . . lead happy and productive lives, contributing to society by hard work and paying taxes, just like you or anybody else. Most of us are virtually invisible in the community, as we tend to distance ourselves from controversial types, like the prostitutes and street-walking drag queens you featured in your articles."[34] While the suggestion that Paige was a "controversial type" intended to disaggregate a trans sex worker through the lateral hostility of trans people who demand normative coherence, her life, within an anti-trans world, was liquidated and returned as meaningless, unable to provoke outrage or even sympathy.

I include this because while perhaps it seems I'm attempting to build a too generalized theory of violence, it can of course never approximate the complexity of the social. Further, even if people disidentify with the kinds of trans life Lauryn Paige was living and the forms of labor she did, that disidentification will not necessarily save them from gender normativity's deadly regulations. In other words, this is an instance where identification and force unravel, and why we must attend to identification as always appearing within a field of violence, which will never pay heed to identity's demands. This is to remember that those who identify as LGBT are not immune to reproducing harm and thus fashioning an analysis around an affirmative identification conceals under the assumption of sameness.[35]

Surplus Violence

Overkill is a term used to indicate such excessive violence that it pushes a body beyond death. Overkill is often determined by the postmortem removal of body parts, as was the case with both Lauryn Paige and Rashawn Brazell. The temporality of violence, the biological time when the heart stops pushing and pulling blood, yet the killing is not finished, suggests the aim is not simply the end of a specific person but the ending of trans/queer life itself. This is the time of trans/queer death—when the utility of violence gives way to the pleasure in the other's immortality. If trans/queers, along with others, approximate *nothing*, then the task of ending, of killing that which is constituted as already dead must go beyond normative times of life. In other words, if Lauryn Paige was dead after the first few stab wounds, then what do the remaining fifty wounds signify?

The legal theory that is offered to nullify the practice of overkill often functions under the name of the trans- or gay-panic defense. Both of these defense strategies argue that the murderer became so enraged after the "discovery" of either genitalia or someone's sexuality they were forced to protect themselves from the threat of trans/queerness. Estanislao Martinez of Fresno, California, used the trans-panic defense and received a four-year prison sentence after admittedly stabbing J. Robles, a Latina trans woman, at least twenty times with a pair of scissors. Importantly, this defense is often used, as in the case of Gwen Araujo, J. Robles, and Lauryn Paige, after the murderer and victim had engaged in sex. The logic of the trans-panic defense as an explanation for overkill, in its gory semiotics, offers us a way of understanding the place of nothingness. Overkill names the technologies necessary for, and the epistemic commitment to, doing away with that which is already gone. Here, trans/queer life is a threat that is so unimaginable that one is *forced* to not simply murder but to push the dead backward out of time, out of history, and into that which comes before. Yet this overkill registers as little in the social—the double bind of inhabiting the place of both menace and void.[36]

In thinking the overkill of Lauryn Paige Fuller and Rashawn Brazell, I return to the ontopolitical category of nothingness—the shadow of liberal democracy. The place of nothingness reemerges in its elegant precision with each case I offer—the repetitious futility of bringing into representation that which escapes it but remains in a para-vitalist order. By resituating this question in the positive, the something more often than not translated as the human is made to appear. Here the category of the human assumes generality, yet is activated, or more precisely weaponized, in the specificity of history and politics. To this end, the human, the something of this query, names the rights-bearing subjects or those who can stand before the law—the beneficiary of equality. The human, then, makes the nothing not only possible but necessary. Following this logic, the work of death, of the death that is already nothing, not quite human, binds the categorical (mis)recognition of humanity. The human resides in the space of life, and under the domain of Man, whereas the trans/queer inhabits the place of compromised personhood and in the zone of death. As perpetual and axiomatic threat to the human, the trans/queer is the negation, through inclusive exclusion, of democracy's proper subject.

Understanding the nothing as the unavoidable double of the human works to counter the arguments that suggest overkill and anti-trans/queer violence at large index a pathological break, and that the severe nature of these killings signals something extreme. In contrast, overkill is that which constitutes, via negation, equality's form, which is lived by many as unfreedom. Or put another way, if the state is the enactment of a majoritarian collective unconscious, then its own intelligibility, or its own will to power, is rendered through the figure of the internal enemy and the mandatory forms of liquidation needed to face this inside/outside threat. Overkill, the calculated practice of gratuitous force, then, is the proper expression to the riddle of the trans/queer *nothingness*. However, the spectacular scene of overkill must not be singularly pathologized as this would, yet again, privatize violence's epistemology under the individual while its structure remains intact. In the end, the killer never works alone. These vicious acts, therefore, must be held as an indictment of the very social worlds of which they are ambassadors. Overkill is what it means, what it must mean, to do violence to that which is *nothing*.[37]

After finishing a graveyard shift washing dishes for minimum wage at a local Waffle House, eighteen-year-old Scotty Joe Weaver stopped by their mom's house to give her some money they owed her before heading home to a green-and-white trailer in the rural town of Pine Grove, Alabama. Scotty Joe was a drag performer in local bars with a fondness and talent for working Dolly Parton. A survivor of cancer and an attempted suicide, Weaver had dropped out of school some years before in hopes of escaping the relentless agony of a childhood lived beyond gender's binary edict. Scotty Joe was excited about a recent move into a new place with their best friend Nichole Kelsay, a trailer that was, according to Scotty Joe's mother, "not much" and was puzzled into a neighborhood of thirty or so mobile homes. Kelsay's boyfriend, Christopher Gaines, had also been staying there along with his friend, Robert Porter.[38]

Returning home in the early morning hours, worn out from a long night's work, Scotty Joe Weaver, alone, took a nap on the couch. As Kelsay, Gaines, and Porter ate pancakes and made last-minute decisions regarding their plan to murder Scotty Joe that they had begun the week before, Scotty Joe slept for the last time. Kelsay, Gaines, and Porter returned to the trailer home in the early afternoon and found Scotty Joe still asleep. Kelsay locked herself in the bathroom as Gaines said to Porter, "OK. Come on. Let's do it."[39]

Robert Porter first struck Scotty Joe Weaver with a blunt object. As blood poured down the back of Weaver's head, Kelsay, Gaines, and Porter tied them tightly to a kitchen chair. Over the next few hours, Scotty Joe Weaver was beaten repeatedly and stabbed with an assortment of sharp objects. Gaines and Porter then strangled Scotty Joe for about ten minutes with a nylon bag until they fell unconscious to the floor. Blood was oozing from Scotty Joe's ears, which, according to the prosecutor, was a sign that they were still alive. Unsure, Gaines kicked Scotty Joe's seemingly lifeless body to see if they had been successful. The details of what happened, and what actually ended Scotty Joe's life, are lost within a collage of accusations and denial. Dr. Kathleen Enstice of the Alabama Department of Forensic Sciences, through her sketches and snapshots at the trial, suggested that Scotty Joe was also stabbed twice in the face and at least nine more times in the chest, with several cuts to the rest of their body, leaving them partially decapitated.

Scotty Joe's body was then, according to a jailhouse phone interview with Gaines, wrapped in a blanket and their head in a towel, then dragged onto the mattress in Scotty Joe's bedroom. Thinking that if the air-conditioning was turned up, the incriminating smell of decomposing flesh might be slowed, Gaines and Porter cooled the room, took the ATM card and $80 in cash that Scotty Joe had, and left. Their original plan was to throw Scotty Joe's body into a nearby river, and the three had even purchased cinder blocks to weigh it to the river's bottom. However, they feared that the body would surface and reveal their attack, so after the murder they returned to the Walmart where the supplies had been purchased and received a refund for the cinder blocks—a detail that affirmed their actions were of little significance beyond a misspent $2.11. After hitting up the local Dairy Queen and Arby's for lunch, they reconvened at Kelsay's mother's house to play some cards and relax. Later that evening Porter and Gaines returned to the trailer to dispose of the body. They stuffed the blanket-wrapped body into the trunk of Gaines's car, then stopped by a gas station and filled an empty Coke bottle with gasoline. About eight miles deep in a nearby pine grove, Porter and Gaines laid out Scotty Joe's body, along with other incriminating evidence, and doused it with the gasoline. In an act of sexualized aggression, the two urinated on the body, then set it afire and drove back to town. Scotty Joe's charred and mutilated remains were later found by a stranger riding an ATV.

Wounds of Intimacy

Scotty Joe and the other victims I've described were forced to embody to the point of obliteration the movement between abject nothingness, a generality that enables one to be killed so easily and frequently that it goes without notice, and at the other end, they approximate a terrorizing threat—a symbol of monstrosity and irreconcilable contradiction. The social reproduces queerness and gender nonnormativity as inescapable dangers, and at the same time beyond the value of sacrifice. Or, put another way, this shuttling necessitates a form of response to maintain its coherence that is more ruthless than that elicited by either indifference or fear.

According to Lum Weaver, Scotty Joe's older brother, Gaines had always had "issues" with Scotty Joe's gender and sexuality. As in the majority of these direct attacks, the assailants knew, and in this case even lived with, their target. This proximity between aggressor and victim undoes the fantasy that strangers are the primary vectors of harm—a fantasy we reproduce for its cover of protection. Here, then, the murder of Scotty Joe must be read as a form of intimate violence, not only because of the relationship the murderers had to Scotty Joe Weaver but also and maybe more importantly because of the technologies of vivisection that were deployed. As Kelsay, Gaines, and Porter had, according to testimony, at least a week to plan the murder of Scotty Joe, it seems logical that, during that time in rural Alabama, they could have produced a gun that would have made the murder much less gruesome. However, the three decided to cut and rip Scotty Joe Weaver to pieces using carnal force. The psychic distance that may be produced through the scope of a hunting rifle, and the possible dissociation it might offer, is the opposite of the bodily strength it takes to plunge a knife into the flesh and bone of a body. The penetrative violence, the moments when Gaines was holding Weaver as he meticulously thrust his knife into their body, stages a kind of terrorizing sexualized intimacy.[40]

If Scotty Joe Weaver was at once so easy to kill, and at the same time so menacing that they had to be destroyed, this intimate overkill might also help us understand why anti-trans/queer violence tends to take this form. Scotty Joe Weaver was, after all, the roommate and "best friend" of one of their killers. However, robbing Weaver would not be enough, killing them would not be enough; the horror of Scotty Joe Weaver's queerness *forced* their killers to mutilate and burn the body. This tender hostility, of ravaging love and tactile brutality, may be an opening for the task of facing the question scribed on a bathroom wall: "What if it feels good to kill or mutilate homos?" The disavowal of the threat through a murderous pleasure signals a much more complicated assembly of desire and destruction. This complex structure of phobia and attachment, not unlike the pleasure and pain Kelsay might have experienced as she helped slaughter her "best friend," asks us to consider anti-trans/queer violence outside the explanatory apparatus that situates it on the side of pure hate, intolerance, or prejudice.

Affective Remains

Scotty Joe Weaver's body, bound in gasoline-soaked fibers, charred and pummeled, as remainder of a trans/queer life, represents what kind of sociality is unlived before such a death. Among the tactics of resistance against the wrath of modernity is our collective attempt to articulate these various forms of vitality that congeal below or against the idea of the human. Such critical theorization, which also live in flesh, collect the spectral figures that remain as modernity's twin. This is perhaps another way of saying that solidarity with Scotty Joe and all those no longer here demands that we work to destroy the conditions of their destruction. This is why we must understand the architecture of violence—its deployment of the human and the human's negativity—so as to not reproduce, as response, harm's continuation.[41]

The liberal articulations of this para-vitality, popularized by the Italian philosopher Giorgio Agamben as bare life, references a stripped-down sociality—a liminality at the cusp of death where one is transposed from human into thing/animal. The temporality of this equation follows the idea that abjection works, in the first instance, through dehumanizing those presumed to be already human. Such a line of thought also announces, via reconciliation, the possibility of return to enfranchisement. In other words, Enlightenment's teleology is restored through legal augmentation. Yet what I've been sketching here, however incomplete, is a form of near life where the "feeling of nonexistence" comes before the question of life might be posed. Near life is a kind of ontocorporal (non)sociality that necessarily throws into crisis the categorical distinction between life/death. This might better comprehend not only the incomprehensible murders of those I've recounted but also the precarity of trans/queer survival in the wake of formal LGBT equality.[42]

Struggling to articulate the phenomenological and psychical limits of Black-ness under colonization, Fanon opens up critical ground for understanding a similar calculation of life that is forced to exist as nonexistence. In *Black Skin, White Masks*, Fanon lays out how recognition (which is also the question of subjectivity) resides between structuring violence and instances of personal attacks. Central to the Western philosophical tradition, which is to say colonial modernity's epistemology, is G. W. H. Hegel's conception of the master/slave (lordship/bondage) dialectic, as it remains one of the most persistent schemes for understanding the encounter that produces self-consciousness. In, but not of, that same intellectual tradition, Fanon clarified how the Hegelian dialectic was an instrument for thinking white recognition and the Enlightenment uni-versalism of its pretext. Under the condition of colonization and its racialized mandates, the dialectic would need to be reconsidered or perhaps totally aban-doned. Hegel, for Fanon, positions the terms of the dialectic (master/slave) outside of history and thus he refuses to account for the historicity of colo-nial domination as central to the question of being. In other words, when the encounter is staged and the drama of negation unfolds, Hegel assumes a pure battle external to the context of arrival. Moreover, by understanding the dia-lectic singularly through the question of self-consciousness, Hegel, for Fanon, misrecognizes the battle as always and only for recognition.[43]

Informed by Alexandre Kojève and Jean-Paul Sartre's rereading, Fanon makes visible the absent figure of the human assumed as the imminent sub-ject of Hegel's formulation. For Fanon, the structure of colonization that he survived under was not a system of recognition but a state of total war. The dialect cannot in the instance of colonization swing forward and offer the self-consciousness of its promise. According to Fanon, "For Hegel there is reciproc-ity; here the master laughs at the consciousness of the slave. What he wants from the slave is not recognition but work."[44] Hegel's dialectic that, through labor, offers the possibility of self-consciousness, for the colonized is frozen in a state of domination and nonreciprocity. The promise of recognition that is dependent on this exchange is suspended in the upside-down world of oc-cupation where the colonized remain, through the epidermalization of their position, as the necessary state of objecthood.[45]

What is at stake for Fanon, which is also why this articulation is helpful for thinking near life, is not only the bodily terror of force; the fantasy of ontolog-ical sovereignty also falls into peril under foundational violence. This state of total war, not unlike the attacks that left Rashawn Brazell, Lauryn Paige Fuller, and Scotty Joe Weaver dead, is at once from without the everyday cultural, legal, and economic practices, and at the same time from within by a consciousness that has been occupied by domination itself. For Fanon, the white imago holds captive the ontology of the colonized. The self/Other apparatus is dismantled, thus leaving the colonized as an "object in the midst of other objects"[46] embodied as a "feeling of nonexistence."[47]

While thinking alongside Fanon, how might we comprehend a phenomenology of racialized anti-trans/queer violence expressed as "nonexistence"? It is not that we can take the specific structuring of Blackness and/or Arabness in the French colonies and assume it would function the same today under U.S. settler colonial regimes of anti-trans/queer violence. However, if both desire and violence are imbricated by colonization and their itinerant afterlives, then such a reading might help make more capacious our understanding of anti-trans/queer violence today, as well as afford a rereading of sexuality and gender nonnormativity in Fanon's texts. His prophetic intervention offers a space of perpetual nonexistence, neither master nor slave, written through the vicious work of epistemic force imprisoned in the cold cell of ontological capture. Here, nonexistence, or near life, forged in the territory of inescapable brutality, demands we only know these murders against the logics of aberration.

Violence, here, returns as irreducible antagonism, which crystallizes the ontocorporal, discursive, and material inscriptions that render specific bodies in specific times as the place of *the nothing*. The figuration of near life should not be understood as the antihuman but as that which emerges in the place of the question of humanity. In other words, this is not simply an oppositional category equally embodied by anyone or anything. This line of limitless inhabitation, phantasmically understood outside the intersections of power, often articulated as equality, leads us back toward rights discourse that seeks to further extend (momentarily) the badge of personhood. The nothing, or those made to live a "damaged life"[48] as Theodor Adorno might have it, is a break whose structure is produced by, and not remedied through, legal intervention or state mobilizations. This also highlights how an analysis of devaluation and/or exclusion, the terms mostly closely associated with domination, misses how those forced to be included and their valuation properly names the forms of modern power we must confront.

Queer Crypts

At 12:48 p.m. on the afternoon of January 8, 1999, the body of Lauryn Paige was found in a concrete ravine near the entrance of the Tokyo Electron Corporation in Austin, Texas. Barely covered by weeds and roadside trash, her body was laid to unrest in the stagnancy of wastewater and debris. In plain view and hidden from sight, Lauryn Paige's tomb holds an open secret with deadly consequences. Thrown in a shallow grave, not worth the cover of earth, the history of Lauryn Paige's unimaginable end indexes the limits of a present. A portrait of a near life, out of time, it terrorizes through its everywhereness. Beyond the pageantry of meaning, this scene pictures the untraceability of anti-trans/queer violence. Both everywhere and nowhere, a series of trash bags, a burning blanket, a concrete ditch, perhaps this is the province of nothingness.[49]

This ditch ought not be our end. Yet I stay in the place of violence, in the muddy isolation of a drainage ditch, precisely because it offers no recuperation, no rescue beyond decomposition. If the normative remedy appears as the empty promise of equality, then our refusal necessitates dwelling in the place of harm as we search for another way out. We remain not because we gain anything from the consumption of pain but because we must name the calm consistency of this violence as the work of its abolition. If we start here, with an understanding that escape is not possible and that against the dreams of liberal democracy there may be no outside to violence, how might we also articulate a kind of near life that feels, in the hollow space of ontological capture, that trans/queer life is still lived, otherwise?

CHAPTER 2 NECROCAPITAL

BLOOD'S GENERAL STRIKE

Capital is dead labor, which, vampire-like,
only lives by sucking living labor, and lives
the more, the more labor it sucks.
—*Karl Marx*

> I found a new home within the hearts of
> my new brothers and sisters, some of whom
> carry the burden of a kind of positivity that
> can only be understood by blood.
> —*Kia LaBeija*

Pray, give money, and donate blood—the
now common refrain returns, once again, as the public response to the spectacle, lived by many as the quotidian, of mass death in the United States. Rattling through news anchors' mouths, these words closed countless segments in the days following the 2016 Pulse nightclub shooting in Orlando, Florida, that left forty-nine people dead and at least another fifty-three wounded. In a performative gesture that offered repair for the breach many people experienced in the aftermath of the attack, thousands did in fact pray, give money, and donate blood. This trinity knots together the metaphysics of the sacred, the work of capital, and the fleshiness of bios through fantasies of togetherness, while its retroactive prescription insists that such slaughter demands no redress beyond the penance of contemplation.[1]

Nonetheless, by way of response to the enormity of the devastation, people lined up, sometimes waiting for many hours, to give blood at local OneBlood donation centers and other mobile blood drive buses throughout Florida. During this short period after the attacks, some 29,000 units of blood were collected. However, because there were relatively few survivors, only 372 units of blood were ever used, of which 214 were used on a single patient. OneBlood, a not-for-profit organization, was able to circulate the remaining 28,000 units through its distribution centers—billing hospitals approximately $210 a unit to cover "lab and personnel" costs, including millions for its CEO's salary and bonuses. Outside the orthodox scene of exchange yet inside its near totality— here capital was accumulated without a proper sale.[2]

Confusion at OneBlood centers over who could give was compounded by chaotic lines and that many who attempted to donate fell under those excluded by Food and Drug Administration (FDA) guidelines, most explicitly "men who have had sex with men" (MSM). Trans women are also often nonconsensually forced into this category by the enduring cis sexism of the medical system. The FDA had officially altered these restrictions from a lifetime ban for MSM to a recommended "12-month blood donor deferral since last MSM contact" by the time of the shooting in 2016.[3] Under this logic, queer people could donate blood as long as they did not have queer sex within the last year. However, they also suggested that "establishments may voluntarily elect more stringent donor deferral criteria," which is what OneBlood did, turning away many donors who had friends and family die in the shooting.[4]

The massacre at Pulse, a gay club gathering a predominately Latinx and Black crowd, was first narrated as an anti-LGBT attack by an assumed heterosexual shooter, unable to cope with the infringement of nonnormative gender/ sexuality, who was forced, to the point of murderous rage, to destroy trans/ queer people and the social worlds they build in nightlife. Later, the event was recast as a terrorist attack by a "radical Muslim"—the child of Afghan parents and husband of a Palestinian—against loyal "Americans," whose victims were LGBT by chance and whose race was assumed to be white. Here, Pulse's specificity faded into obscurity as it became a *random target* after his first proved too secure. Both accounts, however different, are positioned in order to extract a positive valuation of the night's carnage. Instrumentalized, even in death, the murdered are called to make meaning where there is none. Beyond the club's walls, the scene of destruction becomes yet another moment of heteronormativity's primitive accumulation.

In the days following the attack, the shooter, Omar Mateen, was identified by numerous people as a somewhat regular at Pulse, who would cling to the dark of the corners alone. Breaking his anonymity, he would sometimes become aggressively drunk and start trouble. Speaking to Univision, a disguised source by the name of "Miguel" detailed his two-month-long sexual relationship with Mateen. Miguel speculated that the mass killing was in response to Mateen's fear of HIV exposure after having sex with two other men, one of whom, according to Miguel, had disclosed his HIV-positive status. Yet others denied that Mateen was a "closeted homosexual," including the FBI and the jury in the trial of Mateen's wife, Noor Salman, who was charged with aiding and abetting her husband and with obstruction of justice.[5] That trial, which hinged on the question of whether the attack was a premeditated "hate crime," or if it was randomly carried out, would either implicate Salman via a claim to prior knowledge, or not.[6]

The jury in Salman's trial found her not guilty, a rare verdict in a terrorism case. What the defense proved, according to the jury, was that Mateen's attack was not by design anti-LGBT but rather the work of a jihadist who wanted to kill generically as retribution for the United States support for bombings of Iraq and Syria. This verdict exonerated Salman of federal charges of "providing material support to a foreign terrorist organization."[7] This ruling also solidified the renarration of the attacks, absorbing the victims into the white hetero/gender normativity of the state, while almost none of them would otherwise be interpellated as such. The specificity of this violence—its epistemological contours—were exchanged, in the realm of the law, as equally distributed to all *Americans*.[8]

Mateen entered Pulse close to 2 a.m. on June 12, 2016, armed with a rifle and a pistol he had legally purchased, then began indiscriminately shooting into the silhouetted mass of those still dancing. Survivors first thought the loud bursts were notes of the music; then the thumping beats were broken by screams and chaos as people looked for ways to escape, still unsure where the shooting was coming from. At 2:22 a.m. Mateen called 911 to claim his attack: "I pledge my allegiance to [Abu Bakr al-Baghdadi] of the Islamic State." He continued, "What am I to do here when my people are getting killed over there? You get what I'm saying?"[9] As the bathrooms were toward the back of the club, those running from Mateen at the entrance were corralled into one of the few possible hiding places. Working toward total liquidation, Mateen would open the door and look for the feet of the hidden as they contorted their bodies and took shelter, desperate to keep their shoes off the floor and their survival unknown. Hunted, some stayed knotted for the three-hour duration of the attack.

Mateen repeatedly entered the bathrooms, poking at bodies with the barrel of his gun to determine if there was still life, shooting when he believed there to be, and, according to survivors, laughing with each kill. Some played dead, while others, already shot and bleeding, crawled into the stalls to join the hidden—seeking refuge from the spray of bullets. Once in the stalls, many texted or called loved ones begging for help and asking why none had come. Others simply said goodbye. Trapped in their aloneness and dying together, faith waned as the shock steadied. While the police waited outside the club, unwilling to enter and pursue Mateen or offer any protection, at least five of those who had sent pleading texts from the bathroom bled out.[10]

The acute terror for those held captive that night ended after the police blew a hole in the wall, finally gaining entry and shooting and killing Mateen. Paramedics followed. The first responders were tasked with sorting through the mangle of flesh and blood—looking for life where there was little—in the club turned graveyard. In the ensuing hours local Orlando hospitals became overwhelmed with the shot, maimed, or otherwise injured. Arriving ambulances were met with the receding hope of a traumatized community, many of whom were also wounded, still wildly searching for the news of friends' survival. Hope gave way to devastation as many found only coroners asking for body identifications.

While motive—the belief in a coherent psyche organized in relation to diachronic time and space—animates, at least at the level of discourse, U.S. jurisprudence, it offers little here. Further, the transformation of the event from a scene of anti-trans/queer violence to a terrorist attack on *all Americans* fits within, which is to say concretizes, an Islamophobic narrative justifying everything from drone strikes and endless war to indefinite detention and the occupation of Palestine. This while also concealing that anti-trans/queer violence belongs as much to the drive of a New York–born man whose aspiration was to work in law enforcement as it might to a "jihadist." In short, under this recasting, those who were murdered at Pulse were subsumed under a second-order displacement that found them as but a generic screen upon which the state's normativity could be reconstituted.[11]

Attempting to decipher Mateen's intent leads us nowhere—that persistent rub of the uncanny where everything returns with familiar newness and where loss is all we find. What remains, and what is indivisible, is the scene of the dead, scattered across the dance floor where bodies lay abstracted as instruments of measure and entered into evidence. What also remains is a puzzle of Black and Brown flesh, still grasping onto each other in a now failed attempt to patch wounds, stay silent, and become invisible in hopes of surviving the night. In a place of sociality where drugs, music, and sex built transitive worlds through desire's expropriation of normativity's horde, together, they died in a restroom turned execution chamber.

Bloodlines

From the donations that began this scene to the catastrophe that ended in the Pulse restroom, this chapter traces the affective scaffolding and material practices that produce blood as an *exceptional* object. As a commodity that both labors toward the reproduction of *life* and is expressed under the sign of "dead labor," blood is held by an aura unique but not exclusive to it. Here, it is through tracing blood that we expand the proper time of labor not just toward a more exacting comprehension but so that we might better resist our collective exploitation. Attendant to this temporality, we are also able to once again ask who or what occupies the place of the worker. After all, capital's plasticity—its ability to reconfigure and to accumulate in new and ever-expanding ways—also means that we must read with and beyond the typified commodity form and the laborers we assume produce them.[12]

Primarily associated with the postwar emergence of and advancements in genomic research and development, biocapital is one attempt at capturing the specificity of this capitalization of *life*. However, it is clear that apprehending the meaning of biocapital demands that we understand it, in the first instance, as the instantiation of chattel slavery and colonial occupation, or more precisely their copresence. To do any less would be but a partial assessment, which disavows, consciously or not, that enslavement and dispossession are among primitive accumulation's futures. Vital, then, is to read the ways capitalism transforms and is transformed as to neither declare a new epoch, nor discount capitalism's ability to stretch toward continuity, most dramatically in moments of seeming rupture. Following the work of Claudia Jones and the Combahee River Collective to contemporary anarchist and/or socialist feminists who differently read the racial and gendered contours of capitalism's transformations (from cells and workers to networks and supply chains), helps stall the belief that we can understand labor outside of the conditions of its reproduction. This is perhaps another way to confront the ever-present and ever-destructive insistence that "difference," as a code word for race, disability, gender, sexuality, and so on, must be subsumed under a (new or old) materialist analysis. Moreover, such a disavowal not only provides an ahistorical materialism but also produces a subject that maintains that ahistoricism while declaring itself in revolt.[13]

Indeed, returning to the primal scene of biocapital's degradation, among the ruthless functions of slavery was the rendering of humans as commodities—objects that could be exchanged through the generalized equivalence of the money form—and also as workers prohibited from selling their labor power. From the Middle Passage to the auction block, the biological became a domain of speculation, where investors first hedged their bets on the quantity of enslaved Africans that would survive the unsurvivable voyage to the New World, then buyers again wagered on the potential productivity of one's laboring commodity. Here profit was contingent upon a cruel formulation where future returns must be greater than both the initial cost and the annual investment in the slave's reproduction.[14] Rather than an outlier to the massive function of U.S., which is to say global, capitalism, Karl Marx noted that "Direct slavery is just as much the pivot of bourgeois industry as machinery, credits, etc. Without slavery you have no cotton; without cotton you have no modern industry. It is slavery that gave the colonies their value; it is the colonies that created world trade, and it is world trade that is the precondition of large-scale industry."[15] However, this point that slavery was a precondition of modern capitalism (as a moment of primitive accumulation and of that accumulation's unending repetition) has been pushed beyond Marx by Black and other anticolonial feminists. Indeed, as I suggested earlier, it is within this tradition where we are reminded how biocapital, as a project of racial capitalism, functions by culling both the parameters of the category of the worker and the commodity. This is to say, rather than simply a new form of captive worker, the practice of slavery grew the bio-ontologization of race—the solidification of anti-Blackness as *scientific fact*—along with cotton, sugar, rice, and tobacco.[16]

The initial investment, the price paid for an enslaved person, was calculated against a speculated lifetime, the total quantified amount of labor power the buyer expected to steal. This economization transformed a "lifetime" into a predictive and monitored unit of measurement that not only figured investment practices but also cultivated an entire insurance industry for its protection. The Nautilus Insurance Company, which became New York Life, built much of its initial capitalization through policies sold to slave owners. Capitalism's ability to adapt is so nearly complete that even in the event of a slave's death, not only would an owner be able to cash in on the policy but their body parts were sometimes sold, maximizing return and diminishing loss.[17]

The commodification of a body that rendered it flesh, the calculation of "lifetimes," the economization of Black vitality, opened the entirety of an enslaved person to financialization. Yet the stability of this system of racial terror required an alibi in the context of the lie lived as unfreedom, which is not the absence but the most exacting condition of liberal democracy.[18] As Du Bois reminds us, "the true significance of slavery in the United States to the whole social development of America lay in the ultimate relation of slaves to democracy."[19] Indeed, slavery's bio-ontologization was met with the necessary quarantine of value's epidermalization. In other words, anti-Blackness, as expression of social death, not only lived on the skin but was produced through the white world as the psychic and biological interiority of the enslaved herself. Or, as Saidiya Hartman clarifies, "The dual invocation of the slave as property and person was an effort to wed reciprocity and submission, intimacy and domination, and the legitimacy of violence and the necessity of protection."[20] Following this wicked matrix of assumed antagonisms where safety is lived as danger and freedom returns as captivity, blood binds. Chasing its flow, then, as racial signifier, vitalized commodity, and cellular laborer is also a way to comprehend the incomprehensibility of slavery and its afterlives, as they appear with the consistency of their perpetual denial. This is perhaps another way of saying that to understand the making of "bad blood" that was denied donation in the aftermath of Pulse, we must register how blood's surplus value is gathered against Black labor.[21]

This much too quick gloss of the foundations of latest capitalism is necessary as it affords a more precise understanding of, or at least an occasion to ask, how the semiotics of blood accumulates as slavery's afterlife. With this the question remains: What produces blood as a fluid of hyper-signification? Colin Dayan's expansive study of the juridical history of *impurity* as an extraracial production that yields blood as an enchanted substance does much to condense centuries of narrative and legal history. By asking how the law mandates captivity under the very name of freedom, she sketches the links from imprisonment to plantation to penitentiary. Dayan contends that "The site of slavery in the colonies rendered material the conceptual, giving a body to what had been abstraction. Through the stigma of race, the spectral corruption of blood found bodies to inhabit and claim. An idea of lineage thus evolved and turned the rule of descent into the transfer of pigmentation, which fleshed out in law the terms necessary to maintain the curse of color."[22] Here the "spectral corruption of blood" bio-ontologized the fiction of race, at the level of the body, through the discipline of capital. The functions that sized the ability of a convict to either inherit or bequeath property also froze their claim to legal personhood. This positioned them in a state of suspended life, lived as civil death, that found its racial corollary in the enslaving practices of colonization.

Central to maintaining chattel slavery's claim to its own ethical consistency was a sleight of hand that argued both the innate and communicable characteristics of the enslaved. Here, anti-Blackness was maintained through a discursive, which is also to say deadly, incommensurability between the ontological and the transferable. Human/commodity, cloistered/infectious, innate/contingent, life/death, democracy/slavery: a series of seeming opposites demonstrate that rather than a smooth binary system, slavery produced fungibility through the transitivity of power, which reminds us that the true horror of the state form is its radical incoherence, sold as consistency, that does not simply permit these seeming contractions but demands them. For example, civil death resulted from abstracting the effects of an imposition as a typological anchor, then rendering it, through racial paranoia, at the level of species. Yet the reducing of enslaved humans to the abstraction of "species" was coupled, paradoxically, with an ideology that also believed the laboring commodity form might break free from its categorical lockdown and *infect* white civil society.[23]

Through the concept of attainder, the legislating of stripped personhood as "stained or blackened," blood's purity (or its negation as corruption) biologized the epidermalization of racial difference. Stained or blackened and pumping impure blood, but not dead, this early figure of the criminal serves as juridical memory and cultural precedent for both chattel slavery in the United States and contemporary practices of solitary confinement in prisons. However, a pardon, or sovereignty's ability to grant a right of return and "unfreeze" the convict's claim to a social life, became untenable through the logics of racialized slavery. This process imprinted the idea of tainted blood onto the figure of enslaved Africans (and their children), assembling a substitutional arrangement where *corrupt* blood was blackened—the recasting of the circular logic that Black people were enslaved because slaves were Black people.[24] Blood then became a racialized ontological anchor, where through one's very liveliness, Blackness became the color of *bad blood*, unable to flow, antagonistic to kinship and its arbitration of property, and alienated from claims to self-possession. This scheme also helps clarify how mass manumission was not slavery's abolition.[25]

This history of attainder reappears as the rule of hypodescent and in the racial segregation of U.S. blood banks, which continued until as late as 1972. It also echoes in the current restrictions on donations evidenced in the aftermath of Pulse. Blood, then, persists as a disciplining substance of modernity where sexuality enables the threat of contagion through social and other forms of reproduction. This is perhaps a long way of saying that the force of anti-Black racism is preserved through the legal and metaphysical belief that not only was slavery justified but its afterlives, existing as mass destruction, persist to quarantine the possibility of racial contamination in the ruins of de jure segregation. This is a point about miscegenation as well as the way blood, as a stand-in for racial difference, maintains the cultural fantasy of racial biologism precisely in the moment of its disavowal. This twinning action of subjugation and fear, alterity and a suspect intimacy, needs a *scientific* alibi, and it announces itself as such in the curious matter of blood.[26]

Blood Money

Giving the *gift of life* demands a return. Although the idea of blood donation is affectively and legally reliant on its nontransactionality—an act outside compensation or even exchange—gifting is integral to the logics of racial capitalism. In his attempt to bring together the study of consumption and production, Georges Bataille lays out the value of the gift: "The problem posed is that of the expenditure of the surplus. We need to give away, lose or destroy. But the gift would be senseless (and so we would never decide to give) if it did not take on the meaning of an acquisition. Hence giving must become acquiring a power. Gift-giving has the virtue of a surpassing of the subject who gives, but in exchange for the object given, the subject appropriates the surpassing: He regards his virtue, that which he had the capacity for, as an asset, as a power that he now possesses."[27] For Bataille it is the gift giver who acquires the virtue and power of the gift, which surpasses the value of that which was given. The "surplus expenditure" of donors reinscribes both their individual claim to/as excess wealth but also binds them to the living—vitality expressed as collective normativity, the figuration of the human. While some "donors" are compensated, in the U.S. you can only legally be paid for your time, not for the blood. The dividend here, as in the case of those who were able to donate post-Pulse, is on the level of the affective. Blood bans produce the constitutive outside, which is also negativity's inside, that affirms the juridical and social claims to the fiction of the biological. An economy of excess becomes the minimum. This is among the ways the national body is delineated through the inheritance of *pure* blood.[28]

On the public destruction (donation) of this excess, Bataille continues,

> But he would not be able by himself to acquire a power constituted by a relinquishment of power: If he destroyed the object in solitude, in silence, no sort of power would result from the act; there would not be anything for the subject but a separation from power without any compensation. But if he destroys the object in front of another person or if he gives it away, the one who gives has actually acquired, in the other's eyes, the power of giving or destroying. He is now rich for having made use of wealth in the manner its essence would require: He is rich for having ostentatiously consumed what is wealth only if it is consumed.[29]

Through an attention to the expenditure of energy, we can see how the performativity of blood donation is central to its value and the wealth attributed to those who *give life*. To be clear, this is not to suggest that it's a conscious desire that drives people to donate blood. In the aftermath of events like Pulse, where communities impacted are so totally decimated, it does feel to be one of the ways the tear might be mended. Yet Bataille helps trouble the idea that gifts, as a form of exchange and a technology of indebtedness, are opposed to compensation in either the money or other forms.

Given the feelings of exile expressed by many in the wake of the Pulse blood drive, lifting the FDA restrictions would be, it seems, the correct course of action. This demand for biological inclusion continues to be that of mainstream LGBT political organizations as it offers the promise of a unified civil society. Indeed, these restrictions reproduce the idea of contamination, here articulated as the conflation of HIV and trans/queerness, which is a second-order displacement of a preexisting fear of Black freedom. However, rather than operating under a fantasy of bio-unity, this pretense of mimetic similarity cauterizes difference as threat. This is yet another way the violence of civil society and its inclusive mandates capitulate devastation as racial capitalism's nourishment. In other words, the antagonism is not between donation and retention but between endless extraction and extraction's end.[30]

While blood is accumulated, it also accumulates. Through extension, addition, and inversion, blood's escalating significance drags its past into the present. Within this history of signification, what form of labor is expressed in blood? As Marx suggested in the epigraph of this chapter, which also persists as a fundamental for his orthodox readers, that "Capital is dead labor" and that it "only lives by sucking living labor," then an account of dead labor power's surplus value not only expands Marx's thought but reforms it. With this in mind, death continues to be central to the commodity form's rise, and in that centrality, it produces not simply novel forms of labor but new categories of (non)persons whose existence is calibrated as negative value, which ought not be confused with value's liquidation. Or, asked another way: What constitutes the negative value of life/death and its mirrored proxy of human/nonhuman under racial capitalism's creep?

Living Commodity/Dead Labor

If biological matter, including blood, enters the market (donated, "sold" as plasma, resold by OneBlood) and is transformed in that relation into a commodity, who, or what, is the labor that produces it? For Marx, "[a] commodity is, in the first place, an object outside of us,"[31] so then what becomes of the necessary externality of the form when the laborer appears as the commodity? In the context of biocommodities, cell division or other biological functions are as responsible for the labor of reproduction as lab technicians. Indeed, unlike Marx's table where the labor to produce it is assumed to have a beginning and end, without the extracted labor of life, these commodities become waste. Thus, distinct from traditional commodities that *represent* labor power as a product of it, commodified blood both represents labor power and must continue to labor to maintain its status as such. Going further, the person who donated or sold their blood need not be still alive for their blood (or more precisely its matter) to still be working. This is among the unique conditions of laboring commodities—speculative life (even the liveliness of the blood) is not dependent upon the laborer's reproduction. As provocation, the limit of the "worker" here (as well as in other forms of production) is reconstituted via a disarticulation that finds it everywhere and nowhere.

Intensified by the globalization of assembly line production, but not unique to it, the disappearance of the worker as both a coherent class and a physical body, is the precondition of contemporary exchange. For Marx, commodity fetishism describes the process through which the social relations of production are evacuated from commodities—allowing them to appear as independent and self-possessed—outside the webs of their materialization. This "mystical character"[32] is vital to understanding exchange beyond use-value, and is also what allows us to believe a commodity to be a general abstraction, the precondition of its ability to be exchanged for another object. Yet, in the case of blood, rather than concealing its production (its social relations), it declares its labor as its claim to value. Returning to Bataille, this is to say that its value is contingent upon the announcement of the conditions of production as not belonging to the anonymity of abstraction but to a more specific, but perhaps still general, type of labor. In other words, blood's positive value is built, via negation, on its social relations remaining against the spectacular deviance of nonnormativity, here rendered as impurity. Moreover, the laboring commodity disrupts Marx's necessary externalization of the commodity form. Yet rather than an impasse, knowing that the laboring commodity is foundational to racial capitalism, our aim here is to continue to pull at the form, not simply in the name of analysis but to build new practices of anti-capitalist sabotage.[33]

Contagion, then, or more precisely the force against it, drives cultural fantasies, lived as regulatory practices that endow blood with its various forms of value. This suspended threat works through a negative enclosure, in that contagion's imposition opens for extraction all that has not been deemed *dangerous*—a shifting category that, rather than expunging its history, seems to always expand. For example, the FDA guidelines defining the blood donation protocols that excluded MSM after Pulse were developed in the early 1980s, during the first years of the HIV pandemic. It was within that moment that the "4H club," those originally diagnosed as "high risk" for having HIV, were also returned to the social as the mark of imminent and inevitable transmission. "High risk" here names those most impacted by HIV/AIDS, which also affirmed those rendered most *dangerous*: Haitians, homosexuals, hemophiliacs, and heroin users. This motley assemblage of threat produced, through its cruel logic, those most likely to be HIV+ as the sign of impending and lethal infection. Fantasy and science are exchanged in a Manichean structure where the moral fears of migration, Blackness, anticoloniality, drug use, and queerness became vectors of death—the inverse of blood's positive value. Through its narrative retrenchment, death lived, yet again, as the foundational violence of civil society.[34]

This original 4H group haunts not only the virology of contemporary strains of HIV through RNA and its reverse transcription but also the epistemology of blood. HIV is now generally understood to have first multiplied in pre-independence Kinshasa (then Léopoldville) in the Congo, perhaps moving there from Cameroon, where simian immunodeficiency virus (SIV) jumped to humans, creating a new zoonotic disease. While the Belgians' vast atrocities mark the sum of their colonial administration, their procedures of engineering and conquest also proliferated the virus. HIV is both discursively and materially a condition of colonial geographies, as it spread internally via infrastructure projects, namely the expansion of the railroad, while it was also somewhat contained within the colony because of its restrictions on movement. The project's scale demanded a mass labor pool of enslaved and conscripted workers who were trafficked deep into the jungle and fed bushmeat indiscriminately as it was the only readily available and free protein. This, coupled with increased sex work that accompanied the railroad's construction, is the condition under which SIV is believed to have become HIV. Yet, in a fatal twist, it is decolonization that is accused of setting the virus free.[35] According to the most comprehensive epidemiological study, following the assassination of Patrice Lumumba, HIV spread outward with formal decolonization. Here national liberation, in the final instance, is blamed for the pandemic's deadly proliferation to the white world. Further, as Belgian nationals working as nurses and doctors left with the crumbling colonial administration, they were replaced by Haitian health care workers. It is this transition, in the moment of postcolonial chaos and the further transnationalization of labor, through which HIV is traced to Haiti.[36]

Once the virus arrived in Haiti, perhaps in the late 1960s, sex work and unsterile needles used in clinics are again speculated to be the conditions through which HIV was transmitted. While some believe the country's gay transnational tourism industry spread the virus, others argue it was a single "patient zero" who migrated to the U.S. with HIV. However, neither offers more than homophobic conjecture. Yet what we do know is that, like the story of the Congo's decolonization, Haiti must also be understood within the metropole's unending punishment for its protracted liberation. It was the enslaved who set the colonial world aflame as they led the first successful slave revolt in the Western Hemisphere. It was also these insurgents and the generations that followed them that had their freedom held for ransom under France's threat of reenslavement. From the smoldering embers of Saint-Domingue's sugar plantations to the unending U.S.-backed coups, Haiti's victories are ever matched by the structural adjustments of military intervention. Tangled conspiracies of HIV propagation offer nothing here as such wild theories obscure the even more scandalous truth of Haiti's endurance in the face of white retribution.[37]

Queer contagion, including the anxiety triggered by gender nonnormativity, found its viral materiality in the early 1980s. The diagnosis of gay cancer, or

GRID (gay-related immune disorder), the original name for AIDS, was a vengeful nomenclature for the perversion of existing in a world held together, at least in part, by trans/queer undoing.[38] Found by chance, queers began showing symptoms of unexplainable illnesses such as Kaposi's sarcoma (KS) and *Pneumocystis carinii* pneumonia (PCP). Unresponsive to the most aggressive treatments, otherwise healthy, often well-resourced and white, young men were deteriorating and dying with genocidal speed. Without remedy, normative culture celebrated its triumph in knowing the tragic ends they always imagined queers would meet. This, while the deaths of Black, Brown, and Indigenous trans and cis women (queer or otherwise) were unthought beyond the communities directly around them. These women, along with many others, were stripped of any claim to tragedy under the conditions of trans/misogyny.[39]

Among the architects of this silence was then-President Ronald Reagan, who infamously refused to mention HIV/AIDS in public until 1986. By then, at least 16,000 had died in the U.S. alone. Collective fantasies of mass disappearance through the pulsing death of trans/queer people, Haitians, and drug users—the wish fulfillment of a nightmare world concertized the rhetoric that had always been spoken from the lips of power. The true terror of this response to HIV/AIDS was not only its methodological denial but its joyful humor. In Scott Calonico's experimental short film, *When AIDS Was Funny*, a voice-over of Reagan's press secretary Larry Speakes is accompanied by iconic still images of people close to death in hospital beds.[40]

> LESTER KINSOLVING: Over a third of them have died. It's known as "gay plague." [Press pool laughter.] No, it is. It's a pretty serious thing. One in every three people that get this have died. And I wonder if the president was aware of this.
>
> LARRY SPEAKES: I don't have it. [Press pool laughter.] Do you?
>
> LESTER KINSOLVING: You don't have it? Well, I'm relieved to hear that, Larry! [Press pool laughter.]
>
> LARRY SPEAKES: Do you?
>
> LESTER KINSOLVING: No, I don't.

The deadpan of a deadly regime gives way to absurdism as the audio continues —punctuated with giggles, flat jokes, and homophobic asides. This while the state's paradigmatic neglect is buried under the hissing sneers of those too unbothered to even plot.[41]

Further, initial epidemiological studies misclassified trans women as MSM, not simply in opposition to their gender self-determinations but as an act, however unconscious, to again regulate gender under the assumptions of the biological. Indeed, we have no data on the specific experiences of trans women in the first years of the pandemic. However, we do have the ravaging effect the virus has had on the hyper-representation of trans women of color who are living with HIV or who have died from AIDS. This epidemiological conflation—the viral coefficient of transmisogyny—was also buttressed by cis gay men who identified themselves as the primary, if not exclusively, impacted community. To be clear, rather than a personal offense, this practice, which is among the constellations where science, biology, race, and gender convene, helped ensure that generations of trans women, particularly those who are Black, Indigenous, Brown, and/or low-income, were denied necessary information and treatment. This in turn, or once again, reduced them through a pedagogy of disposability—as a warning, beyond sacrifice, for the trespass of existing against the parameters of gender normativity.[42]

These disastrously incomplete accounts are significant, even as surface histories, not because they are the epidemiological fact of AIDS. Rather, they bring into relief the ways HIV/AIDS, as the return of the dispossessed, marks blood's positive value in relation to its outside. While the lifetime bans on blood donation for these initial groups have been somewhat reworked, in 2017 Donald Trump stated in response to the effort to block Haitians from immigrating to the U.S., "They all have AIDS."[43] Further, lifting the FDA ban on donations might loosen the grip these histories have on contagious paranoia: my point is that while the idea of AIDS circulated and cemented these attitudes, it did not, alone, bring them into being. To this end, it is anti-capitalist action, and that action's theorization, which collectivizes the struggle against exploitation's mutant forms. This while also offering us a plan of attack and the representational repertoire to bring it into being.[44]

This idea of contagion, like a border, generalizes scarcity. Contagion, then, along with enclosure and restriction, holds blood in suspense and primes it for speculative valuation. In other words, contagion is how even our blood becomes alienated. Thinking after the dialectics of scarcity and abundance, Marx's optimism in the *Grundrisse* suggested that increased technological innovation would free the worker from the grueling constraints of waged labor. However, scarcity (and its reproduction) is fundamental to capital's outward expansion—the compulsory growth of desiring markets and wanted commodities. "The blood supply is dangerously low," threat and warning come at once with the aim of controlled insufficiency and measured resupply. The crisis of blood, like that of capitalism, is most properly that of overproduction and so abundance, both discursively and as supply, must be marshaled. Speculating on future scarcity (and the production of such shortages) expands the possibility of profits today.[45]

The capacity, either latent or expressed, of contagion works as phobia's evidence smuggled in through virological fact, the twin of (bio)citizenship. In the context of liberal democracy, this troubles formal equality by disrupting the assumption that difference is *only* written on the body. In this I mean to suggest that thinking of the cellular, and specifically the virologic, opens up a way for charting power and difference that shows how the maintenance of fear is about both the aesthetics and the imaginary—the interior of the body via the racialized sexuality of blood. Weaving surface and depth, the force of blood's iconography, as an expression of modernity's drive, reveals blood's positive value and how that valuation reenters as racial capitalism's sanguine life force.[46]

As a material-semiotic, racial allegory, and laboring commodity, blood is a limit concept that patrols the borders as it reproduces the human—normativity's proper subjects. *Bad blood* as the forced imposition of the ontological with the biological, renders the criminal, the enslaved, the Black queer/ trans person, as the disciplining fear necessary to protect white civil society from its own desire. Rather than an analogy that substitutes these categories as coterminous, here, these contaminated histories refract through modernity's economies of extraction, alienation, and dispossession. Put another way, it is not that these categorical exclusions function in isolation, nor that they all bear the same signification, or an identical material weight, but holding them together, at least momentarily, helps name the functions of modern power.

This is to say, along with labor and commodities, charting the appearance of the laboring commodity is vital to describing the forms of old death that live in the New World. It is not by accident, then, that it is autonomous feminists who have organized toward the total reconceptualization of the category of labor to include, as fundamental, reproductive, affective, and its other feminized and racialized forms. As Mariarosa Dalla Costa argues on the seeming contractions of reproduction, "this is where capitalist development, founded on the negation of the individual's value, celebrates its triumph; the individual owner of redundant or, in any case, superfluous labour-power is literally cut to pieces in order to re-build the bodies of those who can pay for the right to live."[47]

While, indeed, blood might be considered redundant, Dalla Costa helps us understand that the extraction of blood—the labor power of a laboring commodity—is not reversed through the compensation of that labor power's reproduction. This is evident in that the average rate for blood plasma "donation" is about thirty dollars, while it can be resold for ten times that amount. Here the open secret of capitalism once again announces itself in the wage, which is but a punishment for the *right* to work.[48]

From the reproduction of laborers so that they might survive to produce another day's commodities—the deadly formula that dictates a wage—to the reproduction of the worker as commodity, the question of the biological as metric and material still reigns. On this relationship Michel Foucault suggests that "this bio-power was without question an indispensable element in the development of capitalism; the latter would not have been possible without the controlled insertion of bodies into the machinery of production and the adjustment of the phenomena of population to economic process."[49] Among the historic consequences of biopower is that it prefigures new forms of capitalism (and capitalism itself) that are dependent on the "insertion of bodies" into the "machinery of production." The reproductive machinery of biopower was the necessary condition that allowed for an ever-expansive mode of accumulation—the market of life, lived also as the work of death. Under this domain of biopower, the "adjustment" is significant because it is not simply the insertion of the biological into capitalism, but it is this relationship that inaugurated the very concept of a population.

In his Collège de France lectures from 1976, Foucault theorized how race became one of the technologies, as illustrated by what he calls state racism, that manages populations by generating them as discrete and knowable. He suggests that "At this point, we have all those biological-racist discourses of degeneracy, but also all those institutions within the social body which make the discourse of race struggle function as a principle of exclusion and segregation and, ultimately, as a way of normalizing society."[50] Foucault's argument is not that this is the origin of racism but that in the early nineteenth century, a new discourse emerges that internalized the figure of the enemy. The social, in turn, required new tactics of protection, and contagion was mobilized as one of its enduring disciplinary ideologies. Racism, here, must not be read as personal bias but was then, as it remains now, one of the primary functions of the biopolitical, which is say the modern state. To this end, the discursive materiality of racialized contagion was, and continues to be, deployed as a coconspirator in a regime where "entire populations are mobilized for the purpose of wholesale slaughter in the name of the life necessity."[51]

It is within this framework that Foucault suggests that blood "owes its value at the same time to its instrumental role . . . and also to its precariousness (easily spilled, subject to drying up, too readily mixed, capable of being quickly corrupted)."[52] Like Dayan's argument about the corruption of blood, Foucault also believes the fragility of blood to be its radical durability. However, for Foucault these older symbolics of blood were transformed into an analytics of sexuality.[53] Foucault goes on to argue that to think in terms of law, death, blood, and sovereignty would be a misreading of the specific kinds of power that are operative in relation to sexuality as a more recently deployed category. This shift from the sovereign to the biopolitical for Foucault accounts for the attention paid to sexuality in the nineteenth century, which becomes dedicated to "the body, to life, to what causes it to proliferate."[54]

However, AIDS, which took Foucault's life in 1984, read through slavery's terror, forces us to rethink Foucault's movement from a symbolic of blood to an analytics of sexuality. In our current time, which is a time of AIDS, the symbolics of blood do more than haunt the analytics of sexuality, although they may also do that. AIDS is the collision of the two—a world where sexuality is feared in the name of blood's ability to transmit. Further, the ongoing condition of colonialism forces a reckoning with how the battle against "internal enemies" is also waged on the level of the cellular. Communicability, the metaphoric and material threat to the idea of bodily (racial/sero) sovereignty, exposes the fragility of these porous claims of individuation. In the time of AIDS, in the time of anti-Black coloniality, the transitivity of blood functions, by disruption and augmentation, as death's return under the name of life. We remain with the query: How does blood continue to figure, not through the protocols of sovereign exception but through the proliferation of that exception in the maintenance of the human?[55]

Graveyards and Factories

Blood circulates as a commodity where some are compensated, however inadequately, for their labor power (as in the case of people selling their blood plasma, or people *donating* their blood); this formulation describes what we might consider to be the positive valuation of the biological. Against this bioeconomy and blood's positive valuation runs another that functions beyond even the thinnest veil of consent (as nonconsent) offered under waged labor. While blood sales and donations are practices of exploitation under capital's logics, those who are excluded from these economies endure a second mode of exploitation. It is not that people living with HIV are outside of these circuits of value; it is the ways they are included that clarify the iterative force of accumulation's capacity. The reproduction of lively capital, the will toward life, is also built upon death's proliferation, where the symbolics of blood and the analytics of sexuality converge.[56]

If biocapital is primarily concerned with speculative or promissory capital via investments in the future, then what is to become of the value of future's end? In Marx's third volume of *Capital*, he suggested, "Yet for all its stinginess, capitalist production is thoroughly wasteful with human material, just as its way of distributing its products through trade, and its manner of competition, make it wasteful of material resources, so that it loses for society what it gains for the individual capitalist."[57] What Marx saw as waste-making in the modes of production is, under biocapital, reincorporated into circuits of exchange. Capital's demand for endless expansion produces waste (human material and/ or distribution of goods) as only a momentary state; these "useless" excesses are perpetually composted into yet another instance of primitive accumulation. Value's potentiality is judiciously recycled while the planet and most of its inhabitants are set aflame. This bounded relationship between the accumulation of wealth by "individual capitalists" and the distributed losses of "society" unveils capitalism's gory fortitude.[58]

Capitalism's totalizing force, its ability to incorporate its outside, where even waste is recirculated, contests the assumption that prohibition is the most profound method of abjection. As this book argues, under contemporary forms of power, inclusion names a method of violence, perhaps differently articulated but equally harmful as that of exclusion. To this end, one of the questions that first instigated this study was my desire to know where blood went after it left my arm at the free clinic. Related, where do the HIV cell lines used in pharmaceutical research and development originate? Resistant to the further surveillance of blood and its criminalization, I wanted to track the abstractions necessary to extract blood (and its viruses), then traffic them through circuits of travel and that travel's revaluation to find them in private labs. Much like the material symbolics of blood, my question is both about where they actually come from (meaning whose body) and what accumulates the various forms of value their cellular labor produces. It's not that those excluded from blood donation are simply outside the commodity chains I've been tracing, it's the ways they are incorporated as value's negativity that matters here.

In order to pay attention to this position, we must also press upon our understanding of both labor and commodities as reference points for the human. If our bodies, as Donna Haraway has helped illustrate, do not stop at our skin, then it seems our labor does not either.[59] I suggest this not to dilute the magnitude of traditional exploitation, nor to create a matrix of equal exchange. In other words, this is not a call for individual compensation, nor is it a belief that owning the means of our cellular production would offer radical transformation. However, an attention to the laboring commodity and to viral labor calls for a materialist analysis that expands beyond itself. This is to suggest that, along with the garment factory, the centrifuge, too, is a space of labor and its alienation that contains within it the possibility of production's communization.[60]

For example, among the repositories for decoupled viruses, most of which have first been procured from unknowing patients, is the National Institutes of Health (NIH) AIDS Reagent Program. This "bank" vigilantly houses unique strains of HIV, SIV, and other pathogens, which are used in research in both the private and public sectors around the world. The program provides reagents, which are cell lines mixed with other compounds, theoretically free of charge. Through an online catalog researchers are able to search by a number of product categories, including antiretroviral compounds, cell lines, and viruses.

Some reagents listed have a "source of origin" and others have a sentence in the attached "Note," yet most have no further biographical information other than, in some cases, the geographic source of the virus, including a number from Haiti and a few who were labeled as "heterosexual transmission" (leaving the others to be assumed to be from "nonheterosexual" contact).[61] One of the oldest was H9/HTLV-IIICC NIH 1983, which has been stored outside the body in liquid nitrogen for over thirty-five years, and given the high mortality rate during those years of the pandemic, we might assume that the body from which the cell line was harvested is no longer alive. In seeming perpetuity, this HIV cell line remains stored in Maryland awaiting its periodic reentry into scientific research as the suspended laborer of pharmaceutical production.

Another reagent, HeLa CD4+ HIV-1 LTR-β-gal cells (MAGI), are HIV and HeLa cells, the now famous "immortal" cell line nonconsensually harvested from Henrietta Lacks. Lacks was a Black woman who had her cancerous cervical cells stored without her knowledge or compensation, which still live many decades after her death, providing the foundation of, and the cellular labor for, much pharmaceutical wealth. Here, HeLa cells and HIV are held in newborn calf serum, amino acids, and other agents, awaiting their reanimation, a mixture of speculative possibility and unmarked graves. Put differently, the reagent and its latent profitability are contingent on the work of those in the lab, as well as that of the assemblage of unnamed cellular laborers.[62]

As a pedagogy, the catalog instructs its readers through classificatory inclusion and the emptiness of reducing the magnitude of the pandemic into instruments of exploration—the raw material of innovation. Scientists can also donate reagents to the program and will in return be given credit for any advancement based on their reagents. The labor of these value-added cell lines can, if used in research that produces a patented drug, enter into a commodity chain. The bank's only condition is that the researcher who donated the cell line must receive proper citation on all innovations produced by their reagent. Within this scheme, or perhaps beyond it, how do we account for the viral labor of this HIV cell line if the body from which it came is disappeared? And what is the relationship between the dead, represented by their still living cellular labor, and the massive wealth they help produce?

This structure of the speculative, banking HIV cell lines for future research, offers an alternative to biocapital's futurity. Here, it is not the blood/virus that is made into waste so that it can enter value chains but the body in which it previously lived. Unlike stem cell banking, the future here is not a bodily future, the individuation of the proper subject but becomes organized as a market future—the disappeared worker returns as a commodity, or at least its potentiality. This speculation is primarily organized by industry needs, perhaps with an attention to a generic common good. Its concern is not the person from which the cell lines came but an abstracted consumer to come—the subject of capital's futurity. Further, the cost of keeping a virus alive for many decades is sizable, yet it is displaced from industry onto the NIH. The state manages the economic risk, while the private sector benefits from its disinvestment in the virus (and its replication) as the body is vanished beyond a few scant notes.

Truvada, the brand name for emtricitabine and tenofovir disoproxil fumarate, a combination of two medications, has radically recalibrated the place of HIV in its adjacent communities with access. Truvada, commonly called pre-exposure prophylaxis, or PrEP, is a pill taken daily that has a strong efficacy for preventing HIV replication if a high enough level of the medication is maintained in the body. While the CDC holds the patent, Gilead Sciences is currently the sole provider of PrEP in the United States. With the market price for the medication typically about $2,000 a month, Gilead's profits, market projections, and capitalization have exploded.[63] Like almost all pharmaceutical innovation in the U.S., the initial science on the efficacy of PrEP was funded almost entirely by public money; this configuration, which often lives under the dreadful name of public-private partnership, again spreads the risk to the public and hoards the profits for private industry—neoliberalism's jouissance. Unfolded, this partnership, and the biocapitalist regime it represents, ensures that the claim to life, even if only a speculative gesture, can exclusively be articulated through the unfreedom of free markets. While a "cure" for HIV would, in effect, decrease Gilead's market share, PrEP not only allows for the capture of those who are HIV+ but has transformed all those who are not into consumers—market saturation as a way of life.[64]

Because of PrEP's prohibitive cost, many of those most impacted by HIV, namely young Black, Indigenous, and/or Latinx trans women and MSM as well as IV drug users, have limited, if any, access. The ongoing legacies of colonial medical disinformation swirls with transphobic epidemiology and the homicidal stigmatization of IV drug use that results in the uninterruption of the pandemic for some, while the *end of AIDS* is habitually proclaimed for others. In a lethal irony, it is the logic of the patent—the argument that innovation is only spurred by the security of private property—that replicates the virus and its differential death. Put plainly, the HIV cells of those taken without their informed consent or compensation, housed in the NIH reagent bank and also laboring in publicly funded labs that produced PrEP, are withheld from the same populations, and perhaps the same people from whom they were initially extracted. The theft of their viral labor helped grow Gilead's incalculable wealth, which includes $36.2 billion in earnings off Truvada alone.[65]

While the reproduction of the worker is necessary under a capitalist order, here not only is the worker's life (in the traditional sense) unnecessary, that they possess a deadly, if untreated, virus is what brings them into the realm of valuation. Of course, with the transnational division of labor, the necessity of the reproduction of a laborer is much contested. However, here, as in the case of Henrietta Lacks, necrocapital names when death is the precondition of captured value. This is not to suggest that necrocapital is in opposition to, or totally divergent from, the general deathworlds that are racial capitalism's biopolitical functions. However, immanent in these shifting conditions is also a way to think beyond the categories of ownership and inclusion as the remedy to exploitation's spread. Returning to the grisly scene of insurers that sold policies on enslaved people, the holder might gain more from a slave's death than their continued labor. It is this co-presence that I'm attempting to apprehend, an economy of immanence and rupture where racial capitalism serves death to many so that it might provide life to markets.[66]

The virology of HIV might best illustrate this form of generativity where the reproduction of death is the precondition of accumulation's extension. The immune system enables the futurity of our bodily possibility and serves as material defense against threat; however, the RNA replication (reproduction) of HIV breaks down cells and causes their death. To this end, the labor of HIV (growth of viral load) is dependent on the death of the body's immune system and, if it's not stopped, the body it is living in as well. Although it is uncertain as to what causes the death of CD4 cells, the most accepted hypothesis is "activation-induced cell death by apoptosis."[67] This suicidal viral logic is dependent on the reproduction of death for its flourishing; the more HIV replicates, the more its capacity to do so is diminished. HIV's speculated future is also the cell's imminent end; reproduction = death.

Captured Value

One response to the violence of stolen labor might be to reenter one's own labor power (HIV replication) into the commodity chains and demand wages for cell work. Another might be, at least at the level of the rhetorical, to collectivize laboring commodities toward a proletarianization of blood. Yet taking control of the means of production, not unlike lifting the blood ban, might do little if the meaning of blood, as among the motors of exploitation, is not, too, confronted. Faced with the enormity of history and that history's repetition, prescription feels already failed. Yet the ongoing legacies of those whose blood lives beyond them gives us a way of thinking with, if not yet forging a shared struggle against necrocapitalism's inevitability.

On October 11, 1992, ACT UP (AIDS Coalition to Unleash Power) vowed to "bring AIDS home" as they staged a political funeral whose target was the unending silence, spoken as inaction, of the U.S. government, and specifically George H. W. Bush's administration. The direct action was organized during, and in accompanied contestation to, an exhibition of the NAMES Project's AIDS Memorial Quilt in Washington, DC. Members of ACT UP felt the quilt gave cover to a racist, ableist, and homophobic culture that might have more emotional attachment to the quilt as object than to the struggle to make it stop growing. While powerful to witness, the quilt, for many AIDS activists, sentimentalized the genocide in the warm familiarity of tactile comfort, and in turn deflated rage through the privatization of collective harm. Further, those who helped plan the action believed that the quilt aestheticized the pandemic for the pleasure of straight life, in effect making cozy the gory devastation of mass death.[68]

"Bringing the dead to your door, we won't take it anymore," the chant beat-matched the thundering drums of the marchers, rhythmically driving the otherwise somber procession. Toward the front, a row of mourners formed, armed with metal urns and wooden boxes raised in defiant irreverence, accompanied by thousands more behind them. Slowly they streamed from the steps of the Capitol building, forming a river of sorrow that collected its edges in a swell of anguish. As they reached the White House fence, those carrying ashes diverged from the crowd in organized hope of arriving before the DC police flanking them on horseback. Screams broke the quiet choreography as protesters rushed the fence while others formed a human barricade—a living wall of loss intent on protecting the pallbearers from the swinging clubs of the mounted cops. Vessels were hurriedly uncapped, and plastic bags of ground bones were ripped open in a frantic gesture to complete the task before the still advancing police. The powdery gray remains of looted people, the ephemera of lifetime's end, took flight in a gust of wind that scattered them onto the green of the lawn. Arms stretched long between bars emptying vials of compressed life, the cathartic shattering of loss's rehearsal. Once emptied, containers were launched over the iron gates and collected on the grass. The ritual ended with riotous mourners pressed against the bars, some covered in ash, creating a pile of the still living. Entangled together, they wailed with miserable rage to announce their devastation and the arrival of the dead (figure 2.1).[69]

Here, it is the bioterror of revenge, not toward expanded death but in hopes of death's end, where the symbolics of blood are returned as a direct action against the murderous state. A general strike of the dispossessed—a stoppage, by way of a refusal to remain entombed. As artist and activist David Wojnarowicz, who died from AIDS a few months before the action, and whose words helped bring it into being, wrote,

> I imagine what it would be like if friends had a demonstration each time a lover or a friend or a stranger died of AIDS. I imagine what it would be like if, each time a lover, friend or stranger died of this disease, their friends, lovers or neighbors would take the dead body and drive with it in a car a hundred miles an hour to washington d.c. and blast through the gates of the white house and come to a screeching halt before the entrance and dump their lifeless form on the front

FIGURE 2.1. ACT UP Ashes Action, 1992. Per the request of their loved ones who passed, members of ACT UP brought their ashes to Washington to throw on the lawn of George H. W. Bush's White House. © Meg Handler.

steps. It would be comforting to see those friends, neighbors, lovers and strangers mark time and place and history in such a public way.[70]

The Ashes Action not only marked time and place, it also interrupted the mechanization of labor as benign and inevitable, by returning the bodies to the scene of their mystification, or, as it was for Wojnarowicz, to the house of their executioner.[71]

The incalculability of this violence, its magnitude and ruthlessness, demands a response that can confront such intensity so that life might extend beyond endless confrontation. Yet, if we believe that entering into contractual relationality with those organizing the profits produced by HIV cell lines will offer us little more than exploitation's continuance, then what is to be done? From the scorched plantations of Haiti to the scattered ashes of ACT UP, the burn recalls the will of collective revolt. Even if the Ashes Action was not able to inaugurate an anti-necrocapitalist present, it continues to stand as testament to forms of disruption that might guide us beyond the misery of our living end. As a protester who spread her father's remains put it, "We have to keep doing this so there are not more boxes of ashes."[72]

The laboring commodity, the deadly formulation that sedimented its presences in the New World as the enslavement of Black people, both relied upon and forcibly redistributed the bio-ontologization of race and sexuality—a circle of interminable death and value. An inheritor of this continuous past, blood captures, as an object of transference, the fantasies and phobias of a world built on racial capitalism's incorporative technologies. It is not that each iteration of blood's meaning is identical but together, they congeal a partial view where inaction and assault meet in the bathroom stalls of Pulse, on the lawn of the White House, in the storage of reagent banks, and in the scene of AIDS. Reading blood as a racial supplement and sexual signifier tells the otherwise absent stories of valuation—a heretical analysis that knows communal life mandates nothing short of capitalism's demise. It also forges, as Kia LaBeija theorizes, a "positivity that can only be understood by blood"—the deproletarianization of the bled. Or, put another way, perhaps capital is dead labor, but dead labor can still strike.

> If the state is ready to kill to
> defend itself from the black, sexual,
> trans body brought before it, do we
> want to be somebody before the
> state, or no-body against it?
> —*Denise Ferreira da Silva*

With the height of trans visibility
has also been the height of trans
violence and trans murders.
—*CeCe McDonald*

"*He-she*, come here!" Defiantly looking
away with her arms and legs crossed, Duanna Johnson refused the hail of
Bridges McRae, an officer with the Memphis Police Department. "*Faggot*, I'm
talking to you!" McRae's demand grew with angered force against Johnson's
resistance. Duanna Johnson had been arrested earlier that evening under "suspicion of prostitution," a charge often levied against Black trans women who
dare to exist in public. On that February night in 2008, in the Shelby County
Jail's intake area, she remained seated in silent protest, refusing to become the
subject, which is to say the object, of Officer McRae's prosaic rage.[1]

Framed within the frame, a closed-circuit television (CCTV) captured the
event. The high-angle shot opens with Johnson sitting in a chair a few feet behind McRae. The silent image shows him standing with his uniformed back

turned as he fills out paperwork at the booking window. The low resolution pixellates the unfolding image as the continuous long shot mediates the frame. More impressionistic than high definition, the image surveils as it disappears. Two other uniformed officers casually talk behind Johnson, while a third waits in line behind them. The camera pictures through its still gaze a tableau vivant of capture: the everydayness of administrative violence.

Enraged by Johnson's audacity, McRae turned away from the window and walked a few steps over to where she remained seated. He reached to snatch her face or possibly her neck, sending her into a fast lean backward in an attempt to escape his grasp. The commotion broke the still of the room and jolted the person sitting behind Johnson out of their seat; it also caught the attention of the other officers. McRae retreated a few inches and readied himself for the real attack. He slipped handcuffs around his leather-gloved right hand, cocked his arm back, using physics and the force of history to ensure the most ruthless swing possible. Aroused by the unfolding cruelty, a crowd of officers moved in closer to get an unobstructed view. James Swain, a fellow officer, entered the frame and circled around behind Johnson. He then pinned her shoulders to the chair, restraining her so she was left with no course of defense from McRae's blows.

After a few more strikes, Johnson's skin gave way and a stream of blood ran down her face. Fearing her suspended death was about to materialize, Johnson sprang to her feet and started swinging her arms like a windmill in self-defense. Seconds later, she returned to her seat, but McRae again punched her in the face. Tired from the attack, or perhaps bored, McRae then reached for the pepper spray that was holstered at his belt and shot directly into Johnson's eyes, nose, and mouth at close range. The cumulative pain collapsed her body as McRae forced his knee into her spine, grinding her further into the tile floor as he cuffed her hands behind her back, celebrating his victory over her ravaged body.

He stood and walked back toward the booking window, leaving Johnson bleeding from head wounds and gassed, as her tortured and bound body flailed in contempt. In a gust of adrenal agony, still shackled, Johnson worked her way back into a chair, unable to escape the toxicity of her own flesh. Disoriented and traumatized, she again stood and paced back and forth with her hands cuffed behind her back, unable to clear the weaponized chemicals and blood from her eyes, nose, and mouth.

The footage ends as an officer with medical supplies examines McRae in the foreground while a nurse enters and walks the length of the room, which is also the length of the frame, passing the still bleeding Johnson and ignoring her to attend to the officer. Unbothered, four officers and the nurse talk with McRae in the foreground of the frame, possibly rehearsing the drama in celebration. Johnson, now in the background, again sits in the row of chairs, just a few seats over from where the beating began. Rhythmically rocking back and forth, she remains manacled and bleeding, still soaked in chemical weapons, with no medical attention, inhabiting the slow death of carceral life.[2]

After the initial beating, Duanna Johnson, along with her lawyer, appeared on local news stations to publicize the abuse that was captured on the CCTV. While Johnson's stated wish for the public to see the tape unties some knots in our viewing, that watching is always an accumulative practice persists. And while I return to the scene and the testimony as an act of solidarity with her, within the generalized field of anti-Black and anti-trans violence there is no space of purity or epistemic escape. In other words, to reproduce the attack by way of its narrativization, to view the video, or to conceal its existence—all bind us to the scene and its repetitious afterlife. How, then, might we account for, or more precisely how might we be accountable to, Duanna Johnson as we consume her image? Left unseen, the video might help mask our own complicity in her attack—its nonspectacle. Here both viewing and not viewing the tape are bound up in the practice of consuming Johnson's image through the dialectics of incorporation and refusal. Rather than knowing in advance, the trouble of representation is a trouble we must attempt to inhabit without the pleasure of assumed innocence. To this end, I choose to narrate it, to bring it yet again into representation, because staying in the space of the visceral—the intolerable fragility of flesh—is perhaps the only place one can dwell when the ethical offers nothing else.[3]

The image, of course, does not begin or end with the tape. Taking the stand in his own defense, Officer McRae claimed the beating was in self-defense and necessary to restrain Johnson because she was "completely out of control" and that her movements made him "startled and scared."[4] The self-defense strategy McRae's attorney constructed was built on Johnson's *inappropriate* physicality as a Black trans woman. During the trial, both McRae and his defense attorney Frank Trapp exclusively referred to Johnson as "he"—rehearsing the "he-she" of his initial assault, the original trigger that, against the enormity of history, Johnson fiercely refused. This misgendering, along with using her deadname, which was not Duanna, held Johnson in the assumptive space of equal justice as truth's negation. There, its arbitrators, including the police and lawyers, produced her as not simply deceitful, a charge one might be able to recover from, but their calculated misnaming and misgendering transformed her into the sign of deception itself. When asked about this by the federal prosecutor, McRae responded, "It's not important. I was just referring to him as he."[5] These linguistic tactics worked to buttress the ways trans women are understood through an assumed danger to the stability of the gender binary, as not only a threat to the order of law but to the very ideas of truth. These *insignificant details*, as McRae might have it, are among the ways transmisogyny's carnivorous anti-Blackness becomes universal.

Even with the incriminating testimony of a fellow officer and the surveillance tape, on the last day of the trial the jury reported that it could not reach a verdict. Concerned with the time and expense the state had already spent, the judge administered an Allen charge to the jurors, ordering them back into deliberation over the weekend. When they returned the following Monday, the jury reported that they were still deadlocked, unable or unwilling to agree on the charges against McRae. In other words, they could not reach consensus on what the video showed; the filmic evidence of McRae's vicious attack faded out of the frame as a disarticulated vision of ambivalence and confusion bewitched the jurors. Thus, the judge officially called a mistrial, reaffirming that the attack was not only legal but also constituted, as limit, the mandate of the law.

Wanting to avoid the cost of another trial and the thin possibility of a guilty verdict, McRae eventually pled guilty in August 2010. His plea deal was for the charges stemming from the beating of Johnson and for tax evasion. On his tax form on file with the Memphis Police Department, he had claimed ninety-nine dependents, resulting in his never paying income tax while he was employed as a police officer. The sentence for both the beating and the tax evasion, which remained joined in the charges, was two years in a minimum-security federal work camp, two years of probation, and a fine of $200. While a guilty verdict would not have offered justice, as it would have only helped build the legitimacy of the practice of imprisonment—a hard lesson that prison abolition asks us to unlearn—reading the impossibility of a conviction is one way to measure what was seen and what was obscured in the very act of viewing by the jury and McRea's other supporters.[6]

Testimony from Duanna Johnson at the trial might have helped stall the frames that pictured her as a force McRae needed to defend himself against. Or perhaps the sentimentality produced by a survivor's words would have, at least momentarily, suspended the white supremacy of the visual and the gender normativity of its syntax so that she might be understood as something other than the twinned curse of danger and disposability. If Johnson were to give voice to the flatness of her image and its accompanying description, and flesh to the fear and pain she survived that night, the jury might have seen otherwise. Yet tragically, Johnson was shot dead on November 9, 2008, just five months after the beating. Not far from the shores of the Mississippi, in North Memphis, her body was found on an otherwise deserted Hollywood Avenue. According to initial reports, she was shot "execution style" in the head at close range and left to bleed out, alone, on the cold pavement.[7]

Subjection's Form

With Duanna Johnson gone, the tape remains as interdiction and inauguration, where aesthetics and violence live on even in death. In the wake of this still unfolding brutality, how might we radically misread, to the point of exhaustion, the visual grammar of the footage to understand both the kinds of force it represents and to work against the seeming inevitability of its reoccurrence? Or, how does the afterlife of the tape both memorialize her beating and subsequent death while also concealing her murder?

The execution of Johnson on that November night should be understood as the tape's extra-diegetic final scene; the unfolding of a narrative structure that is not simply *racist* and *transphobic*, terms too adjacent to name such organized liquidation. Indeed, as I've argued throughout this book, understanding perpetual attack exclusively through the figure of individual is the mechanism by which violence proliferates. This is not to say that the individual officers involved in her beating should be exonerated by the common cover of protocol, or the fiction that also lives under the name of policy. However, if we end at singularity, we, too, have ensured there will be yet another beating tape by refusing to eradicate the conditions of its reproduction.[8]

The video of Johnson's beating continues to haunt because it interrupts, as affirmation, a visual culture replete with such references. The shock of the tape is in its total familiarity; the gap between what we assume to be spectacular and quotidian forms of destruction is always dissipating—revealing disorder's labyrinthian consistency. To this end, tracing the history of moving images is also a way of charting the instantiation of globalized anti-Blackness and the parameters of its gendered mandates. While we must attend to the racist or otherwise phobic depictions that have compromised visual culture from the lynching photograph of the medium's inception to our contemporary digital times, if we stay there we will continue to struggle within a regime that will never offer relief.[9] After all, racist content would have little power if its form were not structured similarly. Or, put differently, we must insist that the filmic is always in relationship to the entire apparatus of viewing—its formalistic qualities, historical referents, techniques of production, dissemination, exhibition, as well as the psychical formations that build the social as such. The image is not simply viewed by us, it also produces the viewer in the process—the image looks back.[10] By reading with the tape of Johnson's beating, we can see the ways optics, as that which both includes and exceeds narrative, produces Johnson as the "no-body" da Silva asked us to think. Yet this no-body is not simply a negative image but the congealment, by way of form and through film's specificity, of the negation of the human. The no-body is forced to withstand the projection of modernity's violence but is also a (non)position from which a counterattack is launched.[11]

Frantz Fanon's often-cited passage detailing his own experience watching a film in a Paris theater sketches these multiple spaces of seeing and being seen that establish the visual as a racialized milieu. Fanon states, "I cannot go to a film without seeing myself. I wait for me. In the interval, just before the film starts, I wait for me. The people in the theater are watching me, examining me, waiting for me."[12] Fanon suggests that the anticipation of Blackness in the cinema is imbued with a form of anti-Blackness that is not only seen but also sensed. Even before the film begins, the racialized gaze is there, constituting him in ruinous anticipation. Stalked by the image to come, he in turn awaits its arrival. Fanon's scheme expands the time of the film, meaning it does not begin or end with the rolling of images. Furthermore, Fanon moves us away from assuming that the most vicious forms of colonial racism appear through depiction alone. It is not that the ways race and gender become tropological in and through film is unimportant, but that they come to figure as both the beginning and the end precludes an analysis that is much more unsettling.

Expanded outward, Fanon's viewing experience becomes an occasion to ask whether there is something about the moving image, as a historically situated medium, that finds its seemingly universal appeal in its racial continuity—its ability to confirm, by way of anxiety's authorization, the fantasies of a racist world. Or is film, beyond representational content, also dependent on a racialized structure that always awaits its viewer, as Fanon was anticipated, in the darkness of the theater? And if this is the case, what remains for the possibility of a Black trans visual culture that attempts to depict—as clandestine disruption—in the interval and outside the image?[13]

Fanon's insights occasion, or perhaps demand, an attention to the psychoanalytics of the moving image. The movie screen and its prosthetics are also spaces for reading with the unconscious as the condensation of the social that it coheres. As a projection of fantasy and fantasy's projection, film becomes a privileged, if not overdetermined, place to think the psyche and the image. The questions of subjectivity, and subjectivity's impossibility, arrive as film becomes a transfer object where the unconscious is not simply represented but also continually reworked. If we are to read the tape of Duanna Johnson's beating beyond, and indeed against, its indexical qualities, then, at least provisionally, considering film as medium becomes another way to ask: What did the jury see?[14]

The Johnson tape and Fanon's observations lay bare not only the force with which the filmic can capture the viewer but also that the image is always a trap. Not least because of anything unique about the specific image, but there are procedures of attachment that make looking pleasurable, even in, and perhaps ultimately in, the displeasure of watching. Sigmund Freud's thoughts on fetishism, as a structure of libidinal aim that allows us to both know and not know, to feel the terror of loss and the comfort of the denial of that same dread, is one way to name the cinematic mechanisms that compel us toward moving images. For Freud, the fetish is a stand-in for the unassimilable sight of sexual difference, which is also the instability of the world experienced as difference itself. The fetish appears as, and in the place of, the maternal phallus, the signifier of difference and its concealment, which returns us to the imaginary space of wholeness at the threshold of subjectivity. For Freud, the fetish becomes an object that protects the viewer from the unbearable *truth* of sexual difference— the visualization of father/not father. In other words, the fetish object becomes a veil so that the child does not have to face the fright of sexual difference and the possibility of castration. The origins of the psychic topography he lays out, also called subjectivity, beginning with the fear of castration as the mark of sexual difference, could be read, at least retroactively, as a second-order displacement. This first displacement, which we might say for Freud was the reality of what he called sexual difference, and what we might call gender, is a stand-in for the aggregation of power, and not necessarily any identification or anatomy. This is not to suggest that Freud specifically, or psychoanalysis at large, should be rescued from its binary gender and colonial grounding. But read otherwise, Freud offers a capacious understanding of gender, which is most often misrecognized under the sign of "sexual difference" as coming into representation in and as power and its differentiation. Both the "disavowal and the affirmation" of that displacement, the structure of the fetish, is not simply an inappropriate object choice but, returning to the case of the cinematic, helps us name the externalization of desire and its incorporation as racialized and gendering processes—it memorializes loss while covering its tracks.[15]

Teasing out the work of subjectivity, Jacques Lacan later suggested, "If the phallus is a signifier then it is in the place of the Other that the subject gains access to it."[16] Here, the splitting of the subject, via the desire for and the desire to be, suggests a doubling that, following Fanon, organizes difference under colonial modernity. This doubling—this being in the place of the Other—sutures the viewer to the film, allowing us to become with the scene. The pleasure of the cinematic arises from our inability to separate ourselves from the image while knowing, in the same moment, that the image's fate is not our own—the comfort of affirmation and disavowal.[17]

This is also the basic structure of anti-Black gendered normativity, or what might be called subjectivity as a production of the colonial encounter. The affirmation, at least on the level of the unconscious, that whiteness both prevails and is protected, not exclusively in the narrative structure (although the Hays codes, at least in the U.S. context, ensured this) but also through the psychic ordering of the scene returns the viewer to this fixity.[18] Further, while there is a kind of racial fetishism that delineates the ways people of color in general, and Black people in particular, are depicted in film, that process, I'm suggesting, is dependent upon a first-order racial fetishism that announces itself as silence in the mechanism of suture and the pleasure of watching. This analysis of the structure of looking, following Fanon, helps us understand how inclusivity, or the appearance of the respectable minoritarian images, is not enough to disrupt cinema's force.[19]

To be clear, psychoanalysis is useful here as an amplifier of normative culture, and not because it offers a cure. It illuminates how the myths that are the foundations of psychoanalysis (and their extraction as analysis) leave us, always, in the colonial context. Fetishism, then, is not a perversion in need of adjustment but a tool to read how its normative grounding is dependent upon its claim to the ordinary (which, as we know from Freud, is also another projection). As an organizing principle of modernity, inasmuch as it helps maintain racist and gender normativity, at least on the battleground of the unconscious, fetishism, then, far from being an anomaly, is any- and everywhere. What's of use here is its structure, which I keep returning to in various ways throughout this book: inclusion/exclusion, presence/absence, limit/outside, visibility/disappearance. All these pairings name not a binary opposition as we might assume but the methodology of normative power's expansive incorruption.[20]

While I have perhaps moved too quickly against the gender essentialism of Freud and his readers, such infidelity is necessary if we are to open these theories beyond themselves. For example, the slippage between the phallus and the penis (through lack, or lack's negation) as that which animates the fetish has given room for the critical insights of feminist film theorists who argue the "maleness" of the viewing position of, at least, Hollywood cinema. Yet what turns differently if we no longer assume the direct connection between "maleness" and penis? What becomes of the castration complex and identification if the racialized gendering it is assumed to produce is further undone? This is not to suggest a fundamental break with the analysis that seeks to name the ways non-trans women are situated within the cinematic. Indeed, perhaps their indictments become stronger, yet differently organized, if we are to focus on the category of gender that accounts for the idea of "man" and "woman," but does not assume it to be exhaustive. Or, asked another way, what becomes of the castration complex when it is not the origin of anxiety but desire?[21]

Feminist film criticism has well argued the "impossibility" of (assumedly white non-trans) women in film as either makers of meaning in the image or as a viewing position from its outside. Turning attention to trans women further complicates the question of the moving image, not because she slips past the trap of "women in film," but because she reminds the viewer, even other trans viewers, of the elaborate force that compels her consistent disappearance. Here I'm not attempting to suggest that a complete or unified theory of a racialized trans analysis might uproot what we already know about the moving image. Rather, while much important work has already been done to consider the impacts of the viewing position of the spectator, what seems operative, and what is truly an impasse that must be confronted, is how we are systematically produced as such. Returning to the structure of the moving image, its raced and gendered contours, is vital if we are to understand how Johnson's image signifies in relation to its formalistic qualities.[22]

On the phallus, Lacan further adjudicates,

> Let us say that these relations will revolve around a being and a having, which, because they refer to a signifier, the phallus, have the contradictory effect of on the one hand lending reality to the subject in the signifier, and on the other making unreal the relations to be signified.
>
> This follows from the intervention of an "appearing" which gets substituted for the "having" so as to protect it on one side and to mask its lack on the other.[23]

Lacan's rereading of Freud places the phallus into the system of signification. Thus, Lacan helps us pivot from an analysis of the unconscious and toward the cinematic through the interplay between being and having, which is mediated as "appearing" and "having." Lacan offers a recasting of the ways seeing is always also a form of possession, pointing to how the incorporation of viewing is central to the reorganization of the subject. This destabilizing of difference is manifest, in the first instance, on the level of the scopic (appearing). Yet in order to bare this moment, the sight of difference is brought into the subject as negation. The appearing is incorporated as protection and also to "mask its lack."[24] This double move of the phallus, as a structure of exhibition and concealment, which we should not conflate with any particular body part or gender, is also an occasion to read race (the disavowal of structuring power under a white world) as not simply supplemental to the psyche, which is to also say the process of viewing (appearing) but indeed, helps illustrate its constitutive presence. In other words, fetishism sutures us to the image via disavowal and displacement, and this fetishism is always racialized as it is gendered in ways that exceed the binary but also renders this expansion invisible.

On the psychoanalytics of the image Christian Metz suggests, "Thanks to the principle of a *moving cutting off*, thanks to the changes of framing between shots (or within a shot: tracking, panning, characters moving into or out of the frame, and so forth), cinema literally *plays* with the terror and the pleasure of fetishism, with its combination of desire and fear."[25] To this end, the anticipatory gaze is comforted from its fear of racial difference—Fanon's "phobogenic object,"[26] or what Hillary Clinton called the Black "super-predator."[27] As loss and reconciliation, the filmic produces Blackness, through form and not simply narrative, as perpetual threat while it simultaneously offers remedy, by way of white coherence. Thus the filmic both produces and mitigates white anxiety. This is not to suggest that film is the only condition of and mirror for anti-Blackness but a reminder of the moving image's dialectical relation to the social that it both constructs and is constructed by.[28]

The visuality that Fanon describes, and I've here attempted to expand, is also enforced by a gender normativity that presides over its own organized inconsistencies. Under a visual regime, binary gender as a force of intelligibility also sutures the viewer—by way of threat and survival, disgust and pleasure—to the suspicious gaze that produces gender nonnormativity (trans and beyond) as a caustic riddle that must be feared and fanatically resolved. In other words, the fetish saves the viewer not from the horror of binary sexual difference but from the violence saved for those who resist the fantasy. Indeed, where anti-Blackness and gender normativity meet, as in the footage of Duanna Johnson, the architecture reveals itself. However, there need not be a Black trans person on screen for anti-Blackness and anti-transness to be operational. The image bleeds off the screen, producing its spectator with every frame, providing not only gendered security as the demand of the white imago but pleasure too, in the sovereign fantasy of psychic and corporal completion.

The Camera and the Police

While I have been concerned with the filmic these assessments must be brought more fully to bear, and perhaps reworked, to weigh upon the specific genre of the Johnson image—the surveillance tape. If the psychic power of narrative cinema resides in its ability to suture the viewer to the image, which I've argued is a process dependent upon anti-Blackness and gender normativity that creates a phantasmatic bind compelling the viewer toward the scene, how might the formalism of surveillance work differently?

Returning to Fanon's passage, the temporality of film is not simply the chronologic measure of change caught between the opening and closing scenes, it's also in the interval and after the scene ends. Stretching the time of the image, and the image of time, allows us to read the murder of Duanna Johnson as the narrative conclusion of the CCTV footage. Further, while Fanon was writing specifically about the cinematic, surveillance as genre, its capacity to formulate worlds and the people that inhabit them, must also be addressed. While analyzing narrative film, Gilles Deleuze was interested in how temporality and fear become organized by what he called a time-image. For Deleuze a time-image is the collapsing of past, present, and future that "makes time frightening and inexplicable."[29] While he was talking about simultaneity in narrative cinema, which was also dependent on the cutting of film, the time-image here might help us understand the specific genre of the tape where past and future are remade not through cutting but by the calmness of the present. Or, if the temporality of the Johnson tape is not dependent on the time-image and its claim to change because it's a continuous shot, perhaps for Johnson there is no moment other than the time of violence. Uncut, the image never allows for her escape.[30]

Fanon's insistence that the time of the image does not align with the opening scene of the film and Deleuze's time-image illustrate the deadly semiotics that await in the interval of both the structure of the visual and the assembly of life outside the theater. To stretch the image beyond its time-code, rather than diminishing the transformative work of the cinematic, compounds the force with which it builds and destroys worlds. This is to say that the filmic is always attempting to contain that which seeps beyond its frames. This blurring of spaces, marked as boundary but acting as gateway, is also an entry point, like dreams, where the unconscious and the image converge.

Surveillance is a technology of anticipation. It's constantly capturing—awaiting a plot to fill its frames and to bring narrative coherence to its image. Surveillance, then, is the gaze one can never escape—the panopticon of *protection*. Indeed, the everywhereness of surveillance is countered by claims to privacy as the definitive attribute of the rights-bearing subject and his demand to go unseen. However, against this belief that privacy is (or at least ought to be) afforded to *proper* subjects, Lauren Berlant reminds us that "there never were free sovereign subjects of politics or the market, but rather monitored subjects who are permitted to pass by and get on with things if their comportment does not go awry."[31] Our relationship to surveillance technology has grown, and radically shifted, yet Berlant's rejection that we were once sovereign subjects outside of administrative monitoring helps us track the expectation of freedom from sight to that of always being seen. Indeed, where critiques of surveillance do surface, they are more often than not organized under a claim of privacy—the demand of liberal democracy from the Fourth Amendment to facial-recognition bans.[32] Now, through the conflations of technology and safety, these calls for privacy reappear as a demand, even for those who might imagine themselves as sovereign subjects, for intensified surveillance as security's adjudication. If the right to privacy is but another displacement intent to protect the idea of freedom for those who have never experienced themselves as anything other, there are those—namely Black, Brown, Indigenous, disabled, trans/queer, and/or houseless—who can never exist out of sight. What differentiates them is how this monitoring has and continues to discipline, returning us to the knot of power's localization we misname identity. Or, put differently, the security camera might see us all, but the meaning of that image is registered in and as an old/new regime of looking. This capturing has the peculiar ability, as it did with the McRae trial, to exonerate some while condemning others.[33]

As Simone Browne makes irreducible, "The historical formation of surveillance is not outside of the historical formation of slavery."[34] With this history and its living present, surveillance footage now exists as a culture of endless innovation where technological precision is mirrored as racial and gendered subjugation. As genera, in terms of both the unconscious and the juridical, surveillance footage claims an unmediated relationship to transparency, and by extension to the Truth. Media literacy and legal pedagogy converge where surveillance footage is taken up as nothing less than an exacting index of fact.[35]

Surveillance footage, the visual regime of our time, operates as *fact* by remaking history (something that is assumed to have happened) and present (something that is happening); the distance between the past event is collapsed into the current moment, producing it as an undeniable event, the unfolding of real time. Not unlike looking out of a window, even as, and perhaps because of its resolution, obstructed view, and bad framing, the view is rendered in the immediacy of the nonaesthetic. This also returns as an aesthetics of banality where we dwell, trapped in our incapacity to believe that things might be any different. Surveillance, then, also names the view of and from everyday misery and the pragmatism that prohibits us from seeing otherwise that locks us in the dread we already know. If, as Deleuze argued, it is narrative cinema's cuts that makes time confusing, it's the unedited consistency of surveillance footage that makes it continuous but also uncanny.

The evidentiary weight of surveillance footage further compels, as it did in McRae's trial, through the scene of its exhibition and its ability to confirm what is already *known*. Screened in the theater of the court, McRae was recast as a heroic protagonist who was protecting the audience from the terror of Johnson's existence. While surveillance footage is typically understood as nonnarrative, it is nonetheless animated by the structure of the cinematic discussed earlier in this chapter. It adheres, as in it resides within an order of signs that brings narrative to the image. For example, when its claim solidifies that of the state, or another institutional force, it consolidates through the rehearsal of its own myths. Yet the question is not how an image satiates normativity's palate, as that has been well discussed. Rather, we must attend to how, in Johnson's case, for example, the jury was able to view the footage of the ruthless beating and chemical attack and arrive at truth's double—an inability to see against the state. When the jury saw Officer McRae beat the chained and seated Johnson, that image disintegrated and its truth returned to the viewer as the image of Johnson's attack and McRae self-defense.

These formalistic qualities of surveillance, written through the historical present of its deployment, construct it as a pedagogy of suspect looking. This is to say, it aligns the viewer, at the level of the unconscious, with the omniscience of police power via its longing for the sight of *criminality* at the edge of each successive frame. The ordering power that is the function of policing, as that which makes the law in and as its enforcement, also names the kind of seeing that surveillance produces. Its continuity is maintained through the persistent specter that is, in the Johnson beating tape, Black trans criminality. While once an obscure form of visual culture, the surveillant gaze, through the propagation of personal cameras from phones and computers to doorbells, might today be the primary viewing position we inhabit.[36] This is not to suggest that surveillance footage, like that of Duanna Johnson, escapes forms of identification but rather than an individual person seen on screen, the viewer of the footage, at least in the first instance, identifies outside the mise-en-scène and with and as the eye of authority. In a nonconsensual sense, we are sutured to surveillance footage, as we are to all moving images, through a fetishistic attachment that affirms the conditions of the social; yet the point of entry is repositioned with and as the very act of looking while witnessing everything and nothing—the spectator sees as the state.

From the acquittal of the officers who beat Rodney King, executed Tony Mc-Dade, and punched Duanna Johnson, the image need not be of the police to do their work. In all three cases, the surveillance footage (handheld VHS, body cam, and CCTV) showed something that could not be seen. In each, a Black person was attacked or murdered by police, beyond even liberal explanations of just cause. Yet the juries in each, and I would argue the social at large, was unable to read the scene as anything other than the necessary self-preservation of normativity, here operating under the name of the police, which rendered Blackness, as officer McRae argued, "completely out of control." Here, reading genera and the gaze as technologies of knowing and instruments of consolidation help us move from the racism of specific images to the structure of visuality.

Until now, I have labored to make a general argument about the racial antagonism of the moving image, and by extension surveillance footage. How and if gender reconfigures these arguments remains a question. In his consideration of the cinematic, Frank Wilderson objects to Judith Butler's often-cited passage that "gender is the repeated stylization of the body, a set of repeated acts within a highly rigid regulatory frame that congeal over time to produce the appearance of substance, of a natural sort of being."[37] Butler here is suggesting a theory of gender that is nonessentialized and only appears as coherent because of its repetitious performance. In response, Wilderson argues, "There is no such narrative as political genealogy and there is no such entity as a 'gender[ed] ontology' unless the subject under discussion is not Black."[38] This impossibility, for Wilderson through a reading of Hortense Spillers, hinges on the transubstitution of body to flesh via the hold of the slave ship. Or, as Wilderson states, "For the body's reification of gender to constitute an essential grammar of suffering there must first be a body there."[39] Here anti-

Blackness is a priori the very idea of gender—the effect of the slave trade as ongoing event whose end might never come negates not simply binary gender but the body, which Wilderson sees as its grammatical prerequisite.

Wilderson's observations function as impediment to the fantasy of white reconciliation, named as agency, by arguing that the condition of slavery prohibits the performativity of gender for those under the sign of Blackness. I agree with him here, and yet what I've been arguing throughout this book is that gender resides, or becomes intelligible in and as a threat, within the very social world that violently confronts its expansion. How, then, do we attend to the differentiation between and among the various ways those rendered flesh are remade as such, or what Patrice Douglass might call "Black gender"?[40] With the endurance of slavery's unfinished abolition, how does gender matter, which is to ask, how does it produce matter given the commodity form's wicked ability to exchange body for flesh?[41]

Reading Spillers somewhat differently, C. Riley Snorton suggests that "captive flesh figures a critical genealogy for modern transness, as chattel persons gave rise to an understanding of gender as mutable and as an amendable form of being."[42] The New World, as the cartographic-historical meeting of chattel slavery and settler colonialism, achieved through the technology of enslavement the "ungendering" of Blackness and the Blackness of ungendering.[43] While perhaps leading in different directions, Wilderson's and Snorton's incisive readings of Spillers converge, by way of expansion, at the impossibility of normative gender (its privileges and impositions) of Black persons.

Indeed, following Snorton's genealogy of transness, that Black trans women experience unique forms and intensities of violence cannot be lost in an attempt to make generalizable either theories of anti-Blackness and/or trans antagonisms. Staying with a Black feminism that argues for the specificity of thinking Blackness and gender as tenuous and yet contingent categories under a modernity that is built, differently, through the exploitation, annihilation, and confinement of both, might offer a way through. With and at times beside this analysis is a collection of emergent and historical interventions, waged at the level of the epistemic, that might be organized under the named Black trans feminism. Which, for Dora Santana, is where the "fugitivity of blackness" and the "unspecified movement of transness"[44] live together. It is within this constellation of thought where we affirm that the assumptive correlation between gender and genitals leads back toward a place of no return.[45]

On the place of Black women under and against chattel slavery, Angela Davis argued that through "the indiscriminate brutal pursuit of profit, the slave woman attained a correspondingly brutal status of equality."[46] Her analysis of the contingent lines of oppression Black women suffered through the institution of slavery suggests both a critical attention to the work of anti-Blackness that, under the demands of racial capitalism, produces a kind of negative equality, which positioned Black women as equally suitable to the disciplinary force Black men were subjected to, not unlike the ungendering that Spillers helps us know. Davis also investigates how sexual violence was uniquely, but not exclusively, saved as a method of torture for enslaved Black women, intent on disciplining them specifically and as proxies for their entire community. Indeed, vital to slavery's continuance, the gender binary was undone, while also re-instrumentalized as a form of sexualized and gendered terror. This is to say that rather than the possibility of being recognized as either a man or woman, slavery rid the gender binary of what slim exceptions might have been afforded to Black women had they any claim to the category of woman, while at the same time accepted them as such, which is to say produced them as objects of white sexual pleasure. Gender, here, did not function as an identification but an imposition thrust upon the flesh of the enslaved as punishment for endurance. It is not that gender in an affirmative sense remained but that sexual violence was a gendering device that appeared at the wish of the master and disappeared once he or she was done.

Here violence and capital collide as a gendered imposition that is anything but a self-description. Extending Davis's observations on the limits of recognition, how might the video of Duanna Johnson augment or disorient this reading? Or, in what ways does Johnson inherit the process of ungendering as negative equality, as near life but also as a "critical genealogy"? McRae's attack, as a representation of the constitutive force Johnson lived and died through, diminished her claims to the protections afforded to white cis womanhood, mirroring the general equivalence, or negative equality, that was normalized through the durational horror of chattel slavery. Yet this argument could be made, via Wilderson, had she not also been a trans woman. I stay with this idea, not in antipathy but as an invitation to connect these points of force so as to not, once again, disappear Duanna Johnson's womanhood, as McRae would have it.

While attendant to the twinning of misogyny and anti-Blackness in the production of the specific degradation that lives under its sign, Davis also elucidates how enslaved Black women operated as militants against their captors and toward the freedom of all Black people. This intervention radically repositions the totality of slavery, as well as tactics of insurgency that might otherwise go missing. Davis does this not through trafficking in liberal claims of uplift nor through the erasure of gender's specificity. Rather, she argues that it was their positioning as Black women, although contingent and provisional, that enabled their covert activities. It was precisely from within zones of reproductive gendered labor, which were also sites of gendered sexual violence (the kitchen, the bedroom, the big house), which occasioned their clandestine attacks that ranged from poisoning and arson to guerrilla warfare.[47]

Here, Davis stays with the ungender of the enslaved, its scales and techniques, while refusing the narrative of a triumphant overcoming and the reconciled humanity of its proper subject, as doing so would rescue the world from slavery's totalizing violence. Gender reenters as an intervention into its disavowal in slavery's epistemologies. For Davis there are gendered directives in the work of ungendering that erupt as moments of recognition but do not adhere to more than their instrumentalization. In other words, with Davis, we can attend to the destructive completeness of a structure of the world, while also gathering the ways that completeness is always incomplete.

Perhaps this is to also say that the arrest, attack, and eventual murder of Duanna Johnson leaves nothing that even the strongest counter-reading might salvage. Yet her initial refusal and windmilling arms mark a form of Black trans persistence that ought not disappear under an assumption that she existed as pure abjection. Following Davis, this is not an attempt to find capacity under the regimes of anti-trans and anti-Blackness, as they collapsed Johnson, like McRae's knee, into the nonspace of permeant attack. Not unlike the position of enslaved women Davis recalibrated, Johnson, too, inherits Black gender as both the parameters of impossibility but also its methodologies of rebellion. It is here, within totality's breakdown, where we might ask, alongside the 2020 Minneapolis uprisings, is another end of the world possible (figure 3.1)?[48]

Clocking

If, for some, gender only functions in a moment of negative equivalence that produces and does not simply echo what is assumed to appear in the social, what, then, might representation offer for a trans visual culture that resides on the side of flourishing? Or, what remains of the possibility of a liberatory moving image if the medium is moored to the conditions of collective detention? As I outlined in the introduction, mainstream LGBT organizations often argue for casting actors whose identities match their roles and, somewhat less common, for funding LGBT directors and crew to control the means of producing their own images. While these are necessary interventions, nevertheless, there

FIGURE 3.1. *Notes on a Burning Kmart,* Minneapolis uprising, 2020.
Photo by Aren Aizura.

is no guarantee that these adjustments will produce anything less dependent or more radically transformative. The representational regime I've been describing is an impasse where a diagnostic is easier to imagine than a corrective by way of speculative prescription. Rather than believing we might be able to "solve" the problem of the image; the charge might be to hold this contraction in the interval of freedom.[49]

As is clear, representation has been produced as the primary site of struggle over diversity in the United States from at least the middle of the last century to our current moment. Positive representation, as a visual common sense, traffics normativity's drive but with a decorative adornment that announces itself as departure. Even with little evidence of its ability to yield a more livable world, positive representation is still offered as the remedy for the years of degraded images that are the history of film. This substitutional logic, where representational change is argued to be analogous to structural change, provides positive representation as both remedy for and evidence of domination's inevitable end—the promise of equality fulfilled. This respectable image, where neoliberal ideas of economic maturity and proper individualism transpose the stunning disturbances of gender, racial, and sexual excess to the failures of our insolvent past, reconfirm the idea of our progression. Yet this assimilatory representation is another impossibility, a disciplining intent on exiling pleasure and abundance, while ensuring hostile images are as much in our future as they might belong to the present.[50]

For example, the last decade has witnessed a vast proliferation of trans representations that are offered as cure to the relentless economic, psychic, affective, and physical violence many trans people endure. These expanding representations are used to undergird dominant culture's argument that progress is inevitably unfolding. Yet, returning to CeCe McDonald's words that begin this chapter, we know that with this increased representation comes sustained or heightened instances of violence. While 2014 was named the "Transgender Tipping Point" by *Time* magazine, each consecutive year since has counted record numbers of murdered trans women of color in the United States.[51] Among our tasks is to attend to the grim reality that the expansion of even "positive" representation might not have simply a neutral corollary to violence but perhaps a causal one as well.[52]

Marsha P. Johnson makes a similar argument about visibility and violence after a 1972 Arthur Bell interview in the *Village Voice*. Referring to a previously published piece, she suggested that the attention brought to the "girlies" (other gender-nonconforming sex workers) increased their harassment and led to their arrest later that week. Linguistic representation in the form of the article produced a broader social understanding of Johnson and her friends, including the geographies and temporalities they lived within which put them more centrally on the police's radar. We have, then, the contradiction of the representational in that it brings us into the world, while also having the capacity to take us out. Here, the distinction (as contradistinction) between being and nonbeing also maps recognition's fugitivity.[53]

Again, rather than an opening toward recognition—a position where one can make a claim instead of exclusively being claimed—representation for Marsha P. Johnson and Duanna Johnson was the prefiguration of their undoings. Duanna Johnson's being read as trans led to her initial arrest under "suspicion of prostitution," a policing practice often referred to as "walking while trans," in which trans women of color are assumed to always be engaging in sex work when they exist in public. Johnson being clocked, or being brought into the general field of representation as negative equality, led to her subsequent beating in the booking room, and perhaps even her murder.

Being clocked, or being seen as trans, is most readily deployed against a person's identity as an attempt to destroy their/our coherence. Clocking adheres with the gripping force of catastrophe by recasting the violent act of misgendering as the ability to name the Other out of existence. Misgendering here is not a minor act of miscalculation but a way to reclaim the domain of gender and one's position as author for those who are most threatened by its fragility. Officer McRae's "he-she" and "faggot," the lacerating words intent on obliteration, enacts the double bind of recognition: being seen by the other brings you into the world—into the field of visibility. But for those already on the edges of vitality, like Duanna Johnson, it is often that which also takes you out of it. Through representation—both the CCTV video and descriptions of Johnson in court—the defense was able to produce a reversal of guilt, where the party harmed is, via the magic of the law, transformed into the assumed aggressor. Johnson, and not the state, is made to hold the burden of proof—the surveillant gaze in action.[54]

Tracing the racial and gendered parameters of recognition from Fanon and da Silva to Snorton and McDonald, how might we reorient the project of recognition, its prohibitions and its access, toward the nondialectical and nondevelopmental? Or, where might relief be found if we abandon the telos of the assumed subject to come? The brutal scene of Duanna Johnson's beating, replayed against the composed testimony of the court, reminds us that recognition is not a smooth space of inevitability, even in struggle. Here, it's the phenomenology of violence that compels us beyond a substitutive logic where life, and life's recognition, is equally distributed.

Fanon turns our attention to the limits of recognition in the colonial context that I more fully explored in chapter 1. By holding on to the dialectics of structure, he also maintains the teleology of subjectivity, even for those deemed nonsubjects. For Fanon, revolutionary violence offers a way through the totalizing constriction of coloniality, the possibility to move from object to subject, however contingent. Given this, how might we push further on Fanon for those who must remain, even in the postcolony, as da Silva might suggest, "no-bodies against the state"? This is perhaps an unfair question to levy against Fanon's thought. Yet this "no-body" as nonidentity, or the negation of the negation of identity—not unlike Spillers's caution against "joining the ranks of gendered femaleness"—might offer "the insurgent ground as female social subject."[55]

From Optics to Opacity

Duanna Johnson's attack and its cinematic afterlife capture the structures of recognition and misrecognition, representation and disappearance, that constitute the field of the visual. While writing from a place of gender self-determination that works toward gender as an "insurgent ground," what is left of our various analytics of recognition and the images that bring us into the world? Or, how might we return to the beating tape: not simply to offer yet another way to imagine what we already know—that anti-Blackness, gender normativity, and violence are tightly bound in the production of flesh and that flesh's destruction—but to ask, yet again, how this bind might be undone.[56] Further, what tactics of production and sabotage might liberate the image from its formalism? This question specifically addresses those trapped in the interval of seeing and being seen where subject and object are collapsed. As a praxis of imagination and survivance, we must pose it without a fantasy of closure. To put it another way, at the center of the problem of recognition lies this: How can we be seen without being known, and how can we be known without being hunted?[57]

Being a "no-body against the state," a position some are already forced to live, stands against the sovereign promise of positive representation and the fantasy of sovereignty as assumed under claims of privacy. Read not as absolute abjection but as a tactic of interdiction and direct action, being a no-body might force the visual order of things to the point of collapse. On the issue of recognition and radical singularity, Édouard Glissant suggests, "From the perspective of Western thought, we discover that its basis is this requirement for transparency.

In order to understand and thus accept you, I have to measure your solidity with the ideal scale providing me with grounds to make comparisons and, perhaps, judgments. I have to reduce."[58] This reduction, which Fanon might call being overdetermined, is, as we know, unequally distributed. Glissant offers a totality of relation in opacity, the work of nontransparency that allows for nondialectic difference—the collectivization of radical singularity. Glissant continues, "Agree not merely to the right of difference but, carrying this further, agree also to the right of opacity that is not enclosure within an impenetrable autarchy but subsistence within an irreducible singularity."[59] We might read the current order of popular trans representation to be a variation of agreeing to only the "right of difference," as transparency is the precondition of visibility politics.

Opacity is useful here not necessarily as a practice of going stealth, residing below or beside the regimes of being seen but not known, although it might be imagined as such for those who find life there. For Glissant it is a method of solidarity without being grasped.[60] Here I'm suggesting it might be one way to theorize a radical trans visuality that attends to the universal and the particular as non-interchangeable. Opacity with representation: an irreconcilable tension that envisions something more than the pragmatism of the transparent and its visual economies of death. ·

The Image to Come

Tourmaline and Sasha Wortzel's 2018 experimental film *Happy Birthday, Marsha!* is a retelling, or more precisely a reassemblage, of the 1969 Stonewall anti-police uprising in New York City.[61] While the film is loosely narrative, in that it introduces us to a number of those who were present that night—including the film's namesake, Marsha P. Johnson—formalistically, it moves as atmospheric. The film's speculative past slides between historical fact and melancholic longing—curating a sense of fantasy and abundance that remains under threat of erasure. In a wash of pastels and low tones the film warmly awaits us.

If for classical narrative cinema the world is made whole by concealment, here the filmmakers highlight artifice by stitching together a number of seemingly disparate media, including digital video and archival VHS footage of Marsha—the cut remains exposed. Through the interruption of narrative as its connective tissue and individual figures as the primary point of dis/identification, we as viewers are guided by the film's ambiance—its soft tonality. Yet, rather than the alienation attributed to the destruction of narrative, pleasure remains and indeed is celebrated as the promise of trans sociality.[62]

FIGURE 3.2. Still from Tourmaline and Sasha Wortzel's 2018 film
Happy Birthday, Marsha!

Even in the film's optimism, for a Black and Brown trans sisterhood, its
somber grain reminds the viewer of the precarity of not only its locations and
characters, but the film itself. Yet *Happy Birthday, Marsha!* does not dissolve
into tragedy, which might be the genre most associated with trans representation. Importantly, it also refuses to become an anthropological study of the fact
of transness whose intended spectators are non-trans—another tenet of much
visual culture about trans people. The film, I believe, holds the contradictions
of life and nonlife, along with the communal rebellion that we already are.[63]

In one emblematic scene, a knocking sound signals the sliding of a rectan-
gular-shaped peephole, which reveals Marsha's obscured face in an otherwise
black frame (figure 3.2). The slivered yet direct image (she is centered and
looking into the camera) captured the clandestine space of gay bars like the
Stonewall Inn in the late 1960s, where charges of homosexuality and *inappro-
priately* gendered clothing were weaponized against trans/queer people along
with those that refused the grasp of normativity's emptiness. The framing of
the image and its use of negative space figure the partiality of its subject as the
doorperson's harassment of Marsha's outfit is countered by her contemptuous
glare and the piercing screech of her silent read. Marsha's eyes ambivalently
meet the security requirement, and a second dissolve reveals the fullness of her
and her friends' images as they, in anticipation of their entrance, announce "It's
gonna be legendary!" The underground of the club offers safe passage, a portal

to a suspended place, where the door provides protection from the outside but also cages Marsha and her friends from the possibility existing beyond it. As Tourmaline, Johan Burton, and I have discussed elsewhere, the image, we argue, works as a trap door. The emptiness of the door and the violence it holds at bay gives way to the shimmering opulence of refracted light as they enter while it also locks them in.[64]

Once inside, violence returns. After a dreamscape and/or counternarrative of Marsha's poetry performance, a police officer unplugs the jukebox while another begins abusing the patrons, including Marsha. In reaction to the police violence that bookends the film, Marsh smashes her glass on the floor after throwing her drink in the officer's face. The film ends with the shattered glass and ruined birthday cake and also in anticipation of the coming riot. However, the weight of harm that is ever-present in the narrative of the film is countered with a kind of spirted presence that appears with the intercut archival footage of Marsha. In other words, the film's conjectural form disrupts not only the cis gaze but also the equally troubling assumption that there is nothing other to Black trans life than violation. The film holds, without the promise of uplift, the dynamism of Marsha's theorization woven in word and gesture—the darting of eyes and in the cadence of delivery. This, while also not disappearing the impending threat that is life under siege.

At world's end, the conditions that produced *Happy Birthday, Marsha!* are remarkable. However, it's the film's formalism, which perhaps is only available under such modes of production, that enables its unfolding. Opacity in *Happy Birthday, Marsha!* is not the emptying out of an image but might be understood as representation's negation, or at least its breakdown. Here, opacity names the doubling, which allows oneself to be unmade by the shattering beauty of trans visual culture, while also knowing that images are never enough. Indeed, my insistence on the potentiality of visual culture is implemented in, as it stands against, the false belief that equates aesthetic austerity with revolutionary social change. *Happy Birthday, Marsha!* resides within and reconfigures a genealogy of trans/queer films that remind us that the corporeal pleasure of the image, its hyper-ornamentation, its anarchic framing and textured light, are tactics for being a no-body against the state. When the demands of civil society are for economic images that slide seamlessly into the cuts of formalism's cinematic traditions, it's the unruly excesses that build a grammar of trans opacity.[65]

While the moving image, including the surveillant gaze, helps grow the cop in our heads, opacity offers us a glimpse, however fleeting, of the sensuous beauty in the ruins of representation's hold. Yet there is no view of freedom to be gleaned from the relentless attack on Duanna Johnson nor its digital after-lives. In the final instance, the only way we might imagine justice for her is by destroying the conditions that enabled, by way of gratuitous reproduction, her undoing. With this destruction, abolition's generativity also insists we summon images where no-bodies can gather, not to become somebodies before the state but to envision, together, the possibility of another end of the world.

Sexual violence has become a way of life.
—*Ashley Diamond*

We must leave our dreams and abandon
our old beliefs and friendships from the
time before life began.
—*Frantz Fanon*

Whirling through identity and identity's
limit, atmospheres yoke the external force of the world and its internalization.
Here, under the cover of sociogeny, we work to defuse the borders that constitute the idea of modernity's singular subject and by effect collapse the barricade
against radical interdependence. Yet as we wade through the mire of neglect
and attack, we know the target is never alone. It is from this nonplace where
we might ask: What form does violence take when it is done to the self? This
is also to ask: What remains of the abstraction of the self, under such orders of
operation? These are the echoes of living with the death that is suicide. Spread
in anxious whispers, suicide and its ideations curate an archive of negotiated
endurance and its release, in a social that is structured against trans/queer life.
Surviving, even in the interval, fashions one as a necessary *problem* of modernity—caught between compulsory disappearance and public capture. This
is to say that modernity needs trans/queer existence to maintain its claim of
gender-normative mastery, as we function as castigated examples at the limit.
Yet we are also that which modernity cannot withstand under threat of prov-

ing its own obsolescence, in that gender can be and is lived otherwise. Suicide is bound to this organizing position, which we might also call the human—the figure of brutality mistaken for freedom. Or, put another way, suicide and its prohibition mark where humanism's contradictions are vividly expressed as near life and differential death.

My aim in this chapter is to diagnose the forces that might push one toward suicide, but to end there would reduce our understanding of suicide's relation to the figure of life. To be sure, the various factors that fall under and extend current discourses on "LGBT youth suicide," a new articulation of an old phenomenon, reminds us what we already know: "it's always open season on gay kids," as Eve Sedgwick argued in 1991.[1] The season continues, yet the subject of Sedgwick's statement, the generic "gay kids," remains inadequate to understand this specificity and that specificity's terrible generalization. "Gay kids" and perhaps even "trans/queer youth" fail to account for what I am here attempting to name. Indeed, this is among the problems we inherit by way of the necessary impossibility of identity as the mandate of subjectivity. My primary interest here is not which populations have higher rates of such practices (although that is important), but to sketch how suicide signifies, how it announces, as finitude, the continuance of an anti-trans/queer social order that is not simply hostile toward so many but is built as hostility itself.[2]

While the recent present has witnessed a stream of data that attempts to account for suicide's persistence, with an attention toward those who fall under the category of "LGBT youth," the epistemic force of this particular form of violation is left obscured. Again, the stories are retold of *troubled outcasts*, unable to adjust to the demands of a social that cannot bear their beautiful disruption—a narrative insistence, played out as legal justification, on singularity and that singularity's nonequivalence. This discursive cloistering locates the suicidal in the abjection of their own making. While perhaps overdetermined by public discourse's pleasurable fascination with trans/queer suicide, its phenomenological contours draw a map of its structuring paradox. At best, suicide is written as the pathological break that, through an ableist dialectic, stands as the *rightful* synthesis of gender and/or sexual nonnormativity written through the white world. Ableism appears here to cauterize suicidal ideation into an individual deficiency and not a response to the ableism that produces it.[3] Indeed, the tragedy of trans/queer existence—the melancholic incorporation of loss, the damned life of those damned to hell—confirms the impossibility of anything other than self-destruction. If we are to face the ways anti-trans/queer violence figures the social, then the surprise is not that suicide is common, it's that it's not inevitable. This point is necessary as we struggle to both depathologize and deindividualize the phenomenon while also holding on to the specificity of those lost and those not yet.

I am not suggesting that trans/queer people do or do not identify as having a psychiatric disability or that there is a relationship between such disabilities and suicide. However, this generalized misdiagnosis serves as cover while concealing ableism's relationality—an equation disability justice organizers know well. To believe in the singularity of suicide relinquishes any claims to context— the conditions of unlivability—that so many are expected to survive. Even worse, the other side of understanding trans/queer suicide as the logical conclusion to a life lived out of relation is that suicide is the wish fulfillment of a murderous culture that insists this "open season" never ends. Suicide becomes murder by other means—perpetrator and victim fall into each other and the social is exonerated. Here, trans/queer suicide and its ideations are analytics, ephemera of a practice of devastation that, once again, forces us against an attachment to the idea of progress as evenly distributed, as for most, it never *gets better.*[4]

What makes suicide different yet not unique is that, unlike most other instances of harm, suicide is produced as a self-contained phenomenon—a psychic drama that dictates its own end, where cause and effect are bowed into a tautological circle. Popular discourse proliferates this pathologization to shore up this loop through the hyper-individuation of suicidal ideations and actions as the province only of those who express them—answering the question before it might be asked. Suicide becomes both the domain of rationality through claims of "personal choice," or what Immanuel Kant called an "emergence from his self-imposed nonage" in that "[n]onage is the inability to use one's own understanding without another's guidance."[5] The capacity to commit suicide can be read paradoxically as the mark of Enlightenment humanism, while it also, in the final instance, memorializes the decisive act of irrationality—self-annihilation—the antihuman. Among the emblematic characteristics of modernity for Kant is self-possession, the capacity to "use one's own understanding," or here, the ability to take one's own life, which also, then, appears as the categorical nonself. What, then, is self-harm if we refuse to assume that we emphatically know the defining limits of either the "self" or "harm" in advance, or beyond the relationality of their appearance? Further, how does suicide figure the consistency of racialized and gendered power that maintains itself by the twinned practices of deadly exile and equally violent inclusion?[6]

A murder without a victim and a victim without a murderer—the compression of suicide rehearses the general way minoritarian violence, including anti-Black, ableist, anti-trans/queer (which often live together), and many more, are produced as self-fulfilling. The legal effect of this logic appears in the success of the trans- and/or gay-panic defense I discussed in chapter 1. This in turn situates trans/queer death not as an organized disaster that breaks with the social but as the unfolding of history—the social's inevitable consolidation. The persistence of anti-Black police violence, which is to say policing, HIV/AIDS, houselessness, poverty (and so on) stands as evidence that the ontological corruption deemed inherent by the social could lead nowhere else. While not interchangeable, the ways these deaths are produced as nonevents helps us notice their commonality.

Autodestruction

As symptoms of occupations of land and psyche, suicide and its ideations appear as often in Frantz Fanon's writing on anticolonial struggle as in the notes from his clinical practice. For Fanon, it was the crushing force of context, here the racist horror of colonization, that was the primary source of suicidal ideation for those under its domain. Central to this schematization was Fanon's insistence that colonization positioned the oppressed as the attached wards of their oppressors, which became dramatized in the scene of suicide. On this point he argued, "At the level of the unconscious, therefore, colonialism was not seeking to be perceived as a sweet, kind-hearted mother who protects her child from a hostile environment, but rather a mother who constantly prevents her basically perverse child from committing suicide or giving free rein to its malevolent instincts. The colonial mother is protecting the child from itself, from its ego, its physiology, its biology, and its ontological misfortune."[7] The perverse child, the violated (non)subject of colonial oversight, is, as Fanon suggests, that which is in need of protection, not from the racist violence that has produced them as such but from the capacity to be overcome by their "malevolent instincts" and to take their own life. Existence here is rendered as the ironic double bind of being "protected" by that which you are in need of being protected from—the other side of phobia. If phobia is the *irrational* fear of that which is materially less able to bring you harm, here Fanon describes the colonial drive to protect, at the level of the unconscious, that which you harm. Protection, here, is not, as he suggests, "kind-hearted," but names a kind of violence saved for those deemed incapable of self-possession—an ableist symbolics of a eugenic common sense that tracks from chattel slavery to solitary confinement and beyond.

Significantly, this prohibition against suicide is not a wish for the psychic well-being of the colonized. Rather, it is a punishment, although not for a specific act but for the offense of being—an "ontological misfortune." This protection operates under the cloak of benevolence—liberalism's deadly incorporation—as limit, into a family drama of rewards and restrictions. In this scheme, life becomes a directed punishment, perhaps even worse than death, inflicted upon those who are already suffering. This fate is nothing other than the productive exercise of power as a totalizing biopolitical force, as explored in chapter 3, whose true might is illustrated not through taking life but by making live.[8]

This scene of phobic attachment also complicates the ways normative power is often made to account for itself. Exile and destruction, or what we might call dehumanization—the steady work of producing nonsubjectivity—are assumed to be the primary ways control is administered and the state reconsolidates itself. Indeed, as I've argued throughout this book, exile and destruction, the psychical and material force of normativity, constitute the ontological capture that is trans/queer vitality. We must constantly be reminded of this if we are to undo the onslaught of jurido-discursive maneuvers that succeed in retelling a story that anti-trans/queer violence is antagonistic to modernity. However, Fanon's insight here again confirms the other function that I've been attempting to describe: that inclusion, in various forms, names not the opposite of exclusion but its entrenchment. For Fanon, the colonist does not simply want to destroy the colonized, although he might want to do that but this wish is coupled with, and compounded by, a governing incorporation, the para-inclusion, as exception, that names the violence of French colonialism as well as U.S. liberal democracy. The perverse children of the colony, trans/queer youth of color, and many others remain as structured negation, the wound that stands as a reminder that settler colonization—the garden of death—must always be replanted.[9]

While Fanon delineates the meaning of suicide and its restrictions so as to bring into relief how the colonial state's "care" arrives as injurious custody, he also helps us understand how suicide, for those in the hold of totalizing power, becomes the only escape. For him, "collective autodestruction in a very concrete form is one of the ways in which the native's muscular tension is set free. All these patterns of conduct are those of the death reflex when faced with danger, a suicidal behavior which proves to the settler (whose existence and domination is by them all the more justified) that these men are not reasonable human beings." Fanon goes on: "In the same way the native manages to by-pass the settler. A belief in fatality removes all blame from the oppressor; the cause of misfortunes and of poverty is attributed to God: He is Fate."[10]

Fanon reads suicide of the oppressed as a practice that dissolves the colonizer's responsibility for the massive violence he perpetuates, closing the circuit he names as "fate" as the outside/inside of coloniality. Fate, then, exists as an object of misappropriated cathexis that allows for the externalization of the drama of suicide—the oppressed are left without choice and thus the oppressors are left without blame. Caught in a trap, their failure to adhere to the demands of the colonizers brings with it death, while surviving means a death in life. Through suicide the colonized are rendered not as "reasonable human beings" as they are overcome with the *irrationality* of autodestruction. Choosing the non-choice of death against a near life under colonial occupation— there is no way out.

Yet Fanon also sees suicide as a kind of freedom, at least at the level of the body, from the tension of, and the price paid for, existing as disruption in the settler colony. Indeed, he goes further to suggest that autodestruction proves the inhumanity of those under the protections of the properly human. Autodestruction is depathologized and rewritten as corporal testimony (muscular tension) that aligns freedom with death as it disturbs the very possibility of existence or even redress within the world. I take his point here, not that he is prescribing suicide as a way out of the terror but that when read retroactively it is not only a leap toward death but also away from the death some are already living.

Following Fanon's two insights, my attention to the question of the universal and the temporalities of life, or more precisely to para-vitality, meet in the scene of trans/queer suicide and its ideations. Suicide here is not an allegory for a theory of non-suicide, nor do I mean to subject it, via ableist pathologization, to a canonizing displacement, which finds it in the final instance to only read the still living. Yet if we follow Fanon's command that we "abandon our old beliefs"—the liquidation of the colonized ontology that marks subjectivity's end—then it also becomes the imperative of its beginning. Here, the time of death—the time of autodestruction—is opened against itself. The temporality that he offers in the epigraph to this chapter, "from the time before life began," suggests a retroactive futurity or even a melancholic utopianism that builds through the revolutionary dream of decolonization. Speaking of a nonreproductive yet speculative future, he finds himself looking back at the present he hopes is unfolding—an anticolonial presencing where the dialectics of horizontality astral project his split self to celebrate the end of the world, as its beginning.

What Jean Améry calls the leap—the death drop—reveals the secret of modernity's cruelty, inasmuch as there are forms of life more unlivable than death. Further, the prohibitions against suicide are not about producing a more livable life for those under distress but are a tactic of maintaining that uninhabitability.[11] Dangerous ground, yet this coiling structure of suicide might help us know beyond that which thrives from our sustained dissolution and the architecture that maintains it. This is not, however, to advance a martyred attachment, nor to suggest that there is anything salvageable in trans/queer (or any) suicide. The personal archive that has known the subject intimately denies me the ability to suggest suicide, or any of the instances of harm I've documented here, can remain exclusively an object of study recalcitrant to the social. On the contrary, suicide demands our attention because, left quiet, it continues to grow as both a limit and an expression of death in waiting.

Staying with suicide in the annals of trans/queer study might seem to be overdetermined given the magnitude of the public discourse that precedes it, yet while we work toward keeping each other alive, what does the persistence of self-negation, and its prohibitions, tell us about the figure of the human as that which stands in opposition to collective vitality? The formation to which I keep returning—a life more unlivable than death, and Fanon's insight that under the totality of racialized hyper-depersonalization, death, at least ontologically, is that which opens into life—allows us to understand modernity as the cumulative death drive turned outward. In this, I mean to suggest that trans/queer suicide, in its tragic repetition, is a forceful analytic, a nonperformance, which reads the world for the filth it is.

The Universe without Universalism

Seth Walsh took a step off a tree stump and into the finitude of self-negation —a death drop. The story of their daily life—the grandchild of conservative Christians who survived relentless physical and psychic attacks by classmates, teachers, and neighbors because they were "out" and "wore girl's stuff" and "shopped in the girls section"—was compounded by the authorial silence, spoken as celebration, by school administrators who found pleasure in Seth's daily torment.[12] Education for the thirteen-year-old was the curricular mandate that fashioned them as a revolt against normativity's claim to its own consistency and beyond even the most basic protections. School taught Seth that they could expect nothing other than the incessant attacks levied by their peers while everyone remained silent. Perhaps their silence—the sound of straight noise—signaled others' fear they might find a similar destiny, or perhaps it was just in soft confirmation. To be clear, the school's administrative inaction must not simply be read as an oversight, the chance incompetence of a system that wanted otherwise. Their abandonment of Seth, and all those like them, instructed the students that the epidemic that needed to be stopped was not youth suicide but gender nonnormativity. Even after Seth's death, their grand-mother, Judy Walsh, a retired schoolteacher, remained caustically ambivalent: "He wasn't happy with his orientation. He read the Bible a lot. This was not the way he wanted to live his life, but that's what he was dealt with."[13]

On September 19, 2010, Seth asked their mother, Wendy, a beautician who was home from work, if they could borrow a pen to write something. Accord-ing to her, Seth was acting "normal," and said they were going to play with the dogs. After some time, Wendy went to check on them and at first thought Seth was picking plums in the backyard but as she walked closer she realized Seth was hanging from a tree by a rope that was stealing the last of their breath. She struggled to pull down her child's small body and tried to revive them. The damage was already too great, and Seth died eight days later in a nearby hos-pital. Along with a traumatized family, Seth left a suicide note scribed with the pen their mother had lent them:

> Mom; Amanda; Shane; Shawn
> I love you. Thank you for having me. It's been a pleasure. I know this will bring much pain. But, I will, hopefully, be in a better place than this shithole. Please, put my body in burial, and visit my used body. And make sure to make the school feel like shit for bringing you this sorrow. This life was a pleasure, mostly having you guys to pull me through the pain.
> Hopefully I become the universe.
> Seth[14]

The surreptitious rage and organizing stillness of Seth's self-eulogy destroys. Both memoir and manifesto, its mixed genera instigate a backward-looking futurity that knows of their own future's impending end. Their poetics figure a para-vitality where they lived the unlivable existence in the "shithole." Here, the terrain upon which they were forced to remain, not unlike the ditch that held Lauryn Paige's body, spatializes the horror of near life. In Seth's traumatic narration, the "shithole" becomes more unbearable than the burial that will follow it.

Unable to sustain even the rawest form of life, Seth calls upon a "better place" as referent for their existence (as nonexistence) to come. Seemingly only available through negation, this better place, which is both a grave and an escape hatch, posits the unknown of metaphysics as more survivable than the harshness of the here and now. In the end, it was their gender nonnormativity, a gift to us all that was returned to them as debt, which tethered them to the ruthless dialectics of sterile indifference and vicious obsession.

Against the mark of a *broken child*—the designation intent on isolating Seth within a non-neurotypical diagnosis of their own fashioning—the note serves as a call to arms against the murderous threads that together strangled them. Seth's demand for those who witness to make the school "feel like shit" centers revenge, and not a liberal call for reconciliation, as their final wish. Their hope remains hostile to the very idea of mitigation through something like anti-bullying laws, or other attempts to overcome the durational misery they suffered. Seth's prose demands a response that does not suture over the very conditions of its arrival under the mystification of legal remedy or a hollow call for a shared humanity—a universalism from which they were held only as its negative.

Becoming the universe, for Seth, was not, it seems, a hope to enter into the assumed protections of the human but for the end of the humanism's continued wrath. My point here is that the human as an icon of modernity, from (at least) Kant to current discourses on trans/queer suicide, including those that circled around Seth's sexuality and gender presentation, names the order of operations for a deadly equation. Sylvia Wynter reminds us that entangled sociality—humanism's double—returns "as the lack of the West's ontologically absolute self-description."[15] This fantasy of Enlightenment's self-description, which for Kant might be named the individual—the human—is the subtext of both the violence Seth endured and its extension as cure. In opposition, Seth's universe refuses the possessed individual of the universal—they hoped to become the shimmering particulate of possibility—the universe.[16]

As a counter-eschatology that moves from death to life, the end of the human returns in the final pages of Fanon's *The Wretched of the Earth*. Dictated to his wife, Josie Fanon, the text was completed while he was suffering from acute myeloid leukemia and was published just months before his death in the United States. It might be said that Fanon's attachment to the language of humanism is emblematic of his colonial sensibilities fashioned by his childhood spent in Martinique, his enlistment in the Free France army, and his continental education, yet in contrast to arguing that at the very moment of its disavowal, humanism returns unscathed, Fanon is perhaps his most deconstructive. It is here while recounting his work with the Front de libération nationale (FLN) that he calls into question the violence of the state form—the mechanical proliferation of the universal. His treatise ends with: "For Europe, for ourselves, and for humanity, comrades, we must turn over a new leaf, we must work out new concepts, and try to set afoot a new man."[17]

Held by the limits of language, Fanon's "new man," much like Seth's "universe," is forged through the practice of revolutionary violence against the colonial order of things, a productive force that opens possibility even as destruction. To be clear, this is not meant to aestheticize either trans/queer suicide or the violence of anticolonial struggle, or a conflation of the two. Yet Seth's text, with Fanon, pushes us beyond the subject of rights as the fiction of the individual and toward a limit where vitality is not predicated upon the grind of modernity. Here, Fanon's "new man" indexes a kind of universe without the wreckage of colonial universality that he well knew was the discursive ground upon which the soldiers of the Fifth Republic stood.[18]

Turned another way, the cis sadism, the cruel drone of everyday life, that Seth lived as everyday death, and that eventually drove them toward suicide—is the demand for subjectivity as the crisis of subjectivity itself. My argument is not that the social always pushes trans/queerness toward death, an analysis that allows us to make a political claim for inclusion in the very categories that, on the level of structure, are antagonistic to survival. In contrast, suicide persists as a limit concept that is harnessed to maintain the idea of the human. Under its domain, suicide, and suicidal ideations, are at times mandated and at other times forcefully prohibited. How then does suicide teach the endurance of humanism and its racialized anti-trans/queer contours as a practice of shuttling abjection?

Forced to Live

Through clandestine cell phone videos smuggled out of her Georgia prison cell, Black trans activist Ashley Diamond narrates the spectacular violence she knows as ordinary life. In the series of twenty-five-second segments that were passed through prison walls and uploaded online, *Memoirs of a Chain Gang Sissy*, Diamond states that for her, "Sexual violence has become a way of life in the Georgia Department of Corrections."[19] The horror of being caged was, for Diamond, calcified and extended by endless sexual attacks, which included being sold and traded by prison guards. Through the space of incarceration, she was returned to that "peculiar institution" that remade her into a laboring

FIGURE 4.1. Screen grab from Ashley Diamond's 2014 digital video series, *Memoirs of a Chain Gang Sissy*.

commodity—rendering her flesh as an object among objects. As feminist insurgents have long argued, the intimacy of sexual violence, like that endured by Diamond, is central to torture's epistemological force as its trespass performs a kind of undoing that links it to but also pushes it beyond corporal punishment. Sexual violence as "a way of life" in her Georgia cell ritualistically transferred her body into an external object—held by anyone other than herself.[20]

The composition of Diamond's serial film frames her image on the far left in direct address to the camera with the majority of the screen filled by a black square (figure 4.1). Perhaps an aesthetic decision, perhaps dictated by the limits of the technology with which she was working, nonetheless the image offers the power of her testimony but also that of her filmmaking. The only episode that is not framed this way is a panning shot of the torsos of the other inmates who were supporting her. Cut in the middle of the series, it's a startling juxtaposition to the consuming black square that threatens to engulf her. At the level of the image, she formalized the subject of her plea as the isolation of her cell is mirrored in the black square that seems to be forcing her back into disappearance. This framing is broken only by the fullness of the shot that includes the other inmates. The menacing space of no-space returns again at the end of the film, reminding the viewer of her proximity to danger.

The cloistering of Diamond's body was not enough to sedate the state's hunger for the totality of her capture. This point cannot be overstated, as the remedy offered for prison violence is almost exclusively the passing of more commanding legal protections, either in form, administration, or both. This reformist approach, as prison abolitionists have helped clarify, is one of the primary ways the prison and its capacity to eviscerate are expanded.[21] If prison, under the liberal state, names the space of suspended rights, then such expansions are structured as antagonistic to itself. After all, in Diamond's case, as it is for imprisonment in general, maintaining a physical and psychical space of total uninhabitability, the destruction of the very possibility of the social, is the unending desire that is incarceration. This is not to suggest that working in solidarity with Diamond and all prisoners so that they might have a better chance of survival is futile, but the question remains: Are the changes we are fighting for now helping to shrink or expand the prison's capacity to kill?[22]

Through a commitment to sustaining its own administrative incoherence —the persistence of disciplinary power shaped toward a state of inconsistency as coherence—the Georgia Department of Corrections (GDOC) orchestrated Diamond's forced gender transition. She was housed in a "men's prison" and denied a uniform that matched her gender—a common practice that relegislates sumptuary laws even after their declared end. The prison administration also withheld the prescribed medication she had been taking for seventeen years before her incarceration, which caused her the shattering pain of transitioning into a body that was not hers. At least at the level of administration, most jails and prisons theoretically adhere to a "freeze frame" policy that allows for imprisoned people to be prescribed medications they were taking before their incarceration. Yet the administrative logic of the prison industrial complex maintains its consistency as inconsistency that always disfavors those caged. While prisons and jails are thought to be highly regulated and controlled environments, one of the reasons prison reforms almost always lead toward worse conditions for those inside is that the system is designed, not unlike racial capitalism, through the incorporation of mandated changes with an openness of interpretation that maintains and grows the reach of the system. To be clear, this is not to suggest that consistency in administration would be the remedy, but tracing the forms power takes is necessary to know how we might confront them. The disarticulation between federal/state (and other) policy and the lived experience of those trapped inside amplifies sovereignty's force as the ability to regulate through discipline and discipline's subtraction. It is not surprising, then, that within the prison, a space of gender's binary production, the dynamic force of Diamond's self-determination was rendered an act of sedition. Diamond clarifies: "The deliberate de-feminization of me is part of the process of my incarceration. It has been from the very beginning."[23]

Entombed in the skin of another, here Diamond was not simply in the "wrong body," a narrative tool used by some, and imposed upon others; she was split into her own antagonism. This "de-feminization" shaped her anew, not to a prior state, as she never was a man but to a future nonself, imprisoned inside a body that was returned to her only as the systematic violence of the state's drive to both destroy her and maintain that destruction. That gender was the site the prison chose for its attack against her illustrates the state's investment in the crude fiction of the binary, but built inside this ideal is a form of revenge endemic to the state itself. This forced transition, her de-feminization as process without end, was a durational experiment in estrangement and that estrangement's capture, not unlike an adrenaline shot to a torture survivor to ensure they know nothing other than the time of pain.

The attack was also managed on the level of her body, as Diamond testified to the physical pain of the transition. In one of the videos she explained how her shape "literally morphed,"[24] and the texture of her skin, "the way it looks and feels,"[25] shifted as the rapid and unmonitored hormonal changes tore through her body. Her flesh became, or more precisely was staged as, the terrain upon which GDOC waged its war against her under the flag of gender normativity. The withholding of her medication weaponized her body against itself; according to her testimonial she had excruciating fatigue, chills, and vomiting. Beyond medical negligence, prisons have long been charged with such brutal practices as withholding medications, treatments, and worse that have resulted in countless fatalities. The penalty of death is administered via calculated neglect, even where the execution chamber has long been empty.[26]

Through underground networks Ashley Diamond built intra-prison solidarity, a dangerous act of cooperation for those inside. She joined forces with other inmates who were either survivors of harm and/or wanted to show up for her, which meant also showing up for themselves. In a number of the videos other prisoners are partially seen, faces obscured for safety, telling their own stories of sexual assault while also substantiating Diamond's torment. As a pedagogy from the inside out, they mocked the prison's already existing "zero-tolerance policy" for sexual assault in their war of position against the state that holds them hostage. This analysis is vital as it shows that the preexisting knot of laws, guidelines, and federal mandates "prevent," at the level of the juridical and administrative, the experiences they are living as fact. "Zero tolerance" is a tautology that is deployed because it forecloses the possibility of critique. Zero, as a nondegree, silences the claim that there could be anything other than what already is. However, their trafficked testimony not only disproves the ability of the prison to offer them any protections; it also illuminates how the law provides cover to the ongoingness of their terror.[27]

In the wake of the repeated sexual and physical abuse she experienced from prison guards and other inmates, coupled with the calculated denial of her medication and her nonconsensual gender transition, Diamond attempted suicide in 2013. Her attempt was unsuccessful, as she was found unresponsive on the floor of her cell. The prison's response to her almost-death was not to follow its own protocols and finally administer her medication, or better yet, to let her out, but to place her in the secured housing unit (SHU).[28]

SHU is a housing category for inmates the state has deemed either too "violent" and/or too "vulnerable" to be placed in the general population. While penance is so integral to the practice of modern imprisonment that penitentiary took its name, it was an Eighth Amendment challenge brought against an Arkansas prison in *Hutto v. Finney*, a 1978 Supreme Court case that surprisingly ruled with prisoners and deemed punitive isolation over thirty days, including placement in solitary confinement, to constitute a cruel and unusual punishment. However, in a maneuver that illustrates the crushing malleability of the state's will, jails and prisons reclassified solitary confinement from a punitive action to an administrative category, which legislated its constitutionality as the same practice by another name. In other words, the stark horror of solitary remained, but the justification that placed one there was rewritten around the Eighth Amendment.[29]

This ruling, which was intended to limit the time prisoners could be isolated, in contrast marked the proliferation of segregation through new administrative policies. Secure housing units (also known as administrative segregation, or ad-seg) are cages within a cage where prisoners exist in hypermediation as physical, aural, and visual contact with staff and other inmates is all but extinguished. Those in SHU are often fed through a slot in the door, communicate with guards only through an intercom system, and are locked in cells for (at least) twenty-three hours a day. Their constitutionally mandated one hour per day out of their cell is spent alone, often indoors, in a similarly small space. Vastly expanded in the aftermath of Attica and other uprisings, SHUs are designed, in part, as an attempt to destroy prisoner organizing and their politicization. Further, those determined by prison officials to have a "gang affiliation" and those who are more likely to be victims of prison violence make up the majority of the SHU population, along with politically active and older prisoners.

Held in an eight-by-ten-foot concrete tomb, Ashley Diamond spent twenty-three hours a day locked down in total isolation. In the damp loneliness of anti-relationality, the scaffolding of the flesh, which many assumed to have disappeared, administered torture as a way of life. SHUs are windowless and lit by fluorescent tubes that never turn off, melting day into night, where doing time means existing outside of it. Beds of poured concrete and rebar offer a sheer blanket shared with rats. With almost no ventilation, the climate is held to maximize distress—blistering hot or freezing cold. In an attempt to break the thick isolation, Ashely would fill the hours, then days, then weeks by singing songs to herself. Like Seth Walsh's "shithole," the SHU is where the metaphoric referent intended to give form to the trans-substitution of flesh as commodity slides into the biopolitical apparatus designed to manage the slow death of carceral life. Here, the architecture of cruelty returns as penance in what is among the most exacting spaces of the management of the human.

A punishment for those beyond the threshold of punishment, SHU is designed to produce complete seclusion. This is to say that the SHU renders a spatial experience of nonrelationality by concentrating one's capacity for a world into anachronistic abandonment—the dreadful time of the human. The intensity of this built environment is so complete and so total that those who survive it are often diagnosed with "SHU syndrome," a post-traumatic stress disorder (PTSD). Its symptoms might include anxiety, hallucinations, disorientation, severe agitation, and more. To this end, among the aims of SHU is to produce a form of incapacitation that renders sociality void and where the only measure is a still beating heart. SHU syndrome ensures that the "time" one does in the hole extends to the entirety of their life, even after release.[30]

Instructive of the state's callous irony, this targeted desocialization is offered as both a punitive placement for those the prison has classified as dangerous to the general population and also protection for trans/queer prisoners who are almost exclusively housed in SHUs. In this way, SHU collapses those who it designates as under threat and those it deems dangerous through a general equivalence of violence. This administrative logic conflates care with durational misery. Protection for trans/queer prisoners (and many others) returns in the form of synchronized assault. This recursive structure, which Fanon also described as the logic of colonial psychiatry, names the limit of the human.

This is to say that the conflation of care with harm, or protection and destruction, is the internal logic of incarceration and not its tragic by-product.[31]

Diamond's time in SHU was a response to the infractions she accumulated from her attempted suicide. In other words, it functioned as a penalty for both her attempt to end the anti-Black and anti-trans violence she was enduring and for surviving it. Imprisoned trans whistleblower Chelsea Manning was similarly disciplined when she was sentenced to fourteen days in solitary confinement following her suicide attempt while in military prison in 2016.[32] Evident in both is a structuring paradox where suicide, or its ideation, lays bare the prohibitions against it, not under the claim of life but precisely through the drawing out of life's subtraction. Here, Diamond's push toward the realm of the human, even through the non-choice of self-negation, was met with the restrictive domain of a "turtle suit"—a device, not unlike a straitjacket, that inhibits mobility—and her time in SHU. Diamond, like the suicidal child of the colony, was produced as being in need of protection, not from the enormity of violence that was swallowing her but from the imminent harm that was herself.

Yet even here in the most impossible of spaces—the dank hardness of custody—she, along with other prisoners, organized a campaign to file her own Eighth Amendment claim against the Georgia Department of Corrections. The suit hinged on the state's refusal to provide the medication that was necessary to address her self- and medically diagnosed "gender dysphoria." This diagnosis, which many trans and disability activists have worked to depathologize as a precondtion of care, was, in another spoiled irony, her only avenue of redress. In other words, while we might rightfully work to dismantle the medicalization of our identities, its continued classification remains the only thin protection for those most subjugated in prisons, psychiatric jails, ICE detention centers, and more.[33]

This ableist non-choice between the further constriction of those most forcibly seized in the crucible of humanism—the prison—to either assume their genders are suspect and in need, without consent, of medical intervention, or a kind of gender self-determination that, through the betrayal that is the state, further diminishes their access to affirming practices. This ruse also lives in the idea that there is a "safe" place to house trans inmates, popularized by the growth of carceral feminism and much prison reform.[34] While indeed prisons both produce and are produced by the gender binary as the image of their own necessity, we must relentlessly affirm that the only safe place for trans women to be housed is outside of prisons.[35] This commitment to an abolitionist trans feminist analysis, which is to say a tradition of Black radicality, is perhaps the only escape route out of the danger that compelled Diamond toward her suicide and that which punished her survival.[36]

Ashley Diamond was released in 2015 after serving four years in prison. Her suit against the Georgia Department of Corrections was settled with a provision that Georgia would update its protocols to be more in line with already existing federal guidelines for inmate health care, including gender-affirmative medications and Prison Rape Elimination Act (PREA) recommendations. While some might claim this as a victory, Diamond and others remind us that these protocols were already in place during her incarceration, and that further attempts to traffic in humanism's promise, via prison reforms, builds its capacity for harm, while offering little to those struggling to survive. In other words, one way to chart the expansion of the prison is by following the attempts to reform it, which leave the institution intact. Further, there is no reparation, no form of collective care or redress available to Diamond that could unmake the agony she endured and the trauma of its persistance.

Return to the Future

The bind that I've been describing in this chapter, between the mandate of trans/queer self-negation, endemic in Seth's education and restricted by Diamond's SHU placement, locates the prison and the school as paradigmatic of the horror that is humanism, and not its lack. The drive of the prison, as it was for the school, was for Ashley Diamond and Seth Walsh to be included into its rotten logics—the intense violence of forcing them into the racial and gendered categories of colonial invention. These two scenes, placed with Fanon's call for a "new man," index a desire to name, and to make "new concepts," so that life might begin at its end. Yet Seth's note and Ashley's organizing must not be misread as arguing for their "humanization." While such demands are assumed to be paramount, what might we understand anew if we read the place of the human as not Enlightenment's fulfilled promise but the terror of a near life? Or perhaps the condition I've been attempting to describe here is not, as we might have understood, that of those beyond the protections the human. The ability to choose to not be human, to not be forcibly placed within, which is also outside, the demands of Enlightenment, is perhaps the position of white cis modernity.[37]

If the subject of humanism is the possessed individual, the Man of logic, freed by capital—and, following Kant, radically independent, cut from the relationality of the social, and returned as the cloistered subject—then we might see how rather than a restriction from the category, as is usually assumed, the totality of subjugation bears upon those who find themselves included as the damned, at the border of human. After all, "free will"—the sign of the human, the ability to pretend to pretend, the distinction between the animal other—is a protective wall but also a cage. Or, sometimes it's safer to go missing than it is to be found.[38]

Seth Walsh's and Ashley Diamond's desire was not for the extension of the cloak of humanism, with its designed ability to be retracted at will as it was in the SHU. They rejected this move for inclusion, which is the architecture of humanism's persistence, and that which the state most readily accommodates. This is also democracy's scam, the fantasy that exclusion is the most perilous position in which one might be held while inclusion is where safety resides. As theoreticians of wreckage and its inversion, Diamond and Walsh, with Fanon, build an insurgent sociality—a universe for the disposed, who are working, not toward juridical equality but toward the end of that which haunts them as catastrophe. Colonial humanism's thirst for the synchronicity of inclusive exclusion—the form of modern power I've been describing in this book—attempts to obscure their message. Yet, against accommodation, their insistence on the fungibility of those shuttered outside/inside its gates exposes, as foundational, modernity's dreadful wrath.

While Diamond's and Walsh's insights are not equivalent to those of Fanon on the question of violence, bringing them together offers more than it disguises. For Fanon, as is perhaps over-attended, revolutionary violence was necessary as it was the precondition for the possibility of being for those under colonial rule. Yet with this schema I also follow Françoise Vergès and others who suggest that Fanon's insistence contains within it the possibility for the expansion of anti-trans/queer and misogynist harm, even under the very name of decolonization. On this point, history continues to affirm. However, with that caveat I return to the formulation—a life more unlivable than death—as it forces us to reimagine the temporality of death for those *doing life*.[39]

Frantz Fanon's directive that begins this chapter and appears as the "conclusion" of *Wretched of the Earth*, to abandon colonial beliefs, or the epistemic, offers us another reading of the scene of autodestruction. Fanon's command that "[we] must leave our dreams, and abandon our old beliefs and friendships from the time before life began" disaggregates not only the assumed time of decolonization but also the coherence of socialities figured under the sign of "life." Or, Fanon's declaration of "abandonment" obstructs the universalizing subject of "life" as that which is distributed to all those who claim it, while also dispatching it as an ellipsis that can only begin at its end. This temporal arrangement of abandoning a life that never was names another kind of autode-struction. Here, the past is figured not only as a spatial temporal marker but as an ontological designation—a cut—that marks the beginning as the end.

How then might the practice of the human, the designation that collects under the sign of self-possession and its scattered temporalities (including the life/death binary), open against the possibility of a universe recalcitrant to the ferocity of colonial universalism? Is there a way to return to the universal as not only a disciplining apparatus that has been deployed under the devastation of Enlightenment's human but also a homeopathic that offers, following Fanon, a time after life began? Perhaps not. However, with them, I remain committed to experiments in collective life that are not dependent on universalism's commitments that return as the targeted violence of liberal democracy.

Angels of History

Tandi Iman Dupree's hypnotic drop from at least fifteen feet marks perhaps the most legendary entrance in ball history. As Bonnie Tyler's introduction to "Holding Out for a Hero" begins, Superman enters the screen from the left and a spotlight casts him in bright contrast as he crosses the stage, miming his search for something or someone of which the audience is still unaware. Not finding what he seeks, Superman exits through a slit in the white curtains, and the camera pans out, revealing a now empty stage awash in red and purple light. As the music builds into Tyler's first verse, Dupree descends upon the stage, landing a split in perfect time with the first lyric. Overwhelmed by her entrance, the crowd erupts into applause and screams as Superman reenters the stage and the two perform a meticulously coordinated dance and lip-sync. The routine is punctuated throughout by Superman lifting Dupree high above his head and throwing her into another version of the split that opened the number (figures 4.2–4.7).

Their ecstatic performance enthralls. Its beauty is in part because it engages the vertical space of the stage, an unusual tactic for drag, which tends to be horizontally oriented. Like her initial drop from the rafters, the space is drama-tized not only by her dancing but also by the skill of her acrobatics. Her body is, time and again, raised and thrown across the stage. The move that reoccurs most vividly in the routine, and that which punctuates with sublime clarity, is the death drop. This gesture, which has softly organized my thoughts, belongs most properly to the grammar of ball culture. While the recursive loop of popu-lar culture has now re/named the move as such, it is, according to many in the ball scene, a dip. Here the dancer begins standing, then slides one leg behind

FIGURES 4.2–4.7. Screen grabs from Tandi Iman Dupree's performance "Holding Out for a Hero."

them as they fall backward, while the other leg is kept straight. In a quick yet controlled transition from standing to flatness, the effect is that of a person dropping dead.[40]

Dupree was primarily a pageant queen, but her 2001 performance at Miss Gay Black America became legendary in the ball scene as it resurfaced a decade later online. The final tableau vivant of the performance finds Dupree again landing a canonical death drop with Superman following with his own dip behind her. The two bodies are puzzled into a joint shape of twisted limbs and exhaustion. As the music fades, Superman spins back into a standing position and grabs one of Dupree's now lifeless arms. The otherwise fast-paced performance ends melancholically, with Superman dragging Dupree's limp form off the stage. Her final drop leaves her without resurrection.

In its theorization of movement and negation, Dupree's ghostly exit exhibited the same choreographed precision as her incendiary arrival. This is to say that its joy is also supplemented by the specter of violence and the risk of collapse. Reading her aesthetics as building a world, and not simply an example of it, is our task. While we might understand Superman as the answer to the "hero" Dupree is holding out for, the way it unfolds offers another possibility. From its opening with Superman searching for her, the drop from the rafters, and their combative dance, which finds her lifeless at the end, the choreography also figures the intimacy of survival and of survival's end. The precarious space above the stage where she, like so many others, was hidden is a place both of sanctuary and of confinement. Her emergence, then, signals the necessary disruption that is Black trans/queer exuberance. The force after life began.

As both a movement of supplication and its repudiation, Dupree's dip recalls the anti-Black and anti-trans/queer violence often waiting within and beyond the club's doors. Death drops in general, and Dupree's specifically, are the gestural movement from Wynter's coloniality of being—the unlivable life in the shithole and the SHU—to Fanon's after "life began." She drops but not alone. The audience's response to her initial drop, and its subsequent iterations, collect a diffracted energy, lived as an ensemble, as a calisthenics of endurance, even when endurance surrenders. Perhaps this is too much significance to grant a singular move, yet there is something undeniably generative here that hinges on the mechanics of the drop and Dupree's exacting repetition of it.

Dupree, Diamond, and Walsh figure the ungovernable, those constituted in and as authority's magnificent decay. Their struggle does not negate the enormity of violence I've been attempting to give language to. However, they, and perhaps we, are engaged in a collective project whose name might never be found, which stands against or at least beside the discipline of Man. Theirs, ours, is not a line of thought defined by its methodologies nor by the protocols of proper research but is an ecstatic experiment in deracination and freedom. As writers, filmmakers, and choreographers, the cases I've included here ought not to be understood as examples, the passive objects of projection, as they are each architects of knowledge. Further, their pedagogical insights on self-negation are vital, not because they fully describe trans/queer existence; on the contrary, they teach us not only that we need another world but that it's already here.

Between the universality of gravity and the gravity of the universe, the death drop reveals both the weight of the body and the weight of history that pulls it down. Seth Walsh's revolutionary demand, Ashley Diamond's trafficked videos, and Tandi Iman Dupree's descent onto the stage, like Walter Benjamin's "angel of history," gathers at least provisionally the emergency we live as rule.[41] The gesture—the dance—the drop—as living archive, as epistemology, writes a poetics of recursive persistence that does not pivot on the narrative of individual survival but knots together an account of resistance unbound by gravity's law. For a life more unlivable than death, and a world no longer, or perhaps never, here, the universe is the quotidian sense of both hope and non-hope. These scenes slide into a messy assemblage of choice as nonchoice, where the energies of life and its sudden withdrawal ask what kind of death is self-negation for those at the limit of the human. While the deadly bind they confront does not dissipate under the will of their aesthetic practices alone, their longing for the time after life begins must not be lost. It is their plea for another place where we, with them, might become the universe, at the end of the world.

CODA **BECOMING UNGOVERNABLE**

> I am not a liberated woman. I'm a transgen-
> der woman and I'm working on becoming
> liberated as we speak.
> —*Miss Major*

It's easy to be free. It's easy to be alive.
—*Tourmaline*

Against the relentless violence this book has attempted to describe and the numerous symptoms of a state that wills death as the promise of life, becoming
liberated, or getting ungovernable, might offer a way out, or at least through
harm's persistence. Here I have argued that the state's spirit, even in its inci-
sively democratic form, contra the pervasive screams of liberalism, is not in
crisis. Indeed, the endless ways our contemporary moments of empire are able
to find new and ever more callous tactics to capture, imprison, and liquidate
under the very name of democracy coheres more than it interrupts. In contrast
to believing these violations are evidence of its decline, I'm suggesting something much more wicked, a wickedness that must be brought into relief if we
are to comprehend, let alone confront it. To restate one of my arguments; racialized anti-trans/queer violence is not antagonistic to the democratic state; it
is among its foundations—a minor claim that demands the end of the world.[1]

To question democracy, even from the left, authorizes suspicious despair
and raw hostility directed toward all that give it language. Yet those produced
as democracy's debris from the global wars waged under its name to the inter-

nal attacks ordered against anyone who dreams of more demand our resolve. This drama was particularly evident in the aftermath of the election of Donald Trump and the subsequent attempts to denounce him and his administration as an outlier in the otherwise smooth space of the United States. The proclamation "This is not normal" codifies the ringing truth of its own lie. Yet the architecture of this reclamation, its nonperformance, enables the force of liberal normativity to pull the center further toward the right in hopes of recovering a now-challenged fantasy of protection that was never there for most. Tragically, we are returned to the dreaded cage of realism, where *less bad* becomes the only name freedom can take. My intent here is not to erase the vicious specificity many are living and dying through in the current nightmare misnamed the United States, but what closures come with reading such habituation as rupture?[2]

Under siege, this declaration of democracy's crisis restages the fictitious pageantry that it has, or might be, any other way. As should be apparent, democracy is not my target because I desire toward the totalitarianism of its assumed opposite. I believe it must be rendered suspect precisely because it is that which is miraculously saved against itself. In other words, even with the weight of history to tell us otherwise, democracy remains that which we cannot release. It returns, time and again, via a messianic attachment to the belief that freedom is always right around the corner. In part, it's because of the hardness with which the concept sticks, from left to right, that leads me to investigate how it might also function as our shared poison.[3]

From the Greek, *dēmos* and *krátos*; democracy—ruled by the people—appears as the antithesis of the nonconsent of existing as an object singularly under administration. It also inaugurated a break with the relentless concentration of autocratic rule by redistributing sovereignty outward. C. L. R. James, in his 1956 article from the *Correspondence* newsletter, which eventually became the shop floor pamphlet "Every Cook Can Govern: A Study of Democracy in Ancient Greece Its Meaning for Today," looked toward ancient Athens for what he understood to be an epicenter of, and possible referent for, the direct democracy of the coming postcolonial future.[4] What persists in James's account is an insistence on the promise of Athenian rule, while knowing that slavery and the subjugation of women were its ground. Throughout his brilliant study he is, however, unable to reconcile this impasse; instead, he pushes past it by setting it aside. "There are many people today and some of them radicals and revolutionaries who sneer at the fact that this democracy was based on slavery. So it was, though we have found that those who are prone to attack

Greek democracy on behalf of slavery are not so much interested in defending the slaves as they are in attacking the democracy."[5] Read at the level of content, his critique of a vanguardism that expresses itself as representational versus direct democracy continues to be necessary. Yet what I want to stay with is that James found Athens useful for him while also knowing its cruelty.[6]

James's reading offers another important insight for the maintenance of a kind of left consensus around the idea of democracy. If both anticolonial freedom fighters as well as conservative defenders of empire argue for democracy's necessity, then what is its substance? Related, how does it become a generalized signifier whose sorcery fills it with cataclysmic emptiness? An apparatus, or at least a tactic, that organizes the collective self is necessary for those of us working toward liberation. Yet the idea that democracy is the antithesis of unfreedom becomes so firmly bound that a cavern of its inversion is opened. How, then, do we get free from democracy's affective stronghold so that we might know the promise of its declaration?[7]

Democracy's durability is built, at least in part, through its mythic past, which, even in ancient Athens, was only mythological. Its triumphant narrative is retold as the overcoming of domination by an internal force that offers nothing other than deliverance. Democracy, the antidote to monarchical rule and the tyrannical violence it engendered, becomes, for those of us on the side of communal life, a dangerous object to question. Yet the distance between that myth of freedom and the distribution of unfreedom reminds us that for Alexis de Tocqueville to find American democracy, he had to study its prisons.[8] More directly, the violence of abstracted nonrepresentative governing is not remedied by our inclusion in that system of administration. There has to be more than the sovereign or sovereignty's simulacrum.

Cataclysms

Critics of the U.S. liberal state help show that, from the moment of its imposition, which is to say the colonial occupation of Indigenous land, it has enacted the idea of the universality of Man while also using that category as measure for the exclusion of all beyond the universe of white propertied manhood. From those who bore the original crest of Man, the "we" of the people, the possessed individual, the subjects before the law, and so on, its double in the form of near life has always been mandated. This constitutive outside perhaps most spectacularly appears in the same mechanism that denies its own limit. On this bind, Fred Moten elucidates, U.S. democracy is "what exists now as crisis management and, on the other hand, the set of acts, dispositions, improvisations, collectivities, and gestures that constitute and will have constituted the crisis."⁹ Autopoietic crisis. Perhaps this is what democracy looks like.¹⁰

The violence that I've archived throughout this book insists that the crisis, as non-crisis, is sure. And while I've clarified how this seeming totality is unsettled by assemblies of radical generativity, I fear that if we preserve our attachment to the democratic form, we will remain trapped inside its walls. One might suggest that democracy, for C. L. R. James, for Jacques Derrida, and for us all, is still to come. Following them, if democracy has been coterminous with its own outside, then through the work of deconstruction and/or the dialectics of struggle its imminence appears—a glimmer of possibility on the horizon, a poetry from the future, an auspicious form whose preservation is paramount. In allegiance with them, I too support saving something, even as a placeholder, from the ever-consumptive present. Yet in contradistinction to democracy's promised futurity, what if we are already living at its limit? If so, then we begin in the dense space of no-space, where the centuries-long experiment has failed, in that it is built as failure for those who were never positioned to win.

On the building of this failure, Lorenzo Kom'boa Ervin suggested in *Anarchism and the Black Revolution* that the "State is a political abstraction, a hierarchical institution by which a privileged elite strives to dominate the vast majority of people."¹¹ Taking this account on the level of structure to be true, I've also worked to augment it with an understanding that this political abstraction is not something external to the social. In other words, the way we reproduce the consistency of the state is through the everydayness of the social—the internalization of the enemy and our reproduction of hierarchy. Yet what does it mean to question democracy, particularly in our contemporary moment, while it's still a banner under which so much is organized? In this ending, I began with the question of democracy, and not simply the liberal state. Critiques of the state, as form and abstraction, often argue that it's not democratic *enough*. In this assessment the potential of the democratic state has fallen into ruin through a force external to it. Countering this, from Plato to James Madison, the other primary anxiety is that the state might become too democratic. The *Federalist Papers* laid out Madison's fear of "mob rule," that the demos, if unrestricted, would be too easily swayed and produce a weak union. Neither accelerating majority rule nor its suspension represents, let alone protects, those positioned in and as the lacunae of normative power. Staying here, in the place of dereliction, pushes on one of the foundations of the democratic ethos, namely how a "we" is cleaved from "the people."¹²

Seditious Life

In defiance of both the liberal statist hypothesis that the social order would, given the direct power, equally distribute life chances, and a libertarian antistatism that believes all structures that do not directly benefit them are impediments to their free market of domination, is the protracted struggle of trans/queer sedition. While this might appear adjacent to a left melancholia or perhaps nihilistic edgeplay, the difference between reconsolidation and resistance, accommodation and refusal, is precisely how we inhabit impossibility. It is not that we have no tradition to look toward that offers beyond the cold desolation that insists, yet again, on democracy's modification as our only chance. Grown through this boundless violence is also an ecstatic vitality, even in death, that builds a collective revolt beyond the reign of pragmatism and its armored logics.[13]

If the attempt to fashion a more perfect democracy is also the order under which its deadly force expands, then ungovernability becomes an abolitionist way of life. The charge of ungovernability, a behavior recast as being, disturbs not just the social but the social's coherence that designates some existence as beautiful disruption. Sylvia Rivera's 1973 climb to the top of a TERF-swarmed stage and her exasperated "Revolution now!" was not just another politic. It opened, by way of desecrating the political, toward a post-politic. In effect, she cleared a path through the resolve of brutality she knew as democracy's nonchoice. Outvoted by the Gay Liberation Front and Gay Activist Alliance, silenced by the Gay Freedom Day's vocal majority, she, along with her STAR sisters, knew there was no home to be found there. It was her unruliness, the inability of either normative culture or the lesbian and gay political order to contain her that she was deeply punished for. However, it was also her riotous theory in action.[14]

Ungovernability finds its legal application in the juvenile court system as a charge for youth who live in refusal. Not surprisingly, Black and Brown trans/queer youth are often judged as such for repudiating the authority of a parent or guardian. These "status offenses," which include truancy, running away, and consuming alcohol, are actions that break the law only because the accused is under legal age. As wards, the legal category of youth produces numerically young people under the jurisdiction of others and who are to some degree also their legal responsibility. This unique relationship became nefariously clear when Kamala Harris chose to aggressively prosecute the parents of Black and Brown truant youth when she was the district attorney of San Francisco.[15]

The assumed protocol via federal guidelines is to keep young people with their legal guardians if they appear in youth courts under status offenses. Yet, for others it is a homophobic and/or transphobic parent who is petitioning to have them removed from their custody and placed in juvenile jail. The non-personhood of trans/queer youth is confirmed through the mark of ungovernability in an attempt to relinquish legal accountability. As is undeniable, trans/queer youth are habitually physically and emotionally terrorized in schools; then, in an attempt to survive, they often refuse to return. Truancy, for most young people, would not find them in juvenile jails, but if their parent or guardian is also invested in their desolation then the lockup is almost certain.

Along with truancy, the sexual practices (even as accusation) of trans/queer youth can find them beyond the governance of their parents' projected cis heterosexuality. In deep Foucauldian realness the court performs its disgust by demanding every titillating detail. The state revels in its forced disclosure. These youth are rendered "incorrigible" because of consensual queer sex, while their straight peers escape the severity of such consequences. Moralism reappears in the *neutral* space of the court to reconfirm the court's affinity to non-neutrality. Trans/queer youth are also sometimes held in contempt for presenting in a way that confirms their gender if that presentation contests the judge's desire. Compounding the cycles of incarceration, if youth that are awaiting trial have been removed from their parents' or guardians' custody, they are often forced to remain incarcerated in pretrial detention. De facto sumptuary laws and sexual morality become relegislated as the conditions of captivity for youth who refuse to remain an "object in the midst of other objects."[16]

"The child's habitual disregard of the lawful and reasonable demands of his caretakers and that the child is beyond their control": thus the Louisiana Children's Code designates ungovernability as twinned evasion.[17] Given the state's foundational violence, being beyond the control of that same system is also an attempt to find safe passage out of it. Indeed, the practices of trans/queer youth, their ability to figure a social world out of the antisociality that envelops them, are not simply a survival strategy, although they are that. A life lived below the incessant charge of *bad choices*, for those without any good ones, scavenges a post-political plan of attack—youth liberation as guerrilla warfare to destitute the state.[18]

Such contemptuous living, even in the small space of habitual disregard, is countered by harm's escalation, here in the form of youth imprisonment. Yet these practices of refusal also open possibility after anything that might resemble options has disappeared. While the state pathologizes and criminalizes young people's ungovernability as yet another symptom of their unwillingness to adhere to white civil society, their methods persist as a rebellion against that which produces them as persons in waiting, at best, while in practice relegating them to democracy's negativity. Or, put another way, these acts stack together to reveal shared tactics of survival—a sociality of *bad kids* who know the goodness of group disruption.

Still Fucking Here

I too was an errant youth. By the age of fourteen I was precariously housed and had already been expelled from school for the second and final time. I was charged with truancy, which was the name they gave my attempt to escape the extended torment of public education. It was then, as it is now, much easier to banish the survivors and to produce us as the problem of our own making than it is to confront violence's grind. My chronic absence was narrated as disruptive, not because I was actively distracting others but because I exposed the fragility of that which kept us in class by escaping it. Indeed, their fear was not for me, a fact they emphatically confirmed but that I might serve as referent for others to join us beyond the school's administration.

My refusal to adhere to the lockdown of normativity's drive, expressed as unavoidable injury, was both the punishment for my escape and the catalyst for its persistence. Alone together, the materiality of my survival was never singular. The intimacy of aid—a sofa, free food, a place to be when there was no other—offered a wayward community, however transitive. Without transcendence, we can't disregard violence's endurance, nor assume flight is always an option. Yet here, I want to hold the beloved networks of care that have always helped us learn, as Tourmaline affirms, that "It's easy to be free." In the quake of her evocative precision, we know our undoing has not been undone; on the contrary, it continues to intensify. Nonetheless, radical dreaming affords us the space of ease, which is how we might learn to feel freedom.[19]

Among the figures whose freedom dreams have allowed for our shared endurance in a world that wishes otherwise is Miss Major. In the 1990s, Major was working at the Tenderloin AIDS Resource Center (TARC) as a street-level service provider for low-income people in the neighborhood. She drove the outreach van and helped run the needle exchange program that provided clean syringes and other supplies to anyone who asked. Needle exchanges were then, and continue to be, semilegal operations where direct action and mutual aid meet in the communal knowledge that distributing resources without expectation keeps us alive. Before the massive tech-fueled gentrification of the

Tenderloin, it was a space of fugitivity where those cast aside came together to build a life out of the wreckage of latest capitalism. The site of the Compton's Cafeteria riots decades before, even under attack, its glorious blight has partially protected it from those who find value in sterility. An unhoused teenager who had, like so many before, sought refuge in the fantasy of San Francisco, I was sitting in the lobby of TARC when a booming laugh broke the ordered chaos of the room. With a swing of a glass door and the slam of a box of condoms on the floor, Major was there.[20]

Major is multiple. She is a Black trans woman by way of the South Side, by way of Deep East, now Little Rock. In the aftermath of at least two bloody uprisings, she was radicalized by Attica survivor Frank "Big Black" Smith in Dannemora prison and on the streets outside the Stonewall. She is the maternal sign for many whose first mothers lost them. Her stories of survival, hooking, and boosting collect a wild history where getting by without getting got grows an ecology beyond the formalism of the state. Sinuous scams, fraudulent documents, and ever-changing identifications, her life on the run brought the world with her—anarchism in action. In 1990s San Francisco, she and most of her girls survived with only scant health care, let alone the coverage necessary to pay for gender-affirming services. Through a dedication to supporting her sisters and daughters, fictitious community college students gleaned financial aid checks for classes never taken to pay for care never otherwise available. Here, ungovernability is not a scene of drifting chaos where power's account of survival always cuts along difference; that is democracy. It is an organized yet improvisational practice in common that revels in pleasure and expropriation, whose aim is to collectivize exposure toward that exposure's abolition.[21]

The Biometrics of Domination

Without consent, the mechanism of being accounted for by being counted against intensifies under the surveillant gaze—democracy's resolve. The walled polis demands your papers, a technology where self-representation is ferociously required to adhere to the genres of state legibility. From public bathrooms and residential hotels to ICE prisons and airports, identification or its lack often dictates movement, or its lack. Many trans organizations remain dedicated to the life-saving task of providing gender markers and name changes that are necessary for people navigating bureaucracy's escalation. Having the option to align one's identification under a regime of state surveillance, especially for those held in highly institutionalized spaces, like shelters and hospitals, is a reform we cannot not fight for.[22]

Along with battling through what Dean Spade might call the violence of administration—democracy's data set reconsolidates the gender binary. Here, by way of boundless accommodation, mainstream LGBT politics has, on occasion, suggested transitioning from medically imposed gender markers to ever-expanding biometrics as criteria in state-issued identification—a deferral of gender as biomedical *truth* and toward retinal scans as that truth's concretization. This idea also accumulates under the growing consensus that facial recognition's artificial intelligence (AI) technology is unable to "accurately" identify many trans, gender-nonconforming, and/or nonwhite people. In response, projects have emerged that demand a *democratization* of AI that can *recognize us all*—equality in and as the gaze of the state. Yet what remains under these attempts to degender identification is that gender normativity and anti-Blackness are designed into the very idea of biometrics. Worse, these demands, in turn, legitimate biometrics, and the state that reads them, as the racial and gendered scientific *truth*, and their proliferation as the path to safety. As we continue to expand gender options on IDs, we must also struggle to end the state that issues them as a practice of territorialization.[23]

While the state's checkpoints remain, collective indeterminacy, or more precisely collectivizing the refusal to be known from without, emerges as a tactic of interdiction. Tourmaline's *The Personal Things* is a stop-motion animated film that layers an interview with Major over the vibrancy of drawings. Opening with a zooming shot of her 1976 Cadillac DeVille crowned with vanity plates that read "TS CUGR," Major announces her cunning irreverence. Major's voiceover declares that "one of the most exciting things to me today is watching a girl go catch the bus in her shit. You know, it's like, yes!" Her joyful laugh cuts through the juxtaposition of the history of how she and other girls could not dress during the day, for fear of absolute violence. Detailing the ways Black trans women were targeted by police for "just breathing," she entangles her optimism with an insistence on harm's ongoingness.[24]

Wanting to reduce the kinds of administrative harassment she lives, Major changed the gender marker on her identification from the assigned "M" to an "F." The camera pans the drawings, creating movement through depth and light, as Major's narration reworks the relationship between the political and the personal. In a radical recasting of the temporality of transition, she then changed them "back to male" because "I want people to know I'm a transgender person and love me for that. Fuck this other stuff." She did not want the state to understand her as a cis woman, and "that was my way to strike back. And you have to find your way to strike back." In effect, her striking back was not a desire to further expand the biometric state, or for a more democratic census but to collapse the very conditions of intelligibility that offer nothing other than life's cessation. She's emphatic that such practices are not available to all, nor is she making a claim to realness or a generalizable prescription but that you have to "get together and abolish what is going on. But it's the personal stuff that gives you the strength to go forward."

Major's perpetual interruptions and illicit practices—the ways she grows a Black trans social life in the ruins of the white world—unsettles the stone precision of the state's biometric drive. This, with the unruliness of trans/queer youth who reject the corporal discipline of education and the emptiness of home, undoes the pledge of incremental personhood. While the scale at which revolutionary change most often becomes known might miss these minor acts, it is their building of another (end of the) world while also allowing for life to fill it that reminds us we never struggle alone. Together, our antiauthoritarianism is a force that wildcats the state in the covert practices of skipping school, jumping turnstiles, and counterfeiting documents. Underground, we creep, undetected, through the dark alleys of recognition and below the frames of democracy's security cameras.[25]

While this book has dwelled for perhaps too long in the space of death, I end with the ungovernable, not because such practices negate violence but because we, those who go on, must hold this incommensurability. If abolition's generativity names a presence of a world as much as it labors to end the one we cannot survive, then ungovernability not only refutes the state; it also figures the ease of living now. This is not to lay claim to the diminishing of modernity's structuring antagonism. If anything, this is an unfinished experiment in collective action—a recursive dream that builds on itself, as pedagogies of rebellion always do. Yet, even in this place of trans/queer celebration that is Major's laugh, we are returned to the banks of the River Jordan, where we await Marsha, Sylvia, and all the others who were stolen from a world that could not bear their opulence. It is in this atmosphere of violence where getting ungovernable is both a trace of, and a map for, "becoming liberated as we speak."

Introduction. River of Sorrow

Epigraph: "Rapping with a Street Transvestite Revolutionary: An Interview with Marcia Johnson," in *Out of the Closets: Voices of Gay Liberation*, ed. Karla Jay and Allen Young (New York: NYU Press, 1992), 114–18. Tourmaline is the eminent researcher and archivist of Marsha P. Johnson. Her uncompensated archival labor, oral histories, and digitizing of those sources has been vital to our collective knowledge. I, and we all, are indebted to her work, much of which has been collected on her blog "The Spirit Was . . . ," https://thespiritwas.tumblr.com/. The title of this introduction comes from Anohni's song about Marsha P. Johnson by the same name. Antony and the Johnsons, "River of Sorrow," from *Antony and the Johnsons* (Durtro, 2000).

Epigraph: Frantz Fanon, *The Wretched of the Earth* (New York: Grove, 2005), 71.

1 Here I am thinking about the ways earth and water in particular, but space in general, hold the histories of their molecular entanglements. See, for example, Tiffany Lethabo King, *The Black Shoals: Offshore Formations of Black and Native Studies* (Durham, NC: Duke University Press, 2019); Dora Silva Santana, "Transitionings and Returnings: Experiments with the Poetics of Transatlantic Water," *Transgender Studies Quarterly* 4, no. 2 (2017): 181–90; and M. Jacqui Alexander, *Pedagogies of Crossing: Meditations on Feminism, Sexual Politics, Memory, and the Sacred* (Durham, NC: Duke University Press, 2005). The violent gentrification of the piers has been met with resistance organized primarily by trans/queer youth of color, including FIERCE! and others. Related, my point here is not to suggest that people do not still build life at the piers but to highlight how New York City supported the massive displacement of those previously in the neighborhood, decimating trans/queer of color social life. For more on this history, see Martin Manalansan, "Race, Violence and Neoliberal Spatial Politics in the Global City,"

Social Text 84–85 23, nos. 3–4 (2005); Christina B. Hanhardt, *Safe Space: Gay Neighborhood History and the Politics of Violence* (Durham, NC: Duke University Press, 2013); *Fenced OUT* (New York: FIERCE, Papertiger TV, and Neutral Zone, 2000), DVD.

2 "Randy Wicker Interviews Sylvia Rivera on the Pier," *Vimeo*, 2011, https://vimeo .com/35975275?cjevent=fab96c0f7da911e983f800ad0a1c0e0d.

3 The ongoing degradation of working-class Black and Brown trans history has, not surprisingly, suppressed much of STAR House's as well, which remains speculative and incomplete at best. See Leslie Feinberg, "Street Transvestite Action Revolutionaries," *Workers World*, September 24, 2006, https://www .workers.org/2006/us/lavender-red-73/; Benjamin Shepard, "Sylvia and Sylvia's Children: The Battle for a Queer Public Space," in *That's Revolting! Queer Strategies for Resisting Assimilation*, ed. Mattilda Bernstein Sycamore (Brooklyn, NY: Soft Skull, 2008), 123–40. See Martin Duberman, *Stonewall* (New York: Plume, 1994), for an oral history of Stonewall. For an early analysis of the links between the rapid gentrification of the Village and Marsha's homelessness, see Steve Watson, "Stonewall 1979: The Drag of Politics," *Village Voice*, June 4, 1979, https:// www.villagevoice.com/2019/06/04/stonewall-1979-the-drag-of-politics/. For another account of this history, see Rachel Corbman, "Sylvia Rivera and Marsha P. Johnson: Listen to the Newly Unearthed Interview with Street Transvestite Action Revolutionaries," New York Historical Society, June 26, 2019, http:// womenatthecenter.nyhistory.org/gay-power-is-trans-history-street-transvestite -action-revolutionaries/. There is much more to be said about the forms of sociality STAR House created. On the question of their reproductive labor and care work, see Nat Raha, "Queer Capital: Marxism in Queer Theory and Post-1950 Poetics" (PhD diss., University of Sussex, 2018), 133–39.

4 A video of Sylvia Rivera's speech is available at https://www.youtube.com/watch ?v=Jb-JIOWUw10. L.O.V.E. (Lesbians Organized for Video Experience), a feminist video collective founded in 1972, owns the only available footage of the rally and her speech. For an early critique of the racism in early LGBT activism, see Third World Gay Revolution (New York City), "What We Want, What We Believe," in *Out of the Closets: Voices of Gay Liberation*, ed. Karla Jay and Allen Young (New York: NYU Press, 1972), 363–67.

5 For a foundational critique of the whiteness of LGBT studies, see Cathy J. Cohen, "Punks, Bulldaggers, and Welfare Queens: The Radical Potential of Queer Politics?," GLQ 3 (1997): 437–65; E. Patrick Johnson and Mae G. Henderson, "Introduction: Queering Black Studies/'Quaring' Queer Studies," in *Black Queer Studies: A Critical Anthology*, ed. E. Patrick Johnson and Mae G. Henderson (Durham, NC: Duke University Press, 2005), 1–17. On this question of writing history and its refusal, see Saidiya Hartman, "Venus in Two Acts," *Small Axe* 26 (June 2008): 1–14. Neoliberalism appears here most vividly through the simultaneous privatization of violence and the inclusion of identities. For example, the attack against Sylvia on the stage in 1973 evidenced the collusion, even then, of lesbian and gay identity with racial and gender norms. Rather than a demand

for the end of coercion, they sought a claim to normativity through the exiling of Sylvia and all gender-nonconforming people of color. This unruliness might also be related to Dora Santana's theorization of "mais viva" as a form of vitality that exceeds capture; see Dora Silva Santana, "Mais Viva! Reassembling Transness, Blackness, and Feminism," *Transgender Studies Quarterly* 6, no. 2 (2019): 210–22. For a much more complete consideration of the ways queer studies holds on to its ideal figures, see Kadji Amin, *Disturbing Attachments: Genet, Modern Pederasty, and Queer History* (Durham, NC: Duke University Press, 2017).

6 I'm not suggesting that homophobic and anti-trans violence are interchangeable, but because of the way the social produces gender and sexuality, their actors do not necessarily make this distinction. Further, both *trans* and *transgender* are, like *queer*, historically and geopolitically located terms. To this end, their deployment always conceals as much as it illustrates. For more on this transnational un/intelligibility, see Aren Z. Aizura, *Mobile Subjects: Transnational Imaginaries of Gender Reassignment* (Durham, NC: Duke University Press, 2018), especially the introduction, "Provincializing Trans."

Those that are most loyal to masking the dependency between gender and sexuality hide under the pitch of "gender critical feminists." TERFs (trans-exclusionary radical feminists), as they are often called by trans activists and others, but a marker they refuse as a slur, understand trans people to be a threat to the sanctity of the categories of women/men, and by extension to sexual identities. Through a eugenicist logic by way of gender essentialism and its fever dreams of biological determinacy, TERFs fortify the border wall between gender and sexuality. "Biology is not bigotry"—their semiotic attempt to disavow charges of transphobia via a reinscription of their own subalternity—is performed as absolute abjection. Through a synchronized sleight of hand, cis womanhood becomes the victim of patriarchy, not because of the misogynist structuring of the social but because of trans women's existence. This is not to suggest that cis women are any more transphobic than cis men. However, what is unique is that TERF anti-trans attacks are launched from inside feminism and under its name. This is the other side of the reality that much if not most physical anti-trans violence is committed by cis men. For a very early interview with Sylvia and Marsha, which includes a discussion with them about men and sexism, see Jeffrey Masters, "Earliest Known Recording of Marsha P. Johnson, Sylvia Rivera Found," *Advocate*, December 29, 2019, https://www.advocate.com/transgender /2019/12/29/earliest-known-recording-marsha-p-johnson-sylvia-rivera-found?. For more on the tensions between queer and trans studies, see Susan Stryker, "Transgender Studies: Queer Theory's Evil Twin," GLQ 10, no. 2 (2004): 212–15.

7 This persistence of a phobic relationship, not to that which is threat but to that which one maintains domination over, is a contour of violence this book charts. Here the imagined boundary between gender and sexuality must not simply be policed, but those of us who cross must be both absorbed into and forcefully excluded from the social fantasy they wish to preserve.

8 On the mainstreaming of the LGBT movement, see Roderick A. Ferguson, *One-*

Dimensional Queer (Cambridge: Polity, 2018); Myrl Beam, *Gay, Inc.: The Non-profitization of Queer Politics* (Minneapolis: University of Minnesota Press, 2018); Lisa Duggan, *The Twilight of Equality? Neoliberalism, Cultural Politics, and the Attack on Democracy* (Boston: Beacon, 2003). A 2019 survey shows that younger people are becoming "less tolerant" of LGBT people. See "Accelerating Acceptance 2019," GLAAD, June 24, 2019, https://www.glaad.org/publications/accelerating-acceptance-2019.

9 I am suggesting the term *anarchism* to provisionally reference the long political tradition of left thought (and action) against the state form. While there are important arguments to be had within this contentious genealogy, what is useful here is its naming of the structuring limits of the settler state as well as a glimpse of how horizontality might offer another path for being in the social. José Esteban Muñoz, *Cruising Utopia: The Then and There of Queer Futurity* (New York: NYU Press, 2009), 1–18. Horizontalism is a theory of collective organizing popular in many antiauthoritarian projects. For one account, see Marina Sitrin, *Horizontalism: Voices of Popular Power in Argentina* (Oakland, CA: AK Press, 2006). On the necessity of collective study, see Stefano Harney and Fred Moten, *The Undercommons: Fugitive Planning and Black Study* (Brooklyn, NY: Minor Compositions, 2013).

10 LGBT politics refers to mainstream, U.S.-based national LGBT organizing, most notably the Human Rights Campaign and the National Gay and Lesbian Task Force.

11 Of course, in a world that aligns life with the normal and relegates the abnormal to the space of death, normality is hard to argue against. However, this push for normativity has the power of further obliteration of the unassimilable. The activist work done by groups like INCITE! Women of Color against Violence shows the connections between interpersonal violence and larger systems of state violence. For more, see Angela Y. Davis, "The Color of Violence against Women," *Colorlines* 3, no. 3 (fall 2000). Dan Savage's 2010 video campaign "It Gets Better," which urges people to make videos stating that LGBT life after youth is filled with less pain and terror, vividly reproduces this logic. See www.itgetsbetterproject.com.

12 "Fictive justice" is a way of talking about how legal precedent forces a kind of "justice" based on analogy. In other words, judgments rely upon previous cases and thus function through a series of abstractions. For a foundational example, see Kimberlé Crenshaw, "Mapping the Margins: Intersectionality, Identity Politics, and Violence Against Women of Color," in *Critical Race Theory: The Key Writings That Formed the Movement*, ed. Kimberlé Crenshaw, Neil Gotanda, Gary Peller, and Kendall Thomas (New York: New Press, 1995), 357. Here Crenshaw shows how the law is unable to apprehend the multiplicity of identity. In relation to trans studies and politics Dean Spade's work continues to invite us to think beyond and against formal equality and rights-based politics as the basis for what he calls a "critical trans politics." Dean Spade, "Introduction: Rights, Movements,

and Critical Trans Politics," *Normal Life: Administrative Violence, Critical Trans Politics, and the Limits of Law* (Durham, NC: Duke University Press, 2015), 1–21. There are also instances when anti-queer violence erupts onto the social screen, for example, the 1998 murder of Matthew Shepard. Shepard, a white, gay, twenty-one-year old college student, it could be argued, was held as referent for all anti-queer violence because of the relative ease of mourning for Matthew. Although this might be true, anti-queer violence must be simultaneously put on public display and made to disappear so that the murders of queers exist outside of national meaning. Mourning for Matthew, through the spectacle of a mocking pain, works to disappear the archive that is queer death.

13 For more on the place of death in trans/queer studies see Jin Haritaworn, Adi Kuntsman, and Silvia Posocco, eds., *Queer Necropolitics* (London: Routledge, 2014).

14 Here I am thinking about the ways groups like the Black Panther Party, American Indian Movement, Black Liberation Army, Weather Underground, Fuerzas Armadas de Liberación Nacional, the George Jackson Brigade, and many other armed leftist groups of the 1970s and 1980s have pushed against the idea that meeting the massive violence of the state with passivism is the best, or only way to build resistance. Also see INCITE! Women of Color against Violence, ed., *Color of Violence: The INCITE! Anthology* (Cambridge, MA: South End, 2006). For more on the question of state violence, race, and sexuality, see Chandan Reddy, *Freedom with Violence: Race, Sexuality, and the US State* (Durham, NC: Duke University Press, 2011). For more on "nonviolence" and state violence, see Peter Gelderloos, *How Nonviolence Protects the State* (Cambridge, MA: South End, 2007). In response to the case of the New Jersey 4, communities, mostly in the Bay Area, organized for their freedom. See "Free the New Jersey 4," https://freenj4.wordpress.com/. For more on the way the attacker produced himself as a survivor of a "hate crime," see Nicole Pasulka, "How 4 Gay Black Women Fought Back against Sexual Harassment—And Landed in Jail," NPR, June 30, 2015, https://www.npr.org/sections/codeswitch/2015/06/30/418634390/how-4-gay-black-women-fought-back-against-a-sexual-harasser-and-landed-in-jail.

15 Karl Marx and Friedrich Engels, "The Holy Family," in *Collected Works*, vol. 4 (New York: International, 1975), 121.

16 This is a concern Foucault also suggested in his criticism of Marxism. See Michel Foucault, *Power/Knowledge: Selected Interviews and Other Writings, 1972–1977* (New York: Vintage, 1980), 58–59. I'm also aware that Marx's statism is the subject of much debate. This tends to circle around readings of the *Communist Manifesto* and his work after the Paris Commune. In short, communism, for some readers of Marx, would dissolve the state form because it would abolish class. However, under my reading of the state as internal to itself, this does not at all seem inevitable. While it might seem redundant, the insistence on "racial capitalism" in this book is always seeking to understand the racial, colonial, and gendered contours of capital.

17 Here I am thinking both with, but perhaps beside, Foucault's investigation of how norms become the force of modernity. See, as one extensive example, Michel Foucault, *Abnormal: Lectures at the Collège de France 1974–1975*, translated by Graham Burchell (New York: Picador, 2003). The concept of negative value is also in conversation with Lindon Barrett's work on Blackness and value. See Lindon Barrett, "Exemplary Values: Value, Violence, and Others of Value," *SubStance* 21, no. 1 (1992): 77–94. For more on the force of normativity and sexuality, see Lauren Berlant and Michael Warner, "Sex in Public," *Critical Inquiry* 24, no. 2 (1998): 547–66. For an anarchist analysis, see Kuwasi Balagoon, "The Continuing Appeal of Anti-Imperialism." *Prison News Service*, no. 65, https://kersplebedeb .com/posts/balagoon-3/.

18 See Ruth Wilson Gilmore, "What Is to Be Done?" *American Quarterly* 63, no. 2 (2011): 245–65.

19 For a discussion of "life chances" in respect to trans low-income and/or people of color, see Spade, *Normal Life*. On homelessness, see Craig Willse, *The Value of Homelessness: Managing Surplus Life in the United States* (Minneapolis: University of Minnesota Press, 2015). A phenomenology reading of anti-trans/queer violence can be found in Gayle Salamon, *The Life and Death of Latisha King: A Critical Phenomenology of Transphobia* (New York: NYU Press, 2018). On anti-Blackness and HIV/AIDS, see Dagmawi Woubshet, *The Calendar of Loss: Race, Sexuality, and Mourning in the Early Era of AIDS* (Baltimore: Johns Hopkins University Press, 2015); and Adam Geary, *Antiblack Racism and the AIDS Epidemic: State Intimacies* (New York: Palgrave Macmillan, 2014). Again, Foucault argues that among the attributes that name modernity is the shift from sovereign power to biopower. Yet rather than "progressing" from the absolute violence of the sovereign, through the racial state, violence is (re)distributed.

20 Walter Benjamin, "Critique of Violence," in *Reflections: Essays, Aphorisms, Autobiographical Writing*, ed. Peter Demetz (New York: Schocken, 1986), 281.

21 For more, see Judith Butler, *Parting Ways: Jewishness and the Critique of Zionism* (New York: Columbia University Press, 2012), 77–78. I am also attentive to multiple definitions of the German *gewalt*. Along with David Lloyd, I'm thinking of it as a continuum of violence and force. David Lloyd, "From the Critique of Violence to the Critique of Rights," *Critical Times* 3, no. 1 (April 1, 2020): 114–15.

22 Jacques Derrida, "Force of Law: The 'Mythic Foundations of Authority,'" in *Deconstruction and the Possibility of Justice*, ed. Drucilla Cornell, Michel Rosenfeld, and David Carlson (New York: Routledge, 1992), 33.

23 Derrida, "Force of Law," 34.

24 Derrida, "Force of Law," 46.

25 Derrida, "Force of Law," 46.

26 For more on the relationship between representational democracy and colonialism, see Glen Coulthard, *Red Skin, White Masks: Rejecting the Colonial Politics of Recognition* (Minneapolis: University of Minnesota Press, 2014). Also see Fred Moten, "Democracy," in *Keywords for American Cultural Studies*, 2nd ed., ed.

Bruce Burgett and Glenn Hendler (New York: NYU Press, 2014), 73–75. Angela Davis made a similar argument about the police, via Frantz Fanon, in her writing while incarcerated. See Angela Y. Davis, "Political Prisoners, Prisons, and Black Liberation," in *If They Come in the Morning: Voices of Resistance*, ed. Angela Y. Davis, Ruchell Magee, and Julian Bond, 27–43 (New York: Third Press, 1971).

27 By abolitionist epistemology I mean those who recognize the ongoingness of capture to expand under calls to reform them. Collectives like Critical Resistance have done much of the work of theorizing a modern abolitionist politic; see http://criticalresistance.org/. Also see Angela Y. Davis, *Are Prisons Obsolete?* (New York: Seven Stories, 2003); Dylan Rodríguez, *Forced Passages: Imprisoned Radical Intellectuals and the U.S. Prison Regime* (Minneapolis: University of Minnesota Press, 2006). For more on the internalization of crime and punishment logics, see Paula X. Rojas, "Are the Cops in Our Heads and Hearts?," in *The Revolution Will Not Be Funded*, ed. INCITE! Women of Color against Violence, 197–214 (Boston: South End, 2009).

28 Frantz Fanon, *Black Skin, White Masks* (New York: Grove, 1967), 31.

29 For more on sociogeny, see Sylvia Wynter, "Towards the Sociogenic Principle: Fanon, Identity, the Puzzle of Conscious Experience, and What It Is Like to Be 'Black,'" in *National Identities and Sociopolitical Changes in Latin America*, ed. Mercedes F. Dúran-Cogan and Antonio Gómez-Moriana (New York: Routledge, 2001), 30–66; C. Riley Snorton, *Black on Both Sides: A Racial History of Trans Identity* (Minneapolis: University of Minnesota Press, 2017), 184–86; David Marriott, "Inventions of Existence: Sylvia Wynter, Frantz Fanon, Sociogeny, and 'the Damned,'" CR: *The New Centennial Review* 11, no. 3 (2011): 45–89.

30 Some selected works in Fanon studies with an attention to gender, sexuality, and/or queerness include T. Denean Sharpley-Whiting, *Frantz Fanon: Conflicts and Feminisms* (Lanham, MD: Rowman and Littlefield, 1997); Darieck Scott, *Extravagant Abjection: Blackness, Power, and Sexuality in the African American Literary Imagination* (New York: NYU Press, 2010); Kara Keeling, *The Witch's Flight: The Cinematic, the Black Femme, and the Image of Common Sense* (Durham, NC: Duke University Press, 2007); David Marriott, *Haunted Life: Visual Culture and Black Modernity* (New Brunswick, NJ: Rutgers University Press, 2007); David Marriott, *Whither Fanon? Studies in the Blackness of Being* (Stanford, CA: Stanford University Press, 2018); William M. Paris, "Humanism's Secret Shadow: The Construction of Black Gender/Sexuality in Frantz Fanon and Hortense Spillers," *philoSOPHIA* 8, no. 1 (2018): 81–99. For important work on Fanon and trans studies, see Snorton, *Black on Both Sides*. I use the term *freedom* here and throughout the text as a placeholder for that which is still to come. In this, I mean to suggest that rather than its liberal deployment as a freedom from, here I am interested in the project of freedom with, a relational experiment in what it might mean to be beyond the human.

31 Fanon, *Black Skin, White Masks*, 180n44. For more on the etymology of "ma commère" in the Antilles, see Charlotte Hammond, *Entangled Otherness: Cross-*

Gender Fabrications in the Francophone Caribbean (Liverpool: Liverpool University Press, 2019), 14.

32 Keguro Macharia, *Frottage: Frictions of Intimacy across the Black Diaspora* (New York: NYU Press, 2019), 47.

33 For other readings of this footnote, see Neville Hoad, *African Intimacies: Race, Homosexuality, and Globalization* (Minneapolis: University of Minnesota Press, 2006), 38–39; Lewis R. Gordon, *What Fanon Said: A Philosophical Introduction to His Life and Thought* (New York: Fordham University Press, 2015), 63–65. For an extended reading of women of color and sexuality in Fanon's work, see Françoise Vergès, "Creole Skin, Black Mask: Fanon and Disavowal," *Critical Inquiry* 23, no. 3 (1997): 578–95. On the question of the Oedipal complex in the Antilles, see Ronald A. T. Judy, "Fanon's Body of Black Experience," in *Fanon: A Critical Reader*, ed. Lewis R. Gordon, T. Denean Sharpley-Whiting, and Renee T. White (Cambridge, MA: Blackwell, 1996), 68–70.

34 That colonialism produces what we come to know as normative gender and sex uality has been well argued by many anticolonial and specifically Native feminists. See, for example, J. Kēhaulani Kauanui, *Paradoxes of Hawaiian Sovereignty: Land, Sex, and the Colonial Politics of State Nationalism* (Durham, NC: Duke University Press, 2018); Tom Boellstorff et al., "Decolonizing Transgender: A Roundtable Discussion," *Transgender Studies Quarterly* 1, no. 3 (2014): 419–39; Joanne Barker, ed., *Critically Sovereign: Indigenous Gender, Sexuality, and Feminist Studies* (Durham, NC: Duke University Press, 2017).

35 Hannah Arendt, *On Violence* (New York: Harcourt Brace, 1970), 18–21.

36 For Arendt, it is essential to separate power, strength, force, and authority from violence. However, I am unconvinced of the usefulness of this idea.

37 The footage from Angela Davis's interview can be found in the film *The Black Power Mixtape*. Göran Hugo Olsson et al., *The Black Power Mixtape 1967–1975: A Documentary in 9 Chapters* (New York: MPI Media Group, 2011).

38 Angela Davis, in Göran Hugo Olsson et al., *The Black Power Mixtape*.

39 Judith Butler offers a philosophical survey of nonviolence, which is, for them, a world-preserving force. Butler argues that, "When any of us commit acts of violence, we are, in and through those acts, building a more violent world." Judith Butler, *The Force of Nonviolence: An Ethico-Political Bind* (London: Verso, 2020), 19. In contrast, I am suggesting that nonviolence is, under the current order, the way we are disciplined into accepting harm as a condition of our own making.

40 C. Riley Snorton and Jin Haritaworn, "Trans Necropolitics: A Transnational Reflection on Violence, Death, and Trans of Color Afterlife," in *The Transgender Studies Reader 2*, ed. Susan Stryker and Aren Z. Aizura (New York: Routledge, 2013), 74. For an extended reading of the work of race, representation, and the production of unfreedom, see David Lloyd, *Under Representation: The Racial Regimes of Aesthetics* (New York: Fordham University Press, 2019), especially the chapter "Representation's Coup," 95–123. Here I am also thinking with Christina Sharpe's conception of "defending the dead." See Christina Sharpe, *In the Wake: On Blackness and Being* (Durham, NC: Duke University Press, 2016), 10–11. Re-

lated to the flatting of the image, the category "trans women of color" now tends to function as a screen for white cis projection that renders all who might identify as such to be both the sign of absolute abjection and radical potentiality. In other words, Marsha and Sylvia are distilled into stand-ins for everything but themselves.

41 Saidiya V. Hartman, *Scenes of Subjection: Terror, Slavery, and Self-Making in Nineteenth-Century America* (New York: Oxford University Press, 1997), 3.

42 Fred Moten, *In the Break: The Aesthetics of the Black Radical Tradition* (Minneapolis: University of Minnesota Press, 2003), 5.

43 For more on the radical potentiality of queerness, see Muñoz, *Cruising Utopia*.

44 "Refuse Powers' Grasp: Introduction," *Arika*, n.d., http://arika.org.uk/events /episode-8-refuse-powers-grasp/introduction.

Chapter 1. Near Life

Epigraph: Frantz Fanon, *Black Skin, White Masks* (New York: Grove, 1967), 139.

Epigraph: Graffiti written on the restroom wall at the University of California, Santa Cruz, 2006.

1 Kelly St. John, "Hayward/Transgender Teen Did Nothing 'to Deserve Death'/But One Accused Killer Said He Vomited on Finding She Was Male," *SFGate*, July 27, 2005, https://www.sfgate.com/bayarea/article/HAYWARD-Transgender-teen -did-nothing-to-2620082.php.

2 Throughout I shift between using trans/queer people's first, last, and sometimes both names. I do this because I want to hold the tension between our assumed familiarity with them, while at the same time I don't want to reproduce them as legalistic objects. I also only use the names and pronouns they used. However, if they are only gendered outside of their own self-description, then I use "they."

3 Kelly St. John, "Chilling Time Line of a Killing / Death of Transgender Teen Described in Grisly Detail," *SFGate*, February 26, 2003, https://www.sfgate.com /bayarea/article/Chilling-Time-Line-of-a-Killing-Death-of-2668044.php.

4 Jaxon Van Derbeken, "Oakland Man Killed by s.f. Cops Had Troubled Past/ Knife Wielder Denounced Gays, Minorities," *SFGate*, October 10, 2002, https:// www.sfgate.com/health/article/Oakland-man-killed-by-S-F-cops-had-troubled -past-2786521.php; Mattilda, A K A Matt Bernstein Sycamore, "Gay Shame: From Queer Autonomous Space to Direct Action Extravaganza," in *That's Revolting! Queer Strategies for Resisting Assimilation*, ed. Mattilda Bernstein Sycamore, 237–62 (Brooklyn, NY: Soft Skull, 2004).

5 For an investigation into the whiteness of the Castro, see Marlon Riggs's experimental documentary *Tongues Untied* (1998). The Castro has a long history of being a space exclusively for gay white men and hostile to everyone else. See Wyatt Buchanan, "Gays at Receiving End of Bias Claim / Investigation at Castro Bar Opens Dialogue about Prejudice," *SFGate*, June 26, 2006, https://www.sfgate .com/news/article/Gays-at-receiving-end-of-bias-claim-2659647.php.

6 For more on the history of the organizing collective Gay Shame, see Mattilda,

"Gay Shame," 237–62; Margot D. Weiss, "Gay Shame and BDSM Pride: Neoliberalism, Privacy, and Sexual Politics," *Radical History Review* 2008, no. 100 (2008): 87–101; Eric Stanley, "The Affective Commons: Gay Shame, Queer Hate, and Other Collective Feelings," GLQ 24, no. 4 (2018): 489–508. Also, most importantly, see their work at gayshame.net. Most of the media coverage that followed Jihad Akbar's murder did not mention that he was queer, which helped produce him as an "outside agitator." See this op-ed from his lover: Tim Silard, "BAGDAD CAFE KILLING / A Year Later the Cops' Wall of Silence Remains / Death at the hands of the SFPD," *SFGate*, October 12, 2003, https://www.sfgate.com/opinion /article/BAGDAD-CAFE-KILLING-A-Year-Later-the-Cops-Wall-2571528.php.

7 Lisa Leff, "Lawyers Debate 'Gay Panic' Defense," *Associated Press*, July 20, 2006, http://www.law.ucla.edu/williamsinstitute/press/LawyersDebateGayPanic Defense.html. During the trial, Nabors also argued that Magidson was a survivor of sexual assault, not because the encounter was nonconsensual but that Araujo's undisclosed trans identity nullified the very possibility of consent. "He (Araujo) did not come clean with being what he really was. I feel like he forced them into homosexual sex, and my definition of rape was being forced into sex." Kelly St. John, "HAYWARD/ Defense Grills Star Witness in Teen Murder Trial/'You're Lying,' Lawyer Says to Man Who Pleaded Guilty," *SFGate*, April 28, 2004, https://www.sfgate.com/bayarea/article/HAYWARD-Defense-grills-star -witness-in-teen-2763861.php.

8 During the investigation into the text messages, Celis was able to resign from the SFPD, which allowed him to end the investigation and keep his pension. See Alex Emsie, "Fallout from SFPD Racist Texts: Officer Resigns amidst Scandal," KQED, March 19, 2015, https://www.kqed.org/news/10454955/racist-texts-prompt -sfpd-internal-investigation. Men who harm and/or kill trans women after long consensual sexual relationships are recast as the victims of their deception when, in reality, transness figures as the site of their desire. There has been much discussion in trans communities around the figure of the "trans-attracted" cis man. While some argue more space needs to be made for these men, in hopes of destigmatizing cis men dating trans women, others argue this once again centers cis men at the expense of trans women. See, for example, Serena Sonoma, "Op-Ed: The Problem with Identifying as 'Trans Attracted,'" *Out*, September 14, 2019, https://www.out.com/transgender/2019/9/14/op-ed-problem-identifying -trans-attracted.

9 Gay Shame's form of organizing might approximate Cathy Cohen's call for a new queer politics. See Cathy J. Cohen; "Punks, Bulldaggers, and Welfare Queens: The Radical Potential of Queer Politics?" GLQ 3, no. 4 (1997): 437–65.

10 I am here thinking with Achille Mbembe when he asks, in a drastically different context, "But what does it mean to do violence to what is nothing?" Achille Mbembe, *On the Postcolony* (Berkeley: University of California Press, 2001), 174.

11 Frantz Fanon, *Peau Noire, Masques Blancs* (Paris: Éditions du Seuil, 2008), 88.

12 Fanon, *Black Skin, White Masks*, 109.

13 Fanon, *Black Skin, White Masks*, 115.

14 By extra-diegesis of difference, I mean to include all signifiers that are ascribed to the visual but are not properly images—for example, the racialization of loudness. From this passage, it also seems that Fanon incorrectly assumed that all Jews are white. However, I'm not suggesting Jewishness makes one nonwhite.

15 For an early definition of the term *queer* as a (non)identity, see Eve Kosofsky Sedgwick, *Tendencies* (Durham, NC: Duke University Press, 1993), xii. For a discussion on Fanon and "homosexuality" that differs from my own, see Terry Goldie, "Saint Fanon and 'Homosexual Territory,'" in *Frantz Fanon: Critical Perspectives*, ed. Anthony Alessandrini (New York: Routledge, 1999), 75–86.

16 The editorial/activist collective Against Equality has helped advance this point.

17 See the National Coalition of Anti-Violence Programs 2010 report on LGBTQ hate violence. Of those murders reported, 79 percent were of people of color and 50 percent were trans women. National Coalition of Anti-Violence Programs, "Reports," https://avp.org/resources/reports/.

18 Lauren Berlant's suggestion that "individuation is a historical process" is useful here for pulling apart the idea of identity while not destroying identification but to complicate how it works under liberalism. See Lauren Berlant, *Desire/Love* (Brooklyn, NY: Punctum, 2012), 16. For more on race, sex, and negativity see Bobby Benedicto, "Agents and Objects of Death: Gay Murder, Boyfriend Twins, and Queer of Color Negativity," GLQ 25, no. 2 (2019): 273–96.

19 I'm here thinking with and at times beside Adorno's reinterpretation of negativity; see Theodor W. Adorno, *Negative Dialectics* (London: Routledge, 2015).

20 William K. Rashbaum, "Body Was Cut Up, Experts Say," *New York Times*, February 26, 2005.

21 "Murder of Gay, African-American Man Reflects Twin Diseases of Racism, Homophobia, NGLTF Says," *National Gay and Lesbian Task Force News & Views*, March 24, 2000. For more on his murder, see Calvin Warren, "Onticide: Afro-Pessimism, Gay Nigger #1, and Surplus Violence," GLQ 23, no. 3 (2017): 391–41.

22 I use the name "A." because the name used in the reports was more than likely her legal name and not the name she went by. "Second Man Convicted of Killing Black Transvestite in Arkansas," *Jet*, July 28, 1997, 18.

23 Saidiya Hartman, "Venus in Two Acts," *Small Axe* 26 (2008): 3.

24 See Kareem Fahim and John Koblin, "A Year after a Teenager Was Dismembered, Still No Answer," *New York Times*, February 13, 2006.

25 This is not to suggest that hate crime statistics or legislation build safety; on the contrary, they strengthen the prison industrial complex, which is the antithesis of trans/queer safety. For a critique of the use of statists, see Dean Spade and Rori Rohlfs, "Legal Equality, Gay Numbers and the (After?) Math of Eugenics," *Scholar and Feminist Online*, spring 2016.

26 "Victims—Hate Crime Statistics, 2017," Federal Bureau of Investigation, n.d., https://ucr.fbi.gov/hate-crime/2017/tables/table-1.xls.

27 "Victims—Hate Crime Statistics."

28 For more on the politics of classification, see Geoffrey C. Bowker and Susan Leigh Star, *Sorting Things Out: Classification and Its Consequences* (Cambridge,

MA: MIT Press, 2000), 255. Furthermore, classification for many trans/queer folks continues to be a practice that reproduces traumatic pain, embarrassment, and humiliation. For an example of the ways the media condenses the murders of trans people, often treating them with a disdain similar to their murderers, see *Long Beach Press Telegram*, November 7, 2004, in which a note stated, "This transsexual woman was found beaten to death in an alleyway near 14th and Paloma streets in Central City neighborhood. She was badly beaten."

29 See "NACJD Home," Institute for Social Research, University of Michigan website, http://www.icpsr.umich.edu/NACJD/, accessed August 22, 2010.

30 See Eric A. Stanley and Nat Smith, eds., *Captive Genders: Trans Embodiment and the Prison Industrial Complex* (Oakland, CA: AK Press, 2011).

31 "It's War in Here," Sylvia Rivera Law Project, April 20, 2007, https://srlp.org/its -war-in-here/. Also see "USA: Stonewalled: Police Abuse and Misconduct against Lesbian, Gay, Bisexual and Transgender People in the U.S.," Amnesty International, September 21, 2005, https://www.amnesty.org/en/documents /AMR51/122/2005/en/.

32 The instances of violence I am attending to in this work are, for the most part, not cross-racial nor cross-class. Among other factors, this seems to be because the victims and murderers share similar social and geographical spaces. Far from believing that white supremacy or classism are not at work here, the question, then, is how they are at work differently.

33 Jordan Smith, "The Lauryn Paige Fuller Story: Of Murder and the Gender Continuum . . . ," *Austin Chronicle*, February 18, 2000, https://www.austinchronicle .com/features/2000-02-18/75904/.

34 "Postmarks: Readers React to Last Week's Cover Story on the Murder of Lauryn Paige Fuller," *Austin Chronicle*, February 25, 2000, https://www.austinchronicle .com/columns/2000-02-25/75972/.

35 Louis Black, "Defending the Lauryn Paige Fuller Murder Story," *Austin Chronicle*, February 25, 2000, https://www.austinchronicle.com/columns/2000-02-25 /page-two/.

36 For a discussion of trans people and discourses of "discovery," see Talia Bettcher, "Evil Deceivers and Make-Believers: On Transphobic Violence and the Politics of Illusion," *Hypatia* 22, no. 3 (2007): 43–65. See "Man Gets Four Years in Prison for Transgender Slaying," *Fox News*, October 1, 2005, https://www.foxnews.com /story/man-gets-four-years-in-prison-for-transgender-slaying. This is not to suggest that justice would be enacted if these defendants were found guilty. For sure, the entirety of the prison industrial complex is itself a form of violence. However, reading the success of these defenses is one way to measure the ways trans/ homophobia is central to the law.

37 Foucault made this point about the birth of state racism. See Michel Foucault, *"Society Must Be Defended": Lectures at the Collège de France 1975–1976*, translated by David Macey (New York: Picador, 2003).

38 Scotty Joe Weaver's body was found on July 22, 2004.

39 See Laura Douglas-Brown, "Ala. Killing May Be Anti-Gay Hate Crime," *Southern Voice*, June/July 2004, http://www.sovo.com/.

40 Organizers working in domestic violence prevention have helped show many of these same contours of intimacy. This is not to argue that these attacks are exclusively enacted by those known to the victim but the regularity with which they are is necessary to account for.

41 I am here referring to a number of theoretical works that are also, in part, attempting to sketch the relationship between modernity and racial and gendered violence. For some examples, see Claude Meillassoux, *The Anthropology of Slavery: The Womb of Iron and Gold* (Chicago: University of Chicago Press, 1991); Orlando Patterson, *Slavery and Social Death: A Comparative Study* (Cambridge, MA: Harvard University Press, 1985); David Wojnarowicz, *Close to the Knives: A Memoir of Disintegration* (New York: Vintage, 1991); Sharon Patricia Holland, *Raising the Dead: Readings of Death and (Black) Subjectivity* (Durham, NC: Duke University Press, 2000); Abdul R. JanMohamed, *The Death-Bound-Subject: Richard Wright's Archaeology of Death* (Durham, NC: Duke University Press, 2005); Judith Butler, *Precarious Life: The Powers of Mourning and Violence* (London: Verso, 2006); Saidiya V. Hartman, *Scenes of Subjection: Terror, Slavery, and Self-Making in Nineteenth-Century America* (New York: Oxford University Press, 1997); Antonio Viego, *Dead Subjects: Toward a Politics of Loss in Latino Studies* (Durham, NC: Duke University Press, 2007); David Marriott, *Haunted Life: Visual Culture and Black Modernity* (New Brunswick, NJ: Rutgers University Press, 2007); Neferti X. M. Tadiar, *Things Fall Away: Philippine Historical Experience and the Makings of Globalization* (Durham, NC: Duke University Press, 2009); Frank B. Wilderson, *Red, White, and Black: Cinema and the Structure of U.S. Antagonisms* (Durham, NC: Duke University Press, 2010); Christina Sharpe, *Monstrous Intimacies: Making Post-Slavery Subjects* (Durham, NC: Duke University Press, 2010); Sayak Valencia, *Gore Capitalism* (South Pasadena, CA: Semiotext(e), 2018).

42 On the "stripped-down" form of life, see Giorgio Agamben, *Homo Sacer: Sovereign Power and Bare Life* (Stanford, CA: Stanford University Press, 1998).

43 Georg W. F. Hegel, Arnold V. Miller, and J. N. Findlay, *Phenomenology of Spirit* (Oxford: Clarendon Press, 1977). For another reading of Hegel's use of reason and its racist contours, see Cedric J. Robinson, *An Anthropology of Marxism* (Chapel Hill: University of North Carolina Press, 2001), 82–83.

44 Fanon, *Black Skin, White Masks*, 220–21, n8.

45 See Alexandre Kojève, *Introduction to the Reading of Hegel*, trans. James A. Nichols, ed. Allan Bloom (New York: Basic Books, 1969); Jean-Paul Sartre, *Being and Nothingness*, trans. Hazel E. Barnes (London: Routledge, 1995). Also see David Marriott, "On Racial Fetishism," *Qui Parle: Critical Humanities and Social Sciences* 18, no. 2 (2010): 215–48.

46 Fanon, *Black Skin, White Masks*, 109.

47 For more on the self/Other collapse Fanon illustrates, see Diana Fuss, *Identifica-*

tion Papers (New York: Routledge, 1995), especially her chapter "Interior Colonies: Frantz Fanon and the Politics of Identification."

48 See Theodor W. Adorno and E. F. N. Jephcott, *Minima Moralia: Reflections on a Damaged Life* (London: Verso, 2005).

49 Smith, "The Lauryn Paige Fuller Story." I am here also thinking with Derrida's idea of the "dead object." See Jacques Derrida, "Fors," foreword to Nicolas Abraham and Maria Torok, *The Wolf Man's Magic Word: A Cryptonymy*, trans. Nicholas Rand (Minneapolis: University of Minnesota Press, 2005), xxxviii.

Chapter 2. Necrocapital

Epigraph: Karl Marx, *Capital*, vol. 1 (London: Penguin, 1990), 342.

Epigraph: Kia LaBeija, "Kia LaBeija's Firsthand Account of Growing Up HIV+," *Vice*, December 1, 2015, https://www.vice.com/en_us/article/bmy3ya/kia-labeijas-firsthand-account-of-growing-up-hiv.

1 See Stephan Hudak, "Blood Banks at Capacity, Donors Urged to Return in Coming Days," *Orlando Sentinel*, June 12, 2016, https://www.orlandosentinel.com/news/breaking-news/os-orlando-nightclub-shooting-blood-donations-20160612-story.html; J. Wheaton, "How to Help Orlando: Donate Money, Blood and, Through It All, Pray," *NewsMax*, June 14, 2016, https://www.newsmax.com/thewire/how-to-help-orlando-shooting-massacre/2016/06/13/id/733604/; Sylvia Cunningham, "Florida Man Feels 'Helpless' after Failed Blood Donation Attempt," *NBC News*, June 13, 2016, https://www.nbcnews.com/feature/nbc-out/florida-man-feels-helpless-after-turned-away-donating-blood-n591346. Donna Jones's conceptualization of life and death in terms of the political is also useful. See Donna V. Jones, *The Racial Discourses of Life Philosophy: Négritude, Vitalism, and Modernity* (New York: Columbia University Press, 2010), 11–18.

2 Dan Tracy, "OneBlood CEO Paid More Than $2 Million in 2013," *Orlando Sentinel*, June 1, 2015, https://www.orlandosentinel.com/business/os-oneblood-blood-bank-ceo-pay-20150522-story.html.

3 U.S. Food and Drug Administration, "Revised Recommendations for Reducing the Risk of Human Immunodeficiency Virus Transmission by Blood and Blood Products—Questions and Answers," February 5, 2018, https://www.fda.gov/biologicsbloodvaccines/bloodbloodproducts/questionsaboutblood/ucm108186.htm.

4 Cunningham, "Florida Man Feels 'Helpless.'" The global traffic in blood products is the larger context within which this story lives; see Ann Marie Kimball, *Risky Trade: Infectious Disease in the Era of Global Trade* (Aldershot, UK: Ashgate, 2006). For an early example of how the media focused on this as an anti-LGBT attack, see Jessica Lussenhop, "Orlando Shooting: Latest Attack on LGBT Community," BBC News, June 13, 2006, https://www.bbc.com/news/world-us-canada-36492127. For a recent news piece that places the Pulse Shooting within the narrative of "world-wide terror," see Peter Bergen, "Why Terrorists Kill: The Striking Similarities between the New Zealand and Pulse Nightclub Shooters,"

CNN, March 18, 2019, https://www.cnn.com/2019/03/18/opinions/why
-terrorists-kill-striking-similarities-bergen/index.html.

5 Noor Salman's indictment can be read here: https://apps.washingtonpost.com
/g/documents/national/the-complete-noor-salman-indictment/2276/.

6 "Orlando Massacre Was 'Revenge,' Not Terrorism, Says Man Who Claims He
Was Gunman's Lover," *Univision*, June 21, 2016, https://www.univision.com
/univision-news/united-states/orlando-massacre-was-revenge-not-terrorism
-says-man-who-claims-he-was-gunmans-lover.

7 Eric Levenson, Nicole Chavez, Martin Savidge, and Ray Sanchez, "Pulse Gunman's Widow Found Not Guilty," CNN, March 31, 2018, https://www.cnn.com
/2018/03/30/us/noor-salman-pulse-trial-verdict/index.html.

8 On the force of loss in the aftermath of Pulse, see Che Gossett, "Pulse, Beat,
Rhythm, Cry: Orlando and the Queer and Trans Necropolitics of Loss and
Mourning," Verso blog, July 5, 2016, https://www.versobooks.com/blogs/2747
-pulse-beat-rhythm-cry-orlando-and-the-queer-and-trans-necropolitics-of-loss
-and-mourning.

9 Mahita Gajanan, "Recording of 911 Calls from Orlando Nightclub Shooter Omar
Mateen Released," *Time*, October 31, 2016, http://time.com/4552365/omar
-mateen-orlando-nightclub-shooting-911-calls/.

10 Adam Goldman and Mark Berman, "'They Took Too Damn Long': Inside the
Police Response to the Orlando Shooting," *Washington Post*, August 1, 2016,
https://www.washingtonpost.com/world/national-security/they-took-too
-damn-long-inside-the-police-response-to-the-orlando-shooting/2016/08/01
/67a66130-5447-11e6-88eb-7dda4e2f2aec_story.html.

11 What is often left out of Mateen's biography is that he was a criminal justice major in college who had previously been in training to become a prison guard until
his expulsion, which led him to armed security work that he continued until his
death.

12 For more on racial capitalism, see Cedric J. Robinson, *Black Marxism: The Making of the Black Radical Tradition* (Chapel Hill: University of North Carolina
Press, 2000); Jodi Melamed, "Racial Capitalism," *Critical Ethnic Studies* 1, no. 1
(2015): 76–85.

13 For a much more complete engagement with the biocapitalism of slavery, see
Alys Eve Weinbaum, *The Afterlife of Reproductive Slavery: Biocapitalism and Black
Feminism's Philosophy of History* (Durham, NC: Duke University Press, 2019).
Other important work on the biological and capitalism includes Melinda Coo-
per, *Life as Surplus: Biotechnology and Capitalism in the Neoliberal Era* (Seattle:
University of Washington Press, 2008); Coleman Nye, "The Commons as Accu-
mulation Strategy: Postgenomic Mutations in Biological Property," *Social Text* 1
37, no. 2 (2019): 1–28.

This tired "race versus class" argument is now recast as a battle against "identity
politics," and while there are many important critiques of identity under a neoliberal ordering, our task is to work to understand how they become weaponized
against us, not to think we can or should disappear difference. While much of the

conversations around the uses and limits of what is now called "identity politics" is not particularly useful for doing the work of organizing, I find this piece to be a good place of departure: Olúfẹ́mi O. Táíwò, "Being-in-the-Room Privilege: Elite Capture and Epistemic Deference," *The Philosopher* 108, no. 4 (2020). For an excellent critique of "new materialism," see Jordy Rosenberg, "The Molecularization of Sexuality: On Some Primitivisms of the Present," *Theory and Event* 17, no. 2 (2014). For another reading of Blackness as commodity form, see Fred Moten, *In the Break: The Aesthetics of the Black Radical Tradition* (Minneapolis: University of Minnesota Press, 2003). On Black socialist feminist theorizing and organizing, see Claudia Jones, *An End to the Neglect of the Problems of the Negro Woman!* (New York: Jefferson School of Social Science, 1949); Combahee River Collective, *The Combahee River Collective Statement: Black Feminist Organizing in the Seventies and Eighties* (Albany, NY: Kitchen Table, 1986); Keeanga-Yamahtta Taylor, ed., *How We Get Free: Black Feminism and the Combahee River Collective* (Chicago: Haymarket, 2017). The Red Nation continues to build a contemporary Native socialist feminist analysis; The Red Nation, "Communism Is the Horizon, Queer Indigenous Feminism Is the Way," September 21, 2020, http://therednation.org /communism-is-the-horizon-queer-indigenous-feminism-is-the-way/.

14   According to W. E. B. Du Bois, this was about $19 a year. See W. E. B. Du Bois, *Black Reconstruction in America 1860–1880* (New York: Harcourt, Brace, 1935).

15   Karl Marx, *The Poverty of Philosophy: A Reply to M. Proudhon's Philosophy of Poverty* (New York: International, 1992), 94–95.

16   Here I am primarily making a theoretical argument. For vital work on the historical dimensions of the question of labor and slavery, see, for example, Jennifer L. Morgan, *Laboring Women: Reproduction and Gender in New World Slavery* (Philadelphia: University of Pennsylvania Press, 2004). For a contested yet endlessly generative analysis, see Eric E. Williams, *Capitalism and Slavery* (Chapel Hill: University of North Carolina Press, 1994). On the managerial practices developed under slavery, see Caitlin Rosenthal, *Accounting for Slavery: Masters and Management* (Cambridge, MA: Harvard University Press, 2018). For one such postcolonial feminist engagement with biocapital, see Kalindi Vora, *Life Support: Biocapital and the New History of Outsourced Labor* (Minneapolis: University of Minnesota Press, 2015). Of course, Spivak's reconceptualization of Marx is among the subtexts of this chapter. Important here is her work on Marx's "use value": Gayatri Chakravorty Spivak, "Scattered Speculations on the Question of Value," *Diacritics* 15, no. 4 (1985): 73–93. While the question of primitive accumulation is much debated, for an expansive reading, see Nikhil Pal Singh, "On Race, Violence, and So-Called Primitive Accumulation," *Social Text 128* 34, no. 3 (2016): 27–50. By bio-ontologization of race, I mean the processes that Frantz Fanon and others have charted that forcefully conflate racist assumptions about Blackness as belonging to the "natural" interiority of Black people. In other words, it is the violent imposition of anti-Blackness at the level of the biological and the psychic.

17   Rachel L. Swarns, "Insurance Policies on Slaves: New York Life's Complicated Past," *New York Times*, December 18, 2018, https://www.nytimes.com/2016

/12/18/us/insurance-policies-on-slaves-new-york-lifes-complicated-past.html.
For a comprehensive account of the sale of slaves after death, see Daina Berry,
*The Price for Their Pound of Flesh: The Value of the Enslaved, from Womb to Grave,
in the Building of a Nation* (Boston: Beacon, 2017).

In the wake of Pulse, companies that insure large Pride celebrations are now
requiring them to purchase extra insurance for their events. This "terrorism" protection also mandates the hiring of more police and a further militarization of
Pride. See Lyanne Melendez, "San Francisco Police Increasing Security for Pride
Weekend," A BC7, June 23, 2017, https://abc7news.com/society/sfpd-increasing
-security-for-pride-weekend/2138120/. For a further analysis, see Tim Arm-
strong, "Slavery, Insurance, and Sacrifice in the Black Atlantic," in *Sea Changes:
Historicizing the Ocean*, ed. Bernhard Klein and Gesa Mackenthun (New York:
Routledge, 2003), 167–86. Finally, see also Edward Baptist, "Toxic Debt, Liar
Loans, Collateralized and Securitized Human Beings, and the Panic of 1837," in
*Capitalism Takes Command: The Social Transformation of Nineteenth-Century
America*, ed. Michael Zakim and Gary John Kornblith (Chicago: University of
Chicago Press, 2012), 69–92.

18 Here I am thinking with Tadiar's concept of "life-time." Neferti X. M. Tadiar,
"Life-Times of Disposability within Global Neoliberalism," *Social Text* 115 31, no. 2
(2013): 19–48.

19 Du Bois, *Black Reconstruction in America*, 13.

20 Saidiya V. Hartman, *Scenes of Subjection: Terror, Slavery, and Self-Making in
Nineteenth-Century America* (New York: Oxford University Press, 1997), 80.

21 On social death, see Orlando Patterson, *Slavery and Social Death: A Comparative
Study* (Cambridge, MA: Harvard University Press, 1982); Claude Meillassoux,
The Anthropology of Slavery: The Womb of Iron and Gold, trans. Alide Dasnosis
(Chicago: University of Chicago Press, 1991).

22 Colin Dayan, "Legal Slaves and Civil Bodies," *Nepantla: Views from the South* 2,
no. 1 (2001): 13.

23 Dayan, "Legal Slaves and Civil Bodies," 22.

24 Dayan, "Legal Slaves and Civil Bodies," 22.

25 Dayan, "Legal Slaves and Civil Bodies," 6. On manumission, see Guyora Binder,
"The New Slavery of Emancipation," *Cardozo Law Review* 17 (1996): 2076.

26 The history of blood banking and blood transfusions is built up alongside and
through practices of war-making and military technology; see Douglas P. Starr,
Blood: An Epic History of Medicine and Commerce (New York: Alfred A. Knopf,
1998), 54, 109, 145. See Philip Handler's letter, "Excessive Anonymity," *Science* 172,
no. 3982 (1971): 427. Also see Harriet Washington, *Medical Apartheid: The Dark
History of Medical Experimentation in Black Americans from Colonial Times to the
Present* (Norwell, MA: Anchor, 2008).

27 Georges Bataille, *The Accursed Share: An Essay on General Economy*, vol. 1, Consumption (New York: Zone, 1991), 69.

28 For more on the idea of gift in relation to the biological, see Kieran Healy, *Last
Best Gifts: Altruism and the Market for Human Blood and Organs* (Chicago: Uni-

versity of Chicago Press, 2006). Lindon Barrett observes how excess is the precondition of value, literary and otherwise. See Lindon Barrett, *Blackness and Value: Seeing Double* (Cambridge: Cambridge University Press, 1998), 25–27.

29 Bataille, *The Accursed Share*, 69.

30 For more of the idea of the national body, see Cathy Waldby, *AIDS and the Body Politic: Biomedicine and Sexual Difference* (London: Routledge, 1996), in particular, her discussion on the "immunological nation-state" (57–60). Also see Thomas E. Yingling, *AIDS and the National Body*, ed. Robyn Wiegman (Durham, NC: Duke University Press, 1997). For activism against the blood ban, see the work of Blood Equality, https://www.blood-equality.com/get-involved/.

31 Marx, *Capital*, vol. 1, 45.

32 Marx, *Capital*, vol. 1, 47.

33 Much of art's value is also contingent on the transparent social relations of its production. However, with artistic production, like blood, this knowing also enables other abstractions. For example, all the assistants who might actually produce the art, like the lab technicians, disappear so that the idea of the artist or the donator might appear.

34 While my analysis focuses on blood's meaning in the United States, its transnational context is also vital. For a reading of blood, Blackness, and sexuality in Canada, see OmiSoore H. Dryden, "Blood Out of Bounds," *No More Potlucks*, July 2015, http://nomorepotlucks.org/site/blood-out-of-bounds-omisoore -h-dryden/.

35 Richard Knox, "Origin of AIDS Linked to Colonial Practices in Africa," *NPR*, June 4, 2006, www.npr.org/templates/story/story.php?storyId=5450391.

36 See Jacques Pépin, *The Origins of AIDS* (Cambridge: Cambridge University Press, 2011); Brandon Keim, "Early Spread of AIDS Traced to Congo's Expanding Transportation Network," *National Geographic*, October 2, 2014, https://news .nationalgeographic.com/news/2014/10/141002-hiv-virus-spread-africa-health/.

37 Will Dunham, "AIDS Virus Invaded U.S. from Haiti: Study," *Reuters*, October 30, 2007, https://www.reuters.com/article/us-aids-usa/aids-virus-invaded-u-s-from -haiti-study-idUSN2954500820071030. See also Paul Farmer, *AIDS and Accusation: Haiti and the Geography of Blame* (Berkeley: University of California Press, 2006); Karma Chávez, "ACT UP, Haitian Migrants and Alternative Memories of HIV/AIDS," *Quarterly Journal of Speech* 98, no. 1 (2012): 63–68. For a discussion of Haiti and the question of unfreedom, see Susan Buck-Morss, "Hegel and Haiti," *Critical Inquiry* 26, no. 4 (2000): 821–65; C. L. R. James, *The Black Jacobins: Toussaint l'Ouverture and the San Domingo Revolution* (New York: Vintage, 1963).

38 See Lawrence K. Altman, "New Homosexual Disorder Worries Health Officials," *New York Times*, May 11, 1982, http://www.nytimes.com/1982/05/11/science /new-homosexual-disorder-worries-health-officials.html.

39 This is not to suggest that the ways HIV/AIDS destroyed those we have the most accessible accounts of, namely white gay cis men, are any less horrific. Yet it's important to hold this history alongside all the other histories we are never able to know.

40 Access to the video can be found at Vanityfair.com. See Richard Lawson, "The Reagan Administration's Unearthed Response to the AIDS Crisis Is Chilling," *Vanity Fair*, December 1, 2015, https://www.vanityfair.com/news/2015/11/reagan-administration-response-to-aids-crisis. For an early, yet still timely, reading of the signification of AIDS, see Paula A. Treichler, "AIDS, Homophobia, and Biomedical Discourse: An Epidemic of Signification," *October* 43 (1987): 31–70. While not specifically about HIV/AIDS, see Mel Chen, *Animacies: Biopolitics, Racial Mattering, and Queer Affect* (Durham, NC: Duke University Press, 2012), for a discussion of points of contact where race and sexuality meet through a biopolitics of contagion. For an account of drug users' activism around HIV/AIDS in New York City, see Christina B. Hanhardt, "'Dead Addicts Don't Recover': ACT UP's Needle Exchange and the Subjects of Queer Activist History," GLQ 24, no. 4 (2018): 421–44.

41 See Centers for Disease Control and Prevention, "A Cluster of Kaposi's Sarcoma and Pneumocystis carinii Pneumonia among Homosexual Male Residents of Los Angeles and Range Counties, California," *Morbidity and Mortality Weekly Report* 31, no. 23 (June 18, 1982): 305–7, https://www.cdc.gov/mmwr/preview/mmwrhtml/00001114.htm.

42 The first large epidemiological study of trans women and HIV was not published until 2008. See J. H. Herbst, E. D. Jacobs, T. J. Finlayson, et al., "Estimating HIV Prevalence and Risk Behaviors of Transgender Persons in the United States: A Systematic Review," AIDS *and Behavior* 12, no. 1 (2008): 1–17. Also see Stefan D. Baral et al., "Worldwide Burden of HIV in Transgender Women: A Systemic Review and Meta-Analysis," *The Lancet* 13, no. 3 (2013): 214–22, https://www.thelancet.com/journals/laninf/article/PIIS1473-3099(12)70315-8/fulltext.

43 Edwidge Danticat, "Trump Reopens an Old Wound for Haitians," *New Yorker*, December 29, 2017, https://www.newyorker.com/news/news-desk/trump-reopens-an-old-wound-for-haitians.

44 Provincializing HIV/AIDS activism (along with the distribution of resources) continues to be a problem with deadly consequences; see Nishant Shahani, "How to Survive the Whitewashing of AIDS: Global Pasts, Transnational Futures," QED: *A Journal in* GLBTQ *Worldmaking* 3, no. 1 (2016): 1–33.

45 Karl Marx, *Grundrisse: Foundations of the Critique of Political Economy* (New York: Penguin, 1993), 706–7. For an account of how scarcity is produced through underdevelopment, primarily in the United States, see Manning Marable, *How Capitalism Underdeveloped Black America: Problems in Race, Political Economy, and Society* (Chicago: Haymarket, 2018). Marable's discussion of capital's production of "subproletarians," which limits collective class consciousness, is of particular interest. Also see Walter Rodney, *How Europe Underdeveloped Africa* (London: Bogle-l'Ouverture, 1972).

46 For more on biological citizenship, see Nikolas S. Rose, *Politics of Life Itself: Biomedicine, Power, and Subjectivity in the Twenty-First Century* (Princeton, NJ: Princeton University Press, 2007). Citing a number of surveys, many people in the U.S. still feel that receiving a blood transfusion is "risky" and some go so far as

to suggest there is significant risk of getting HIV from the act of blood donation. This point shows how the general public conflates blood and HIV. See Cathy Waldby and Robert Mitchell, *Tissue Economies: Blood, Organs, and Cell Lines in Late Capitalism* (Durham, NC: Duke University Press, 2006), 51.

47 Mariarosa Dalla Costa, "Capitalism and Reproduction," libcom.org, March 12, 2012, https://libcom.org/library/capitalism-reproduction-mariarosa-dalla-costa.

48 For an important critique of the "Wages for Housework" campaign, see Angela Davis, "The Approaching Obsolescence of Housework: A Working-Class Perspective," in *Women, Race and Class* (New York: Random House, 1981), 222–44. Also see Antonio Negri, "Value and Affect," *boundary 2* 26, no. 2 (1999): 77–88. See Michael Hardt, "Affective Labor," *boundary 2* 26, no. 2 (1999): 89–100. Disability justice scholars and organizers have pushed against the "right to work" discourses in asking why we don't fight for a right not to work. Sunny Taylor, "The Right Not to Work: Power and Disability," *Monthly Review* 55, no. 10 (1949): 20.

49 Michel Foucault, *The History of Sexuality: An Introduction*, vol. 1, translated by Robert Hurley (New York: Vintage, 1999), 140.

50 Michel Foucault, *Society Must Be Defended: Lectures at the Collège de France, 1975–1976* (New York: Picador, 2003), 61.

51 Foucault, *The History of Sexuality*, vol. 1, 137.

52 Foucault, *The History of Sexuality*, vol. 1, 147.

53 Foucault, *The History of Sexuality*, vol. 1, 149.

54 Foucault, *The History of Sexuality*, vol. 1, 147–50.

55 An extensive consideration of how Blackness reforms Foucault's conception of biopolitics is offered in Alexander G. Weheliye, *Habeas Viscus: Racializing Assemblages, Biopolitics, and Black Feminist Theories of the Human* (Durham, NC: Duke University Press, 2014). For an earlier analysis of colonialism and Foucault's work, see Ann L. Stoler, *Race and the Education of Desire: Foucault's History of Sexuality and the Colonial Order of Things* (Durham, NC: Duke University Press, 1995). On the work of the dead within the frame of life, see Achille Mbembe, "Necropolitics," *Public Culture* 15, no. 1 (2003): 11–40.

56 See Melinda Cooper, *Life as Surplus: Biotechnology and Capitalism in the Neoliberal Era* (Seattle: University of Washington Press, 2008). Here she argues that the dual motor of biocapital produces through an excess of waste "a promissory surplus of life and an actual devastation of life in the present" (58).

57 Karl Marx, *Capital*, vol. 3 (London: Penguin, 1991), 180.

58 Capital's ability to reincorporate waste is also evident in tech's "gig economy." For example, if you require a car to get to work and it is otherwise idle, "ride shares" (which are not sharing anything) were built on the premise that your unused car, along with your unused labor time after work, could be reinstrumentalized. This gigification of unwaged work also allows for the depression of waged work as second and third jobs are normalized.

59 Donna J. Haraway, "A Cyborg Manifesto: Science, Technology, and Socialist-

Feminism in the Late Twentieth Century," in *Manifestly Haraway*, ed. Donna J. Haraway and Cary Wolfe (Minneapolis: University of Minnesota Press, 2016), 61.

60 I make this point not to suggest that bioeconomies, like blood or organ sales, are fundamentally more violent than capitalism's more traditional functions. The belief that the bioeconomy is more exploitative can naturalize the other ways capitalism harms.

61 NIH HIV Reagent Program, "Home," http://hivreagentprogram.org.

62 On the racial and gender dynamics of the "case" of Henrietta Lacks, see Jayna Brown, "Being Cellular: Race, the Inhuman, and the Plasticity of Life," GLQ 21, nos. 2–3 (2015): 321–41; Rebecca Skloot, *The Immortal Life of Henrietta Lacks* (New York: Crown, 2010).

63 Sefali Luthra and Anna Gorman, "Rising Cost of PrEP to Prevent HIV Infection Pushes It Out of Reach for Many," NPR, June 30, 2018, https://www.npr.org /sections/health-shots/2018/06/30/624045995/rising-cost-of-prep-a-pill-that -prevents-hiv-pushes-it-out-of-reach-for-many.

64 For more on the global pharmaceutical industry, see Adriana Petryna, Andrew Lakoff, and Arthur Kleinman, eds., *Global Pharmaceuticals: Ethics, Markets, Practices* (Durham, NC: Duke University Press, 2006). In 1980 the Bayh-Dole Act "streamlined" federal patent regulations and allowed universities and industry to keep many of their patents for inventions funded by governmental monies. This deregulation and subsequent privatization of the pharmaceutical industry helped propel the era of Reagan economics.

65 For an incomplete graph of HIV infections, see HIV.gov, "U.S. Statistics," https://www.hiv.gov/hiv-basics/overview/data-and-trends/statistics. The CDC actually owns the patent; however, they are not litigating against Gilead over infringement. See Michela Tindera, "Gilead Said PrEP to Prevent HIV Was 'Not a Commercial Opportunity.' Now It's Running Ads for It," *Forbes*, August 7, 2018, https://www.forbes.com/sites/michelatindera/2018/08/07/gilead-said-prep-to -prevent-hiv-was-not-a-commercial-opportunity-now-its-running-ads-for-it/. For more on the anti-Blackness of HIV/AIDS, see Adam M. Geary, *Anti-Black Racism and the AIDS Epidemic: State Intimacies* (New York: Palgrave Macmillan, 2014). Also see Cathy J. Cohen, *The Boundaries of Blackness: AIDS and the Breakdown of Black Politics* (Chicago: University of Chicago Press, 1999). The current practices of criminalizing and incarcerating people under "HIV disclosure laws" are another way to track the anti-Blackness of HIV/AIDS in our current moment. See, for one example, the case of Michael Johnson, "Free Michael Johnson and End the Criminalization of HIV," https://freemichaeljohnson.org/.

66 On the concept of deathworlds, see Mbembe, "Necropolitics."

67 Jean Claude Ameisen, "Programmed Cell Death and AIDS: From Hypothesis to Experiment," *Immunology Today* 13, no. 10 (1992): 388–91.

68 For an account of the action, see James Wentzy, "The Ashes Action," *Vimeo*, 1992, https://vimeo.com/158801570. Also see the video of their debriefing after the ac-

tion, "ACT UP Ashes Action Defriefing," *YouTube*, https://www.youtube.com
/watch?v=OeofFyWZWXI. For more on the quilt, see Marita Sturken, *Tangled
Memories: The Vietnam War, the AIDS Epidemic, and the Politics of Remembering*
(Berkeley: University of California Press, 1997).

69 For more on the affective politics of ACT UP, see Deborah B. Gould, *Moving Politics: Emotion and ACT UP's Fight against AIDS* (Chicago: University of Chicago
Press, 2009).

70 David Wojnarowicz, "Postcards from America: X-Rays from Hell," in *Close to the
Knives: A Memoir of Disintegration* (New York: Vintage, 1991), 122.

71 For an account of loss and mourning, see Dagmawi Woubshet, *The Calendar of
Loss: Race, Sexuality, and Mourning in the Early Era of AIDS* (Baltimore: Johns
Hopkins University Press, 2015). For more on the mass strike, see Rosa Luxemburg, "The Mass Strike," in *The Essential Rosa Luxemburg: Reform or Revolution
and the Mass Strike*, ed. Helen Scott, 111–82 (Chicago: Haymarket, 2008).

72 This quote is from an unnamed speaker at the post-action ACT UP meeting:
"ACT UP Ashes Action Defriefing," *YouTube*, https://www.youtube.com
/watch?v=OeofFyWZWXI.

Chapter 3. Clocked

Epigraph: "Refuse Powers' Grasp: Introduction." Arika, n.d., http://arika.org.uk
/events/episode-8-refuse-powers-grasp/introduction. For a more extensive theorization of "no-bodies," see Denise Ferreira da Silva, "No-Bodies," *Griffith Law
Review* 18, no. 2 (2009): 212–36.

Epigraph: Miss Major Griffin-Gracy, CeCe McDonald, and Toshio Meronek,
"Cautious Living: Black Trans Women and the Politics of Documentation," in
Trap Door: Trans Cultural Production and the Politics of Visibility, edited by Tourma-
line, Eric A. Stanley, and Johanna Burton (Cambridge, MA: MIT Press, 2017), 26.

1 Lawrence Buser, "Mistrial Declared in Police Beating Case Involving Transgender Prisoner," *Memphis Commercial Appeal*, April 19, 2010.

2 For more on the beating of Duanna Johnson, see Matt Richardson, *The Queer
Limit of Black Memory: Black Lesbian Literature and Irresolution* (Columbus:
Ohio State University Press, 2013), 163–66.

3 The double bind of representation as it lives within the context of global capital
is further excavated in C. Riley Snorton and Hentyle Yapp, eds., *Saturation: Race,
Art, and the Circulation of Value* (Cambridge, MA: MIT Press, 2020).

4 "Former Cop Claims Self-Defense in Transsexual Beating Trial," Fox 13
Memphis, April 13, 2010, https://web.archive.org/web/20100503052406/http://
www.myfoxmemphis.com/dpp/news/local/041310-former-cop-claims-self
-defense-in-transsexual-beating-trial.

5 Lawrence Buser, "Ex-Officer: Transgender Prisoner Was Aggressor," *Memphis
Commercial Appeal*, April 14, 2010, https://www.pressreader.com/usa/the
-commercial-appeal/20100414/281758445485075.

6 Here I am writing with prison abolitionists who argue that "jailing killer cops"

fails to build justice for communities that have been systematically abused by the police, while it also reconfirms that the system has the ability to do so. As always, Mariame Kaba offers a way to think through these seeming contractions; Mariame Kaba and John Duda, "Towards the Horizon of Abolition: A Conversation with Mariame Kaba," *The Next System*, November 9, 2017, https://thenext system.org/learn/stories/towards-horizon-abolition-conversation-mariame -kaba; Morgan Bassichis, Alexander Lee, and Dean Spade, "Building an Abolitionist Trans and Queer Movement with Everything We've Got," in *Captive Genders: Trans Embodiment and the Prison Industrial Complex*, ed. Eric A. Stanley and Nat Smith (Oakland, CA: AK Press, 2015). Also see Jay Stanley, "We Need to Move beyond the Frame of the 'Bad Apple Cop,'" *ACLU*, March 19, 2015, https://www .aclu.org/blog/national-security/we-need-move-beyond-frame-bad-apple-cop.

7   Joey L. Mogul, Andrea J. Ritchie, and Kay Whitlock, *Queer (In)Justice: The Criminalization of LGBT People in the United States* (Boston: Beacon, 2011), 142. For more on the negotiated settlement, see Jessica G., "Death of Memphis Woman Is Shrouded in Mystery," *Jezebel*, November 18, 2008, https://jezebel.com /death-of-memphis-woman-is-shrouded-in-mystery-5091918.

8   See Eric A. Stanley and Nat Smith, eds., *Captive Genders: Trans Embodiment and the Prison Industrial Complex* (Oakland, CA: AK Press, 2011).

9   For more on lynching photography and the relationship between modernity and the medium, see Jacqueline D. Goldsby, *A Spectacular Secret: Lynching in American Life and Literature* (Chicago: University of Chicago Press, 2006); David Marriott, *On Black Men* (New York: Columbia University Press, 2000).

10 Stuart Hall clarifies this point during his interview in Julien's film. See Isaac Julien, *Frantz Fanon: Black Skin, White Masks* (San Francisco: California Newsreel, 1996).

11 With the proliferation of personal technologies (camcorders, camera phones), a genre of the visual has emerged that both references the tropes of cinema and creates new viewing sensibilities. Perhaps inaugurated by the release and reproduction of the 1991 beating video of Rodney King, now every few days a new video surfaces visualizing the multiple forms of harm the police, or their ambassadors, perform against Black people. See Robert Gooding-Williams, ed., *Reading Rodney King/Reading Urban Uprising* (New York: Routledge, 1993). In particular, see Ruth Wilson Gilmore, "Terror Austerity Race Gender Excess Theater," in Gooding-Williams, *Reading Rodney King*, 23–38. Also see Christina Sharpe, "Blackness, Sexuality, and Entertainment," *American Literary History* 24, no. 4 (2012): 827–41; Nicole R. Fleetwood, *Troubling Vision: Performance, Visuality, and Blackness* (Chicago: University of Chicago Press, 2011).

12 Frantz Fanon, *Black Skin, White Masks* (New York: Grove, 1967), 140.

13 For a vital theorization of Fanon's interval, see Kara Keeling, "'In the Interval': Frantz Fanon and the 'Problems' of Visual Representation," *Qui Parle* 13, no. 2 (2003): 91–117. Also see David Marriott, *Haunted Life: Visual Culture and Black Modernity* (New Brunswick, NJ: Rutgers University Press, 2007).

14 Jean-Louis Baudry, "Ideological Effects of the Basic Cinematographic Apparatus," in *Narrative, Apparatus, Ideology*, ed. Philip Rosen (New York: Columbia

University Press, 1986), 286–98. Baudry's assertion that "The cinema can thus appear as a sort of psychic apparatus of substitution, corresponding to the model defined by dominant ideology" is helping guide my thoughts about the power of film here (296). Also see Christian Metz, *The Imaginary Signifier: Psychoanalysis and the Cinema* (Bloomington: Indiana University Press, 1986).

15 Sigmund Freud, "Fetishism," in *Collected Papers*, vol. 5 (London: Hogarth, 1924–50), 198–204, https://cpb-us-w2.wpmucdn.com/portfolio.newschool. edu/dist/9/3921/files/2015/03/Freud-Fetishism-1927-2b52v1u.pdf. For a reading of fetishism and phobia, see David Marriott, "On Racial Fetishism," *Qui Parle* 18, no. 2 (2010): 215–48. Also see Patricia Gherovici, "Psychoanalysis Needs a Sex Change," *Gay and Lesbian Issues and Psychology Review* 7, no. 1 (2011): 3–18.

16 Jacques Lacan, *Feminine Sexuality*, ed. Juliet Mitchell and Jacqueline Rose, trans. Jacqueline Rose (New York: W. W. Norton, 1985), 83.

17 For a detailed analysis of the work of suture in cinema, see Kaja Silverman, *The Subject of Semiotics* (New York: Oxford University Press, 1983). On Fanon's use of Lacan, see Derek Hook, "Fanon via Lacan, or: Decolonization by Psychoanalytic Means . . . ?," *Journal of the British Society for Phenomenology* 51, no. 4 (2020): 305–19; Françoise Vergès, "Creole Skin, Black Mask: Fanon and Disavowal," *Critical Inquiry* 23, no. 3 (1997): 578–95.

18 The Hays codes refers to the Hollywood Production Code that banned "immorality" in film.

19 For more on racial fetishism, see David Eng, *Racial Castration: Managing Masculinity in Asian America* (Durham, NC: Duke University Press, 2001); Anne Anlin Cheng, *The Melancholy of Race: Psychoanalysis, Assimilation, and Hidden Grief* (New York: Oxford University Press, 2001); Kobena Mercer, "Looking for Trouble," *Transition* 51 (1991): 184–97.

20 This ambivalence as methodology might mirror Fanon's sustained engagement with psychoanalysis as both produced by, and a remedy for, the terror of colonial occupation. Ranjana Khanna offers a deep and sweeping historical/theoretical reading of the points of convergence among gender, colonialism, and psychoanalysis. See Ranjana Khanna, *Dark Continents: Psychoanalysis and Colonialism* (Durham, NC: Duke University Press, 2003).

21 See Teresa de Lauretis, *Narrative, Apparatus, Ideology*, edited by Philip Rosen (New York: Columbia University Press, 1986), 286–98. See also Laura Mulvey, "Visual Pleasure and Narrative Cinema," in *Film Theory and Criticism: Introductory Readings*, edited by Leo Braudy and Marshall Cohen (New York: Oxford University Press, 1999), 833–44. For an early analysis of Black women's spectatorship as well as resistant ways of viewing, see bell hooks, "The Oppositional Gaze: Black Female Spectators," in *Black Looks: Race and Representation* (Boston: South End, 1992). Fanon was himself somewhat ambivalent about the limits of Freud's work. See Ato Sekyi-otu, *Fanon's Dialectic of Experience* (Cambridge, MA: Harvard University Press, 1996), 6–7.

22 De Lauretis gets us somewhere toward this direction if we read her suggestion that we move from a less rigid, less structural reading practice toward one that is

positioned in and as relationality. For an earlier account of psychoanalysis and transsexuality, see Jay Prosser, *Second Skins: The Body Narratives of Transsexuality* (New York: Columbia University Press, 1998).

23 Lacan, *Feminine Sexuality*, 83–84.

24 Lacan, *Feminine Sexuality*, 84.

25 Christian Metz, "Photography and Fetish," *October* 34 (1985): 87–88.

26 Fanon, *Black Skin, White Masks*, 129.

27 See Hillary Clinton's remarks in Anne Gearan and Abby Phillip, "Clinton Regrets 1996 Remark on 'Super-Predators' after Encounter with Activist," *Washington Post*, February 25, 2016, https://www.washingtonpost.com/news/post-politics /wp/2016/02/25/clinton-heckled-by-black-lives-matter-activist/.

28 Freud lays out the difference between phobia and anxiety in his analysis of the case of Little Hans. See Sigmund Freud, "Analysis of a Phobia of a Five-Year-Old Boy," in *The Pelican Freud Library*, vol. 8: *Case Histories 1* (New York: Penguin, 1977), 169–306.

29 Gilles Deleuze, *Cinema 2: The Time-Image* (Minneapolis: University of Minnesota Press, 1989), 101.

30 See Marriott, "On Racial Fetishism."

31 Lauren Berlant, *Cruel Optimism* (Durham, NC: Duke University Press, 2011), 243.

32 For one recent example, see San Francisco's banning of the use of facial-recognition technologies. While I support this ban, it was argued under a claim of privacy infringement, which in turn helped normalize the various other ways specific populations are hyper-surveilled, like unhoused people, sex workers, and people in jails and prisons. Gregory Barber, "San Francisco Bans Agency Use of Facial-Recognition Tech," *Wired*, May 14, 2019, https://www.wired.com/story /san-francisco-bans-use-facial-recognition-tech/.

33 Simone Browne's excellent study of the technological history of surveillance, which is always intensified against the twinning of black criminality and as their mutual substitution, confirms the networks between anti-Blackness and visual accounting. See Simone Browne, *Dark Matters: On the Surveillance of Blackness* (Durham, NC: Duke University Press, 2015).

34 Browne, *Dark Matters*, 50.

35 For more on how various technologies of state surveillance enforce gender normativity, see Toby Beauchamp, *Going Stealth: Transgender Politics and U.S. Surveillance Practices* (Durham, NC: Duke University Press, 2019).

36 On the ways the police are a limit concept that constructs the law through its enforcement, see the work of prison abolition activists, including Critical Resistance (http://criticalresistance.org/); TGI Justice Project (http://www.tgijp .org/about.html); BreakOUT! (http://www.youthbreakout.org/).

37 Judith Butler, *Gender Trouble: Feminism and the Subversion of Identity* (New York: Routledge, 1990), 45.

38 Frank B. Wilderson III, *Red, White, and Black: Cinema and the Structure of U.S. Antagonisms* (Durham, NC: Duke University Press, 2010), 341.

39 Wilderson, *Red, White, and Black*, 313.

40 Patrice D. Douglass, "Black Feminist Theory for the Dead and Dying," *Theory and Event* 21, no. 1 (2018): 106–23.

41 For more on the place of gender in Afro-pessimism, see Selamawit D. Terrefe, "Speaking the Hieroglyph," *Theory and Event* 21, no. 1 (2018): 124–47. On Black gender also see Treva Carrie Ellison, "Black Femme Praxis and the Promise of Black Gender," *Black Scholar* 49, no. 1 (2019): 6–16.

42 C. Riley Snorton, *Black on Both Sides: A Racial History of Trans Identity* (Minneapolis: University of Minnesota Press, 2017), 57.

43 Hortense Spillers, "Mama's Baby, Papa's Maybe: An American Grammar Book," *Diacritics* 17, no. 2 (1987): 64–81.

44 Dora Silva Santana, "Mais Viva! Reassembling Transness, Blackness, and Feminism," *Transgender Studies Quarterly* 6, no. 2 (2019): 219.

45 See, for example, Combahee River Collective, *The Combahee River Collective Statement* (Albany, NY: Kitchen Table, 1986); much of the writing in Barbara Smith, ed., *Home Girls: A Black Feminist Anthology* (New York: Kitchen Table, 1983); Patricia Hill Collins, *Black Feminist Thought: Knowledge, Consciousness, and the Politics of Empowerment* (Boston: Unwin Hyman, 1990).

46 Angela Y. Davis, "Reflections on the Black Women's Role in the Community of Slaves," *Massachusetts Review* 13, no. 1 (1972): 99.

47 See Snorton, *Black on Both Sides*, for a discussion on the ways cross-dressing was a vital tool for escape.

48 "Another end of the world is possible" appeared as graffiti in Minneapolis and other cities during the 2020 uprising sparked by the murder of George Floyd by the Minneapolis Police Department. The phrase is a reworking of the slogan "another world is possible," which was popularized in anti-globalization protests of the 1990s.

49 This is not to argue that trans/queer actors should not be cast for such roles but rather noting the limits of that kind of inclusion. Related, on this point, we might want to understand the demand to hire trans/queer actors as, primarily, a demand around labor. For one example of the discussion that accompanies almost any successful LGBT characters, see Ryan Gilbey, "Playing It Straight: Should Gay Roles Be Reserved for Gay Actors?" *The Guardian*, January 14, 2019, https://www.theguardian.com/stage/2019/jan/14/gay-roles-actors-assassination-gianni-versace-bohemian-rhapsody.

50 The ease with which conservatives now seem to argue for positive representation is one of the ways we might want to monitor the work it does.

51 Katy Steinmetz, "The Transgender Tipping Point," *Time*, May 29, 2014, https://time.com/135480/transgender-tipping-point/. With the growth of social media, the ability to collect and build a more representative count of anti-trans/queer violence and murder is easier. While this might account for some of the growing numbers, it cannot account for the forms the violence takes, or their persistence.

52 For an early critique of "positive representations" and the assumption that all viewers consume the image in the same ways, see Teresa de Lauretis, *Alice*

Doesn't: Feminism, Semiotics, Cinema (Bloomington: Indiana University Press, 1984), 37–39.

53 Bob Kohler, "Rapping with a Street Transvestite Revolutionary: An Interview with Marcia [*sic*] Johnson," in *Out of the Closets: Voices of Gay Liberation*, ed. Karla Jay and Allen Young (New York: Jove, 1977), 112–21.

54 For more on the reversal of defense, see Judith Butler, "Endangered/Endangering: Schematic Racism and White Paranoia," in *Reading Rodney King*, edited by Gooding-Williams, 15–23. On becoming the nonsubject of knowledge, see Sylvia Wynter, "No Humans Involved: An Open Letter to My Colleagues," *Forum NHI: Knowledge for the 21st Century* 1, no. 1 (fall 1994): 42–73.

55 Hortense Spillers, *Black, White, and in Color: Essays on American Literature and Culture* (Chicago: University of Chicago Press, 2003), 229.

56 I am here thinking about the relationship between image, language, and meaning. See Stuart Hall, *Representation: Cultural Representations and Signifying Practices* (London: SAGE, 1997). Of importance here is how gender self-determination is a collective project. For more, see Eric A. Stanley, "Gender Self-Determination," *Transgender Studies Quarterly* 1, no. 1 (2014): 89–91.

57 For an example that both foregrounds the radical potential of trans visual cultures/histories while also reworking the forms it most readily arrives in, see Chris Vargas's project MOTHA (Museum of Transgender Hirstory and Art) at http://www.sfmotha.org/.

58 Édouard Glissant, *Poetics of Relation* (Ann Arbor: University of Michigan Press, 1997), 190.

59 Glissant, *Poetics of Relation*, 190.

60 Glissant, *Poetics of Relation*, 193.

61 Tourmaline and Sasha Wortzel, dirs., *Happy Birthday, Marsha!* (New York, 2017).

62 For more on the ways coherence is produced in classic cinema, see Silverman, *The Subject of Semiotics*, 206–7.

63 I am here suggesting that *Happy Birthday, Marsha!* atmospherically produces a kind of Blackness that, following Fred Moten, indexes an "open collective being." Fred Moten, "The Subprime and the Beautiful," *African Identities* 11, no. 2 (2013): 238.

64 Tourmaline, Eric A. Stanley, and Johanna Burton, eds., *Trap Door: Trans Cultural Production and the Politics of Visibility* (Cambridge, MA: MIT Press, 2017).

65 While films made by and for trans/queer people might seem evidently to attend to the problem of representation, we cannot assume that visual culture alone will ultimately transform the social into something more livable, although without it we are already lost. That said, freeing production is necessary if we are to ever get free. To this end, I am still deeply committed to the demands of Third Cinema. See Fernando Solanas and Octavio Getino, "Toward a Third Cinema," *Cinéaste* 4, no. 3 (1970): 1–10.

Chapter 4. Death Drop

Epigraph: Ashley Diamond, "Memoirs of a Chain Gang Sissy pt6," *YouTube*, August 6, 2014, https://www.youtube.com/watch?v=jpgoEVE5YDQ&list=PLUWy oTsP1yJ-fLk903fv1oNtZsRH3Fuwv&index=6.

Epigraph: Frantz Fanon, *The Wretched of the Earth* (New York: Grove, 1963), 311.

1 Eve Kosofsky Sedgwick, "How to Bring Your Kids Up Gay," *Social Text* 29 (1991): 18.

2 By recent media attention I'm roughly periodizing this from 2010, the year Rutgers University student Tyler Clementi commitment suicide after a video of him having sex with a man was nonconsensually streamed online by his roommate, to the present. For a nuanced account see Yasmin Nair, "The New Yorker Sheds More Light on the Clementi- Ravi Story," February 7, 2021, https://yasminnair .com/the-new-yorker-sheds-more-light-on-the-clementi-ravi-story/. For another investigation into the phenomena, see Jasbir K. Puar, *The Right to Maim: Debility, Capacity, Disability* (Durham, NC: Duke University Press, 2017), especially the chapter "Introduction: The Cost of Getting Better," 1–31.

3 There is a robust and ongoing conversation within disability justice communities around the practice of physician-assisted suicide. Some believe that it upholds an ableist worldview that suggests that living with a disability is worse than death, while others believe this falls into an anti-choice argument that relinquishes a person's choice over what happens to their body. See Leah Smith, "Why I'm Not Buying Death with 'Dignity,'" Center for Disability Rights, n.d., http://cdrnys .org/blog/disability-dialogue/the-disability-dialogue-why-im-not-buying-death -with-dignity/. Also see Robert McRuer, "Capitalism and Disabled Identity: Sharon Kowalski, Interdependency, and Queer Domesticity," in *Crip Theory: Cultural Signs of Queerness and Disability* (New York: NYU Press, 2006), 77–102.

4 Here I am thinking about conceptions of disability as well as disability justice organizing as relational. For more, see Jen Deerinwater, "Indigenous Lives and Disability Justice," Disability Visibility Project, March 17, 2019, https://disability visibilityproject.com/2019/03/17/indigenous-lives-and-disability-justice/. Gay media personality Dan Savage popularized the phrase *It gets better* through YouTube videos, then the founding of a nonprofit. In this project he asked people to create videos addressed to "LGBT youth" promising them that as they grow older, life "gets better." Not surprisingly, many thought the campaign was dishonest (at best) and obscured the differences that often lead to premature death.

5 Immanuel Kant, "What Is Enlightenment?," trans. Mary C. Smith, http://www .columbia.edu/acis/ets/CCREAD/etscc/kant.html.

6 For another account of what the end of humanism might bring, see Achille Mbembe, "The Age of Humanism Is Ending," *Mail and Guardian*, December 22, 2016, https://mg.co.za/article/2016-12-22-00-the-age-of-humanism-is-ending.

7 Fanon, *The Wretched of the Earth*, 168.

8 Michel Foucault, *"Society Must Be Defended": Lectures at the Collège de France,*

1975–1976, trans. David Macey (New York: Picador, 2003), 241; Michel Foucault, *The History of Sexuality*, vol. 1: *An Introduction*, translated by Robert Hurley (New York: Pantheon, 1978), 136.

9 French colonial subjects were considered citizens, a point that Fanon suggested was more psychically harmful than outright exclusion. For a discussion of how settler colonialism is an ongoing project of state making, see Patrick Wolfe, "Settler Colonialism and the Elimination of the Native," *Journal of Genocide Research* 8, no. 4 (2006): 387–409.

10 Fanon, *The Wretched of the Earth*, 54.

11 Jean Améry, *On Suicide: A Discourse on Voluntary Death* (Bloomington: Indiana University Press, 1999), 1.

12 After Seth Walsh's death, federal investigators concluded that the school district did not do enough to protect them from the years of harassment. Brody Levesque, "Federal Investigators: Calif. School's Response to Anti-Gay Bullying 'Inadequate,'" *LGBTQ Nation*, July 2, 2011, https://www.lgbtqnation.com/2011/07/federal-investigators-california-schools-response-to-anti-gay-bullying-inadequate/.

13 Bryan Alexander, "The Bullying of Seth Walsh: Requiem for a Small-Town Boy," *Time*, October 2, 2010, http://content.time.com/time/nation/article/0,8599,2023083,00.html. Judy Walsh uses "he" pronouns for Seth; however, I do not know how they understood themselves.

14 A video of Walsh's mother reading the note can be seen at "Seth Walsh 1997 2010," *YouTube*, September 19, 2012, https://www.youtube.com/watch?v=DpdSEhDw7nA.

15 Sylvia Wynter, "Unsettling the Coloniality of Being/Power/Truth/Freedom: Towards the Human, after Man, Its Overrepresentation—An Argument," *CR: The New Centennial Review* 3, no. 3 (2003): 282.

16 For more on the racial and gendered parameters of humanism, see Alexander G. Weheliye, *Habeas Viscus: Racializing Assemblages, Biopolitics, and Black Feminist Theories of the Human* (Durham, NC: Duke University Press, 2014); Mel Chen, *Animacies: Biopolitics, Racial Mattering, and Queer Affect* (Durham, NC: Duke University Press, 2012).

17 Fanon, *The Wretched of the Earth*, 316. For more on the history and context of his writing, see Leo Zeilig, *Frantz Fanon: The Militant Philosopher of Third World Revolution* (London: I. B. Tauris, 2014), 179–83.

18 Radical organizers, including those directly impacted by the legal system, have long been at the forefront of the critique of rights. See Dean Spade, *Normal Life: Administrative Violence, Critical Trans Politics, and the Limits of Law* (Brooklyn, NY: South End, 2011). Chandan Reddy's work is also key for understanding the paradoxes of liberalism and the law. See Chandan Reddy, *Freedom with Violence: Race, Sexuality, and the US State* (Durham, NC: Duke University Press, 2011), especially the chapter "Rights-Based Freedom with Violence: Immigration, Sexuality and the Subject of Human Rights," 143–81. Also, see Duncan Kennedy,

"The Critique of Rights in Critical Legal Studies," in *Left Legalism/Left Critique*, ed. Wendy Brown and Janet Halley (Durham, NC: Duke University Press, 2002), 178–228.

19 The quote comes from Diamond, "Memoirs of a Chain Gang Sissy pt6."

20 As feminist organizers have long argued, sexual violence is used to reduce one's capacity toward life. For a discussion of sexual violence in prisons and its relation to Abu Ghraib, see Angela Y. Davis, *Abolition Democracy: Beyond Empire, Prisons, and Torture* (New York: Seven Stories, 2011), 52–55. Also see Judith Butler, *Frames of War: When Is Life Grievable?* (London: Verso, 2008). Here I am thinking with Marx on the formation of the commodity and its externality; Karl Marx, *Capital*, vol. 1 (London: Penguin, 1990), 125.

21 "Gender-responsive prisons," or trans pods, are spaces of incarceration that are offered, via carceral feminism, to be "better" for trans and gender-nonconforming people. However, as abolitionists have shown, they expand the system's capacity to house people, which in turn increases incarceration. For a critique, see Vanessa Huang, "Gender Wars: State Changing Shape, Passing to Play, and Body of Our Movements," in *Captive Genders: Trans Embodiment and the Prison Industrial Complex* (Oakland, CA: AK Press, 2015), 315–26.

22 These kinds of demands are sometimes called "non-reformist reforms" by prison abolitionist organizers. See Mariame Kaba and John Duda, "Towards the Horizon of Abolition: A Conversation with Mariame Kaba," *Next System Project*, November 9, 2017, https://thenextsystem.org/learn/stories/towards-horizon-abolition-conversation-mariame-kaba.

23 Gina Tron, "Ashley Diamond on Being a Transgender Woman in a Men's Prison," *Hopes&Fears*, n.d., http://www.hopesandfears.com/hopes/now/politics/214755-ashley-diamond-on-caitlyn-jenner. The Department of Justice eventually sided with Diamond in her claim that she must receive her hormone treatments; however, this judgment highlights that federal law does not dictate the everyday practices of imprisonment. Mitch Kellaway, "DOJ Tells State Prisons: Denying Trans Inmates Hormone Therapy Is Unconstitutional," *Advocate*, April 8, 2015, https://www.advocate.com/politics/transgender/2015/04/08/doj-tells-state-prisons-denying-trans-inmates-hormone-therapy-uncons.

24 Ashley Diamond, "Memoirs of a Chain Gang Sissy pt2," *YouTube*, August 6, 2014, https://www.youtube.com/watch?v=hMOLoATbh-c.

25 Ashley Diamond, "Memoirs of a Chain Gang Sissy pt3," *YouTube*, August 6, 2014, https://www.youtube.com/watch?v=PQMAlwuDrDc.

26 The ACLU has numerous settled and pending cases against jails, prisons, and ICE detention centers over their deadly medical care. As just one example, see "Prison Health Care on Trial," ACLU Michigan, n.d., https://www.aclumich.org/en/cases/prison-health-care-trial. I'm suggesting that these deaths are "countless" because coroners are also often prison employees. Families of those who die in custody are left with little information and are tasked with fighting for justice for the dead.

27 Here the possibility of gender as a field of knowing is dramatized by the inter-

diction of identification and intelligibility in the raw violence of the state. While some anti-trans "feminists" bemoan the conspiracy that trans people are forcing everyone to transition into a gender against their consent, it is, of course, trans people, and specifically those in spaces of deadly regulation like prisons, who bear the weight of gender normativity. While this book is concerned with gender, I remain disloyal to a positive definition that argues we can know its conclusion in advance. The California Coalition for Women Prisoners (CCWP) is currently organizing a powerful #MeToo Behind Bars campaign around sexual assault of trans/queer people inside. See "#MeToo Behind Bars—Lawsuit and Grassroots Campaign," CCWP, n.d., https://womenprisoners.org/our-programs/metoo -behind-bars-lawsuit-and-grassroots-campaign/.

28 Diamond's attempt, it seems, was a wish to live and not to die. This structure of suicide as an expression of the life drive is further explored in Huey P. Newton, *Revolutionary Suicide* (New York: Harcourt Brace Jovanovich, 1973).

29 For a thorough examination of the historical and philosophical meaning of soli- tary, see Lisa Gunther, *Solitary Confinement: Social Death and Its Afterlives* (Min- neapolis: University of Minnesota Press, 2013).

30 Stuart Grassian, "Psychiatric Effects of Solitary Confinement," *Washington Uni- versity Journal of Law and Policy* 22 (2006): 325–83.

31 Jails and prisons without a specifically designated "LGBT pod" often place trans/queer prisoners in SHU, where they serve the entirety of their sen- tences. However, many trans/queer survivors argue that, along with the hyper- depersonalization of SHU, rather than offering them "more safety," it provides heightened privacy for guards and others to sexually and physically assault them without witnesses. This is not to suggest that LGBT pods (or "queen tanks" as they are often called) are a solution to the relentless violence of prison. On the contrary, racist, gendered, ableist, and sexualized violence is not an administra- tive accident or oversight but is what structurally maintains the prison as a space of total war.

32 Jessica Glenza, "Chelsea Manning Gets 14 Days in Solitary Confinement for Suicide Attempt," *The Guardian*, September 23, 2016, https://www.theguardian .com/us-news/2016/sep/23/chelsea-manning-solitary-confinement -suicide-attempt.

33 "Settlement Reached in SPLC Case That Highlighted Plight of Transgender Pris- oners," Southern Poverty Law Center, February 12, 2016, https://www.splcenter .org/news/2016/02/12/settlement-reached-splc-case-highlighted-plight -transgender-prisoners; Kellaway, "DOJ Tells State Prisons"; Dylan Cowart, "Transgender Prisoners Face Sexual Assault and Discrimination at Pittsburgh Jail," *Speak Freely* (blog), ACLU, November 13, 2017, https://www.aclu.org/blog /lgbt-rights/criminal-justice-reform-lgbt-people/transgender-prisoners-face -sexual-assault-and; Samantha Michaels, "'3 Years of Torture Is Enough': A Trans- gender Inmate Sues Georgia Prisons," *Mother Jones*, March 2, 2015, https://www .motherjones.com/politics/2015/03/transgender-inmate-sues-georgia-prisons -torture/; Deborah Sontag, "Ashley Diamond, Transgender Inmate, Is Out of

Prison but Far from Free," *New York Times*, September 25, 2015, https://www
.nytimes.com/2015/09/25/us/ashley-diamond-transgender-inmate-out-of
-prison-but-not-fully-free.html. This is not to say that gender dysphoria is not
real, but that our access to medical care should not be tethered to it.

34 Carceral feminism is generally understood to be the practice of arguing for
the expansion of policing and imprisonment under the name of feminism or
gender justice. For a good analysis, see Victoria Law, "Against Carceral Feminism," *Jacobin*, October 17, 2014, https://www.jacobinmag.com/2014/10
/against-carceral-feminism/.

35 See CeCe McDonald, "Foreword," in *Captive Genders: Trans Embodiment and the
Prison Industrial Complex*, ed. Eric A. Stanley and Nat Smith, 1–3 (Oakland, CA:
AK Press, 2015).

36 For more on the concept of gender self-determination as a collective practice,
see Eric A. Stanley, "Gender Self-Determination," *Transgender Studies Quarterly* 1,
nos. 1–2 (2014): 89–91.

37 Here I am less invested in periodizing Enlightenment than following Foucault,
understanding it as an "attitude." See Michel Foucault, "What Is Enlightenment?"
in *The Foucault Reader*, ed. Paul Rabinow (New York: Pantheon, 1984), 32–50.

38 As one of the foundations upon which the U.S. liberal state was theoretically organized, John Locke's links between property and self-possession (property in
the self) are also among the motors that both support and mandate the kinds of
individualism whose legacy we are still living. See John Locke, *Two Treatises of
Government* (Cambridge: Cambridge University Press, 1988). I'm borrowing the
concept of "pretend to pretend" from Derrida. See Jacques Derrida, "The Animal
That Therefore I Am (More to Follow)," *Critical Inquiry* 28, no. 2. (2002): 401.

39 Françoise Vergès, "Creole Skin, Black Mask: Fanon and Disavowal," *Critical Inquiry* 23, no. 3 (1997): 578–95.

40 While focusing on Detroit, Bailey offers an important account of the ballroom
scene. See Marlon M. Bailey, *Butch Queens Up in Pumps: Gender, Performance,
and Ballroom Culture in Detroit* (Ann Arbor: University of Michigan Press, 2013).

41 Walter Benjamin, *Illuminations*, ed. Hannah Arendt, trans. Harry Zohn (New
York: Schocken, 1969), 257.

Coda. Becoming Ungovernable

Epigraph: Jayden Donahue, "Making It Happen, Mama: A Conversation with
Miss Major," in *Captive Genders: Trans Embodiment and the Prison Industrial Complex*, ed. Eric A. Stanley and Nat Smith, 301–13 (Oakland, CA: AK Press, 2015).

Epigraph: Tourmaline, "Filmmaker and Activist Tourmaline on How to Freedom
Dream," *Vogue*, July 2, 2020, https: //www.vogue.com/article/filmmaker-and
-activist-tourmaline-on-how-to-freedom-dream.

1 The thinking in this coda has benefited from conversations with Lauren Berlant
and Dean Spade, as well as organizing in various antiauthoritarian projects over
the last decades.

2　For an anarchist critique of democracy see CrimethInc. ex-Worker's Collective, "From Democracy to Freedom," 2016, https://crimethinc.com/2016/04/29 /feature-from-democracy-to-freedom.

3　The concept of the "bad object" might be useful here. See Lauren Berlant, *Cruel Optimism* (Durham, NC: Duke University Press, 2011).

4　For one reading, see Matthew Quest, "Direct Democracy and the Search for Identity for Colonized People: The Contemporary Meanings of C. L. R. James's Classical Athens," *Classical Receptions Journal* 9, no. 2 (2017): 237–67.

5　C. L. R. James, *A New Notion: Two Works by C. L. R. James*, ed. Noel Ignatiev (Oakland, CA: PM Press, 2010), 190. For more on James's critique of vanguardism see Laura Harris, *Experiments in Exile: C. L. R. James, Hélio Oiticica, and the Aesthetic Sociality of Blackness* (New York: Fordham University Press, 2018), 24–25. This is also not to suggest that James was not critical of the state form, as he wrote about the dangers of state-capitalism as well as Stalinism. C. L. R. James, *World Revolution, 1917–1936: The Rise and Fall of the Communist International*, ed. Christian Høgsbjerg (Durham, NC: Duke University Press, 2017).

6　Importantly, Angela Davis, in her inaugural lecture at UCLA in 1969, opened with the contractional of ancient Greece as well. Angela Y. Davis, *Lectures on Liberation* (New York: Committee to Free Angela Davis, 1971). Perhaps this position is a form of "staying with the trouble" in the thickness of struggle as Donna Haraway offers; Donna J. Haraway, *Staying with the Trouble: Making Kin in the Chthulucene* (Durham, NC: Duke University Press, 2016).

7　The January 6, 2021, storming of the Capitol was also organized under the demand of "democracy," as was the resistance to it. Such confrontations force us to return to the relationship between fascism and the idea of the democratic. If "the people" are intent on building a deathworld, then how does democracy's form fail to offer those excluded from the "we"? This question is not simply theoretical but, I believe, asks us to think expansively about how we reimagine the social.

8　Alexis de Tocqueville, *Democracy in America* (New York: Harper Perennial, 2006).

9　Fred Moten, "Democracy," in *Keywords for American Cultural Studies*, 2nd ed., ed. Bruce Burgett and Glenn Hendler (New York: NYU Press, 2014), 74.

10　On the question of neoliberalism and the democratic form, see Wendy Brown, *Undoing the Demos: Neoliberalism's Stealth Revolution* (Cambridge, MA: MIT Press, 2015).

11　Lorenzo Kom'boa Ervin, *Anarchism and the Black Revolution*" (1993), *Anarchist Library*, March 19, 2009, https://theanarchistlibrary.org/library/lorenzo-kom -boa-ervin-anarchism-and-the-black-revolution.

12　This also rehearses Plato's critique of excessive democracy. Plato, *The Republic* (New York: Basic Books, 1968). See James Madison, "The Union as a Safeguard against Domestic Faction and Insurrection," *Federalist Papers* no. 10, https:// billofrightsinstitute.org/founding-documents/primary-source-documents/the -federalist-papers/federalist-papers-no-10/.

13　I am here referencing Benjamin's "left-wing melancholia"; see Walter Benjamin,

"Left-Wing Melancholy," in *The Weimar Republic Sourcebook*, ed. A. Kaes, M. Jay, and E. Dimendberg (Berkeley: University of California Press, 1994), 305. For an example of how a critique of democracy in America is also evidence of "dogged hope," see W. E. B. Du Bois, "Why I Won't Vote," *The Nation*, October 20, 1956.

14 You can hear Jean O'Leary's anti-trans speech, which followed Sylvia Rivera's, here: "L039A Jean O'Leary Speech at 1973 Gay Rally with Watermark," LoveTapesCollective, posted June 6, 2019, https://www.youtube.com/watch?v=USWWUVEFLUU.

15 Molly Redden, "The Human Costs of Kamala Harris' War on Truancy," *Huffington Post*, March 27, 2019, https://www.huffpost.com/entry/kamala-harris-truancy-arrests-2020-progressive-prosecutor_n_5c995789e4b0f7bfa1b57d2e. Much of the research on ungovernable trans/queer youth of color comes from Wes Ware, "'Rounding Up the Homosexuals': The Impact of Juvenile Court on Queer and Trans/Gender Non-Conforming Youth," in *Captive Genders: Trans Embodiment and the Prison Industrial Complex*, ed. Eric A. Stanley and Nat Smith, 97–104 (Oakland, CA: AK Press, 2015).

16 Frantz Fanon, *Black Skin, White Masks* (New York: Grove, 1967), 109.

17 Angela Irvine, Shannan Wilber, and Aisha Canfield, "Lesbian, Gay, Bisexual, Questioning, and Gender Nonconforming Girls and Boys in the California Juvenile Justice System: A Practice Guide" (Oakland, CA: Impact Justice and the National Center for Lesbian Rights, 2017), https://perma.cc/3L9T-TMSB. In a recent study, an intake officer suggested that nine out of ten LGBT young people in juvenile jail were there because of their assumed ungovernability. Katayoon Majd, Jody Marksamer, and Carolyn Reyes, "Hidden Injustice: Lesbian, Gay, Bisexual, and Transgender Youth in Juvenile Courts" (San Francisco: Legal Services for Children, National Juvenile Defender Center, and National Center for Lesbian Rights, 2019), 4, http://www.nclrights.org/wp-content/uploads/2014/06/hidden_injustice.pdf.

18 Youth liberation was until the recent past a strong current in left social movements. While young people are still central to much organizing, the idea of "youth liberation" has been subsumed under the idea of "youth leadership development." I'm also here thinking with the anonymous anarchist collective, the Invisible Committee's definition of ungovernable. See The Invisible Committee, *Now*, translated by Robert Hurley (Cambridge, MA: MIT Press, 2017), 48.

19 I am inspired by Ren-yo Hwang's work on forms of care that persist in spaces of hyper-institutionalization. See Ren-yo Hwang, "Deviant Care for Deviant Futures: QTBIPoC Radical Relationalism as Mutual Aid against Carceral Care," *Transgender Studies Quarterly* 6, no. 4 (November 1, 2019): 559–78. I am also attendant to Rinaldo Walcott's point that flight is not coterminous with freedom; see Rinaldo Walcott, "Freedom Now Suite: Black Feminist Turns of Voice," *Small Axe* 22, no. 3 (2018): 151–59.

20 On the connections between trans/queer politics and needle exchange, see Christina B. Hanhardt, "'Dead Addicts Don't Recover': ACT UP's Needle Exchange and the Subjects of Queer Activist History," *GLQ: A Journal of Lesbian*

and *Gay Studies* 24, no. 4 (2018): 421–44. For more on the history of Compton's and the Tenderloin, see Susan Stryker and Victor Silverman, dirs., *Screaming Queens: The Riot at Compton's Cafeteria* (San Francisco: Frameline, 2010).

21 Toshio Meronek's extensive oral history of Major pieces many of her stories together, including her time with "Big Black." See Toshio Meronek, *Miss Major Speaks* (London: Verso, forthcoming). Also see the documentary about her life, *Major!*, directed by Annalise Ophelian (San Francisco: Floating Ophelia Productions, 2016). Another example of how *co-exposure* (a term Lauren Berlant offered me) is built is a fare dodgers' union where public transit riders all pay a small union fee while refusing to pay for public transportation. If one of them gets ticketed, the union dues are tapped to pay for that ticket. See https://planka .nu/eng/.

22 I am here, as I often am, thinking with Donna Haraway's concept of the "informatics of domination." Donna Haraway, "A Cyborg Manifesto: Science, Technology, and Socialist-Feminism in the Late Twentieth Century," in *Simians, Cyborgs and Women: The Reinvention of Nature* (New York: Routledge, 1991), 149–81.

23 Dean Spade has helped us know how "administrative violence" functions through and as the state. Dean Spade, *Normal Life: Administrative Violence, Critical Trans Politics, and the Limits of Law* (Durham, NC: Duke University Press, 2015); Amrita Khalid, "Facial Recognition AI Can't Identify Trans and Non-Binary People," *Quartz*, October 16, 2019, https://qz.com/1726806/facial-recognition -ai-from-amazon-microsoft-and-ibm-misidentifies-trans-and-non-binary -people/. For a "policy redesign" that rightfully articulates the need for gender markers to be removed from state-issued IDs but then argues for the use of other "biometric markers," see Heath Fogg Davis, *Beyond Trans: Does Gender Matter?* (New York: NYU Press, 2017), 51–53. Ruha Benjamin continues to produce work that shows how race is coded into tech, or what she has called "engineered inequalities." See Ruha Benjamin, *Race after Technology: Abolitionist Tools for the New Jim Code* (Cambridge: Polity, 2019).

24 Tourmaline, dir. "*The Personal Things*," *YouTube*, November 21, 2016, https:// www.youtube.com/watch?v=vzafzVv2G2E. Here I am also thinking about joy as an insurgent strategy. See Alfredo M. Bonanno, *Armed Joy*, https://theanarchist library.org/library/alfredo-m-bonanno-armed-joy.

25 Here I am influenced by Ralowe T. Ampu's provocative configuration of the "root queen." Ralowe T. Ampu, "Hotel Hell," in *Captive Genders: Trans Embodiment and the Prison Industrial Complex*, ed. Eric A. Stanley and Nat Smith, 105–18 (Oakland, CA: AK Press, 2015).

BIBLIOGRAPHY

Abraham, Nicolas, and Maria Torok. *The Wolf Man's Magic Word: A Cryptonymy.* Translated by Nicholas Rand. Minneapolis: University of Minnesota Press, 2005.

"Accelerating Acceptance 2019." GLAAD, June 24, 2019. https://www.glaad.org /publications/accelerating-acceptance-2019.

Adorno, Theodor W. *Negative Dialectics.* London: Routledge, 2015.

Adorno, Theodor W., and E. F. N. Jephcott. *Minima Moralia: Reflections on a Damaged Life.* London: Verso, 2005.

Agamben, Giorgio. *Homo Sacer: Sovereign Power and Bare Life.* Stanford, CA: Stanford University Press, 1998.

Aizura, Aren Z. *Mobile Subjects: Transnational Imaginaries of Gender Reassignment.* Durham, NC: Duke University Press, 2018.

Alexander, M. Jacqui. *Pedagogies of Crossing: Meditations on Feminism, Sexual Politics, Memory, and the Sacred.* Durham, NC: Duke University Press, 2005.

Ameisen, Jean Claude. "Programmed Cell Death and AIDS: From Hypothesis to Experiment." *Immunology Today* 13, no. 10 (1992): 388–91.

Améry, Jean. *On Suicide: A Discourse on Voluntary Death.* Bloomington: Indiana University Press, 1999.

Amin, Kadji. *Disturbing Attachments: Genet, Modern Pederasty, and Queer History.* Durham, NC: Duke University Press, 2017.

Arendt, Hannah. *On Violence.* New York: Harcourt Brace, 1970.

Armstrong, Tim. "Slavery, Insurance, and Sacrifice in the Black Atlantic." In *Sea Changes: Historicizing the Ocean*, edited by Bernhard Klein and Gesa Mackenthun, 167–86. New York: Routledge, 2003.

Bailey, Marlon M. *Butch Queens Up in Pumps: Gender, Performance, and Ballroom Culture in Detroit.* Ann Arbor: University of Michigan Press, 2013.

Balagoon, Kuwasi. "The Continuing Appeal of Anti-Imperialism." *Prison News Service*, no. 65. https://kersplebedeb.com/posts/balagoon-3/.

Baptist, Edward. "Toxic Debt, Liar Loans, Collateralized and Securitized Human

Beings, and the Panic of 1837." In *Capitalism Takes Command: The Social Transformation of Nineteenth-Century America*, edited by Michael Zakim and Gary John Kornblith, 69–92. Chicago: University of Chicago Press, 2012.

Baral, Stefan D., Tonia Poteat, Susanne Stromdahl, Andrea L. Wirtz, Thomas E. Guadmuz, and Chris Beyrer. "Worldwide Burden of HIV in Transgender Women: A Systemic Review and Meta-Analysis." *The Lancet* 13, no. 3 (2013): 214–22. https://www.thelancet.com/journals/laninf/article/PIIS1473-3099 (12)70315-8/fulltext.

Barker, Joanne, ed. *Critically Sovereign: Indigenous Gender, Sexuality, and Feminist Studies*. Durham, NC: Duke University Press, 2017.

Barrett, Lindon. *Blackness and Value: Seeing Double*. Cambridge: Cambridge University Press, 1998.

Barrett, Lindon. "Exemplary Values: Value, Violence, and Others of Value." *SubStance* 21, no. 1 (1992): 77–94.

Bataille, Georges. *The Accursed Share: An Essay on General Economy*, vol. 1: *Consumption*. New York: Zone, 1991.

Baudry, Jean-Louis. "Ideological Effects of the Basic Cinematographic Apparatus." In *Narrative, Apparatus, Ideology*, edited by Philip Rosen, 286–98. New York: Columbia University Press, 1986.

Beam, Myrl. *Gay, Inc.: The Nonprofitization of Queer Politics*. Minneapolis: University of Minnesota Press, 2018.

Beauchamp, Toby. *Going Stealth: Transgender Politics and U.S. Surveillance Practices*. Durham, NC: Duke University Press, 2019.

Benedicto, Bobby. "Agents and Objects of Death: Gay Murder, Boyfriend Twins, and Queer of Color Negativity." GLQ: *A Journal of Lesbian and Gay Studies* 25, no. 2 (2019): 273–96.

Benjamin, Ruha. *Race after Technology: Abolitionist Tools for the New Jim Code*. Cambridge: Polity, 2019.

Benjamin, Walter. "Critique of Violence." In *Reflections: Essays, Aphorisms, Autobiographical Writing*, edited by Peter Demetz, 291–319. New York: Schocken, 1986.

Benjamin, Walter. *Illuminations*. Edited by Hannah Arendt. Translated by Harry Zohn. New York: Schocken, 1969.

Benjamin, Walter. "Left-Wing Melancholy." In *The Weimar Republic Sourcebook*, edited by A. Kaes, M. Jay, and E. Dimendberg, 304–6. Berkeley: University of California Press, 1994.

Berlant, Lauren. *Cruel Optimism*. Durham, NC: Duke University Press, 2011.

Berlant, Lauren. *Desire/Love*. Brooklyn, NY: Punctum, 2012.

Berlant, Lauren, and Michael Warner. "Sex in Public." *Critical Inquiry* 24, no. 2 (1998): 547–66.

Berry, Daina. *The Price for Their Pound of Flesh: The Value of the Enslaved, from Womb to Grave, in the Building of a Nation*. Boston: Beacon, 2017.

Bettcher, Talia. "Evil Deceivers and Make-Believers: On Transphobic Violence and the Politics of Illusion." *Hypatia* 22, no. 3 (2007): 43–65.

Binder, Guyora. "The Slavery of Emancipation." *Cardozo Law Review* 17 (1996): 2063–101.

Boellstorff, Tom, Mauro Cabral, Micha Cárdenas, Trystan Cotten, Eric A. Stanley, Kalaniopua Young, and Aren Z. Aizura. "Decolonizing Transgender: A Round-table Discussion." *Transgender Studies Quarterly* 1, no. 3 (2014): 419–39.

Bonanno, Alfredo M. *Armed Joy: The Anarchist Library*, n.d. https://theanarchist library.org/library/alfredo-m-bonanno-armed-joy.

Bowker, Geoffrey C., and Susan Leigh Star. *Sorting Things Out: Classification and Its Consequences*. Cambridge, MA: MIT Press, 2000.

Brown, Jayna. "Being Cellular: Race, the Inhuman, and the Plasticity of Life." *GLQ: A Journal of Lesbian and Gay Studies* 21, nos. 2–3 (2015): 321–41.

Brown, Wendy. *Undoing the Demos: Neoliberalism's Stealth Revolution*. Cambridge, MA: MIT Press, 2015.

Browne, Simone. *Dark Matters: On the Surveillance of Blackness*. Durham, NC: Duke University Press, 2015.

Buck-Morss, Susan. "Hegel and Haiti." *Critical Inquiry* 26, no. 4 (2000): 821–65.

Butler, Judith. *The Force of Nonviolence: An Ethico-Political Bind*. London: Verso, 2020.

Butler, Judith. *Gender Trouble: Feminism and the Subversion of Identity*. New York: Routledge, 1990.

Butler, Judith. *Parting Ways: Jewishness and the Critique of Zionism*. New York: Columbia University Press, 2012.

Butler, Judith. *Precarious Life: The Powers of Mourning and Violence*. London: Verso, 2006.

Centers for Disease Control and Prevention. "A Cluster of Kaposi's Sarcoma and Pneumocystis carinii Pneumonia among Homosexual Male Residents of Los Angeles and Range Counties, California." *Morbidity and Mortality Weekly Report* 31, no. 23 (June 18, 1982): 305–7. https://www.cdc.gov/mmwr/preview /mmwrhtml/00001114.htm.

Chandler, Nahum. *X—The Problem of the Negro as a Problem for Thought*. New York: Fordham University Press, 2014.

Chávez, Karma. "ACT UP, Haitian Migrants and Alternative Memories of HIV/ AIDS." *Quarterly Journal of Speech* 98, no. 1 (2012): 63–68.

Chen, Mel. *Animacies: Biopolitics, Racial Mattering, and Queer Affect*. Durham, NC: Duke University Press, 2012.

Cheng, Anne Anlin. *The Melancholy of Race: Psychoanalysis, Assimilation, and Hidden Grief*. New York: Oxford University Press, 2001.

Cohen, Cathy J. *The Boundaries of Blackness: AIDS and the Breakdown of Black Politics*. Chicago: University of Chicago Press, 1999.

Cohen, Cathy J. "Punks, Bulldaggers, and Welfare Queens: The Radical Potential of Queer Politics?" *GLQ: A Journal of Lesbian and Gay Studies* 3, no. 4 (1997): 437–65.

Collins, Patricia Hill. *Black Feminist Thought: Knowledge, Consciousness, and the Politics of Empowerment*. London: Routledge, 1990.

Combahee River Collective. *The Combahee River Collective Statement: Black Feminist Organizing in the Seventies and Eighties.* Albany, NY: Kitchen Table, 1986.

Cooper, Melinda. *Life as Surplus: Biotechnology and Capitalism in the Neoliberal Era.* Seattle: University of Washington Press, 2008.

Coulthard, Glen. *Red Skin, White Masks: Rejecting the Colonial Politics of Recognition.* Minneapolis: University of Minnesota Press, 2014.

Cowart, Dylan. "Transgender Prisoners Face Sexual Assault and Discrimination at Pittsburgh Jail." *Speak Freely* (blog), ACLU, November 13, 2017. https://www .aclu.org/blog/lgbt-rights/criminal-justice-reform-lgbt-people/transgender -prisoners-face-sexual-assault-and.

Crenshaw, Kimberlé. "Mapping the Margins: Intersectionality, Identity Politics, and Violence Against Women of Color." In *Critical Race Theory: The Key Writings That Formed the Movement,* edited by Kimberlé Crenshaw, Neil Gotanda, Gary Peller, and Kendall Thomas, 357–83. New York: New Press, 1995.

da Silva, Denise Ferreira. "No-Bodies." *Griffith Law Review* 18, no. 2 (2009): 212–36.

Davis, Angela Y. *Abolition Democracy: Beyond Empire, Prisons, and Torture.* New York: Seven Stories, 2011.

Davis, Angela Y. *Are Prisons Obsolete?* New York: Seven Stories, 2003.

Davis, Angela Y. "The Color of Violence against Women." *Colorlines* 3, no. 3 (fall 2000).

Davis, Angela Y. *Lectures on Liberation.* New York: Committee to Free Angela Davis, 1971. https://archive.org/details/AngelaDavis-LecturesOnLiberation.

Davis, Angela Y. "Reflections on the Black Women's Role in the Community of Slaves." *Massachusetts Review* 13, nos. 1/2 (1972): 81–100.

Davis, Angela Y. *Women, Race and Class.* New York: Random House, 1981.

Davis, Angela Y., Ruchell Magee, and Julian Bond. *If They Come in the Morning: Voices of Resistance.* New York: Third Press, 1971.

Davis, Heath Fogg. *Beyond Trans: Does Gender Matter?* New York: NYU Press, 2017.

Dayan, Colin. "Legal Slaves and Civil Bodies." *Nepantla: Views from the South* 2, no. 1 (2001): 3–39.

Dayan, Colin. *The Story of Cruel and Unusual.* Cambridge, MA: MIT Press, 2007.

Deerinwater, Jen. "Indigenous Lives and Disability Justice." Disability Visibility Project, March 17, 2019. https://disabilityvisibilityproject.com/2019/03/17 /indigenous-lives-and-disability-justice/.

de Lauretis, Teresa. *Alice Doesn't: Feminism, Semiotics, Cinema.* Bloomington: Indiana University Press, 1984.

de Lauretis, Teresa. *Narrative, Apparatus, Ideology.* Edited by Philip Rosen. New York: Columbia University Press, 1986.

Deleuze, Gilles. *Cinema 2: The Time-Image.* Minneapolis: University of Minnesota Press, 1989.

Derrida, Jacques. "The Animal That Therefore I Am (More to Follow)." *Critical Inquiry* 28, no. 2 (2002): 369–418.

Derrida, Jacques. "Force of Law: The 'Mythic Foundations of Authority.'" In *Decon-*

struction and the Possibility of Justice, edited by Drucilla Cornell, Michel Rosenfeld, and David Carlson, 3–67. New York: Routledge, 1992.

de Tocqueville, Alexis. Democracy in America. New York: Harper Perennial, 2006.

Douglass, Patrice D. "Black Feminist Theory for the Dead and Dying." Theory and Event 21, no. 1 (2018): 106–23.

Duberman, Martin. Stonewall. New York: Plume, 1994.

Du Bois, W. E. B. Black Reconstruction in America 1860–1880. New York: Simon and Schuster, 1999.

Duggan, Lisa. The Twilight of Equality? Neoliberalism, Cultural Politics, and the Attack on Democracy. Boston: Beacon, 2003.

Ellison, Treva Carrie. "Black Femme Praxis and the Promise of Black Gender." The Black Scholar 49, no. 1 (2019): 6–16.

Eng, David. Racial Castration: Managing Masculinity in Asian America. Durham, NC: Duke University Press, 2001.

Ervin, Lorenzo Kom'boa. Anarchism and the Black Revolution (1993). Anarchist Library, March 19, 2009. https://theanarchistlibrary.org/library/lorenzo-kom -boa-ervin-anarchism-and-the-black-revolution.

Fanon, Frantz. Black Skin, White Masks. New York: Grove, 1967.

Fanon, Frantz. Peau Noire, Masques Blancs. Paris: Éditions du Seuil, 2008.

Fanon, Frantz. The Wretched of the Earth. New York: Grove, 1963.

Farmer, Paul. AIDS and Accusation: Haiti and the Geography of Blame. Berkeley: University of California Press, 2006.

Feinberg, Leslie. "Street Transvestite Action Revolutionaries." Workers World, September 24, 2006. https://www.workers.org/2006/us/lavender-red-73/.

Fenced OUT. DVD. New York: FIERCE, Papertiger TV, and Neutral Zone, 2000.

Ferguson, Roderick A. One-Dimensional Queer. Cambridge: Polity, 2018.

Fleetwood, Nicole R. Troubling Vision: Performance, Visuality, and Blackness. Chicago: University of Chicago Press, 2011.

Foucault, Michel. Abnormal: Lectures at the Collège de France 1974–1975. Translated by Graham Burchell. New York: Picador, 2003.

Foucault, Michel. The History of Sexuality: An Introduction, vol. 1. Translated by Robert Hurley. New York: Vintage, 1999.

Foucault, Michel. Power/Knowledge: Selected Interviews and Other Writings, 1972–1977. New York: Vintage, 1980.

Foucault, Michel. "Society Must Be Defended": Lectures at the Collège de France 1975–1976. Translated by David Macey. New York: Picador, 2003.

Foucault, Michel. "What Is Enlightenment?" In The Foucault Reader, edited by Paul Rabinow, 32–50. New York: Pantheon, 1984.

Freud, Sigmund. "Analysis of a Phobia of a Five-Year-Old Boy." In The Pelican Freud Library, vol. 8: Case Histories 1, 169–306. New York: Penguin, 1977.

Freud, Sigmund. "Fetishism." In The Standard Edition of the Complete Works of Sigmund Freud, vol. 21, edited by James Strachey, 147–57. London: Hogarth, [1927] 1953–74.

Fuss, Diana. *Identification Papers*. New York: Routledge, 1995.

Geary, Adam. *Antiblack Racism and the AIDS Epidemic: State Intimacies*. New York: Palgrave Macmillan, 2014.

Gelderloos, Peter. *How Nonviolence Protects the State*. Cambridge, MA: South End, 2007.

Gherovici, Patricia. "Psychoanalysis Needs a Sex Change." *Gay and Lesbian Issues and Psychology Review* 7, no. 1 (2011): 3–18.

Gilmore, Ruth Wilson. "What Is to Be Done?" *American Quarterly* 63, no. 2 (2011): 245–65.

Glissant, Édouard. *Poetics of Relation*. Ann Arbor: University of Michigan Press, 1997.

Goldie, Terry. "Saint Fanon and 'Homosexual Territory.'" In *Frantz Fanon: Critical Perspectives*, edited by Anthony Alessandrini, 75–86. New York: Routledge, 1999.

Goldsby, Jacqueline D. *A Spectacular Secret: Lynching in American Life and Literature*. Chicago: University of Chicago Press, 2006.

Gooding-Williams, Robert, ed. *Reading Rodney King/Reading Urban Uprising*. New York: Routledge, 1993.

Gordon, Lewis R. *What Fanon Said: A Philosophical Introduction to His Life and Thought*. New York: Fordham University Press, 2015.

Gossett, Che. "Žižek's Trans/Gender Trouble." *Los Angeles Review of Books*, September 13, 2016. https://lareviewofbooks.org/article/zizeks-transgender-trouble/.

Gould, Deborah B. *Moving Politics: Emotion and ACT UP's Fight against AIDS*. Chicago: University of Chicago Press, 2009.

Grassian, Stuart. "Psychiatric Effects of Solitary Confinement." *Washington University Journal of Law and Policy* 22 (2006): 325–83.

Gunther, Lisa. *Solitary Confinement: Social Death and Its Afterlives*. Minneapolis: University of Minnesota Press, 2013.

Hall, Stuart. *Representation: Cultural Representations and Signifying Practices*. London: SAGE, 1997.

Hamilton, Alexander, et al. *The Federalist Papers*. Edited by Ian Shapiro. New Haven, CT: Yale University Press, 2009.

Hammond, Charlotte. *Entangled Otherness: Cross-Gender Fabrications in the Francophone Caribbean*. Liverpool: Liverpool University Press, 2019.

Handler, Philip. "Excessive Anonymity." *Science* 172, no. 3982 (1971): 425–27.

Hanhardt, Christina B. "'Dead Addicts Don't Recover': ACT UP's Needle Exchange and the Subjects of Queer Activist History." *GLQ: A Journal of Lesbian and Gay Studies* 24, no. 4 (2018): 421–44.

Hanhardt, Christina B. *Safe Space: Gay Neighborhood History and the Politics of Violence*. Durham, NC: Duke University Press, 2013.

Haraway, Donna J. "A Cyborg Manifesto: Science, Technology, and Socialist-Feminism in the Late Twentieth Century." In *Manifestly Haraway*, edited by Donna J. Haraway and Cary Wolfe. Minneapolis: University of Minnesota Press, 2016.

Haraway, Donna J. *Staying with the Trouble: Making Kin in the Chthulucene*. Durham, NC: Duke University Press, 2016.

Hardt, Michael. "Affective Labor." *boundary 2* 26, no. 2 (1999): 89–100.

Haritaworn, Jin, Adi Kuntsman, and Silvia Posocco, eds. *Queer Necropolitics*. London: Routledge, 2014.

Harney, Stefano, and Fred Moten. *The Undercommons: Fugitive Planning and Black Study*. Brooklyn, NY: Minor Compositions, 2013.

Harris, Laura. *Experiments in Exile: C. L. R. James, Hélio Oiticica, and the Aesthetic Sociality of Blackness*. New York: Fordham University Press, 2018.

Hartman, Saidiya V. *Scenes of Subjection: Terror, Slavery, and Self-Making in Nineteenth-Century America*. New York: Oxford University Press, 1997.

Hartman, Saidiya V. "Venus in Two Acts." *Small Axe* 26 (June 2008): 1–14.

Hartman, Saidiya V. *Wayward Lives, Beautiful Experiments: Intimate Histories of Social Upheaval*. New York: W. W. Norton, 2019.

Healy, Kieran. *Last Best Gifts: Altruism and the Market for Human Blood and Organs*. Chicago: University of Chicago Press, 2006.

Hegel, Georg W. F., Arnold V. Miller, and J. N. Findlay. *Phenomenology of Spirit*. Oxford: Clarendon Press, 1977.

Herbst, Jeffrey H., Elizabeth D. Jacobs, Teresa J. Finlayson, Vel S McKleroy, Mary Spink Neumann, Nicole Crepaz, "Estimating HIV Prevalence and Risk Behaviors of Transgender Persons in the United States: A Systematic Review." *AIDS and Behavior* 12, no. 1 (2008): 1–17.

Hoad, Neville. *African Intimacies: Race, Homosexuality, and Globalization*. Minneapolis: University of Minnesota Press, 2006.

Holland, Sharon Patricia. *Raising the Dead: Readings of Death and (Black) Subjectivity*. Durham, NC: Duke University Press, 2000.

Hook, Derek. "Fanon via Lacan, or: Decolonization by Psychoanalytic Means . . . ?" *Journal of the British Society for Phenomenology* 51, no. 4 (2020): 305–19.

hooks, bell. *Black Looks: Race and Representation*. Boston: South End, 1992.

Hwang, Ren-yo Hwang. "Deviant Care for Deviant Futures: QTBIPOC Radical Relationalism as Mutual Aid against Carceral Care." *Transgender Studies Quarterly* 6, no. 4 (November 1, 2019): 559–78.

INCITE! Women of Color against Violence, ed. *Color of Violence: The INCITE! Anthology*. Cambridge, MA: South End, 2006.

The Invisible Committee. *Now*. Translated by Robert Hurley. Cambridge, MA: MIT Press, 2017.

Irvine, Angela, Shannan Wilber, and Aisha Canfield. "Lesbian, Gay, Bisexual, Questioning, and Gender Nonconforming Girls and Boys in the California Juvenile Justice System: A Practice Guide." Oakland, CA: Impact Justice and the National Center for Lesbian Rights, 2017. https://perma.cc/3L9T-TMSB.

"It's War in Here." Sylvia Rivera Law Project, April 20, 2007. https://srlp.org/its-war-in-here/.

James, C. L. R. *The Black Jacobins: Toussaint l'Ouverture and the San Domingo Revolution*. New York: Vintage, 1963.

James, C. L. R. *A New Notion: Two Works by C. L. R. James*. Edited by Noel Ignatiev. Oakland, CA: PM Press, 2010.

James, C. L. R. *World Revolution, 1917–1936: The Rise and Fall of the Communist International*. Edited by Christian Høgsbjerg. Durham, NC: Duke University Press, 2017.

JanMohamed, Abdul R. *The Death-Bound-Subject: Richard Wright's Archaeology of Death*. Durham, NC: Duke University Press, 2005.

Johnson, E. Patrick, and Mae G. Henderson. "Introduction: Queering Black Studies/ 'Quaring' Queer Studies." In *Black Queer Studies: A Critical Anthology*, edited by E. Patrick Johnson and Mae G. Henderson, 1–17. Durham, NC: Duke University Press, 2005.

Jones, Claudia. *An End to the Neglect of the Problems of the Negro Woman!* New York: Jefferson School of Social Science, 1949.

Jones, Donna V. *The Racial Discourses of Life Philosophy: Négritude, Vitalism, and Modernity*. New York: Columbia University Press, 2010.

Judy, Ronald A. T. "Fanon's Body of Black Experience." In *Fanon: A Critical Reader*, edited by Lewis R. Gordon, T. Denean Sharpley-Whiting, and Renee T. White, 53–73. Cambridge, MA: Blackwell, 1996.

Julien, Isaac, dir. *Frantz Fanon: Black Skin, White Masks*. San Francisco: California Newsreel, 1996.

Kaba, Mariame, and John Duda. "Towards the Horizon of Abolition: A Conversation with Mariame Kaba." *The Next System Project*, November 9, 2017. https:// thenextsystem.org/learn/stories/towards-horizon-abolition-conversation -mariame-kaba.

Kant, Immanuel, and Mary J. Gregor. *Practical Philosophy*. Cambridge: Cambridge University Press, 1996.

Kauanui, J. Kēhaulani. *Paradoxes of Hawaiian Sovereignty: Land, Sex, and the Colonial Politics of State Nationalism*. Durham, NC: Duke University Press, 2018.

Keeling, Kara. "'In the Interval': Frantz Fanon and the 'Problems' of Visual Representation." *Qui Parle* 13, no. 2 (2003): 91–117.

Keeling, Kara. *The Witch's Flight: The Cinematic, the Black Femme, and the Image of Common Sense*. Durham, NC: Duke University Press, 2007.

Kennedy, Duncan. "The Critique of Rights in Critical Legal Studies." In *Left Legalism/Left Critique*, edited by Wendy Brown and Janet Halley, 178–228. Durham, NC: Duke University Press, 2002.

Khanna, Ranjana. *Dark Continents: Psychoanalysis and Colonialism*. Durham, NC: Duke University Press, 2003.

Kimball, Ann Marie. *Risky Trade: Infectious Disease in the Era of Global Trade*. Aldershot, UK: Ashgate, 2006.

King, Tiffany Lethabo. *The Black Shoals: Offshore Formations of Black and Native Studies*. Durham, NC: Duke University Press, 2019.

Kojève, Alexandre. *Introduction to the Reading of Hegel*. Translated by James A. Nichols. Edited by Allan Bloom. New York: Basic Books, 1969.

Lacan, Jacques. *Feminine Sexuality*. Translated by Jacqueline Rose. Edited by Juliet Mitchell and Jacqueline Rose. New York: W. W. Norton, 1985.

Law, Victoria. "Against Carceral Feminism." *Jacobin*, October 17, 2014. https://www
.jacobinmag.com/2014/10/against-carceral-feminism/.

Lenin, Vladimir. *The State and Revolution*. New York: Penguin, 1993.

Lloyd, David. "From the Critique of Violence to the Critique of Rights." *Critical
Times* 3, no. 1 (April 1, 2020): 109–30.

Lloyd, David. *Under Representation: The Racial Regimes of Aesthetics*. New York: Fordham University Press, 2019.

Locke, John. *Two Treatises of Government*. Cambridge: Cambridge University Press,
1988.

Luxemburg, Rosa. *The Essential Rosa Luxemburg: Reform or Revolution and the Mass
Strike*. Edited by Helen Scott. Chicago: Haymarket, 2008.

Macharia, Keguro. *Frottage: Frictions of Intimacy across the Black Diaspora*. New York:
NYU Press, 2019.

Majd, Katayoon, Jody Marksamer, and Carolyn Reyes. "Hidden Injustice: Lesbian,
Gay, Bisexual, and Transgender Youth in Juvenile Courts." San Francisco: Legal
Services for Children, National Juvenile Defender Center, and National Center
for Lesbian Rights, 2019. https://www.nclrights.org/wp-content/uploads/2014
/06/hidden_injustice.pdf.

Manalansan, Martin. "Race, Violence and Neoliberal Spatial Politics in the Global
City." *Social Text 84–85* 23, nos. 3–4 (2005): 141–55.

Marable, Manning. *How Capitalism Underdeveloped Black America: Problems in Race,
Political Economy, and Society*. Chicago: Haymarket, 2018.

Marriott, David. *Haunted Life: Visual Culture and Black Modernity*. New Brunswick,
NJ: Rutgers University Press, 2007.

Marriott, David. "Inventions of Existence: Sylvia Wynter, Frantz Fanon, Sociogeny,
and 'the Damned.'" CR: *The New Centennial Review* 11, no. 3 (2011): 45–89.

Marriott, David. *On Black Men*. New York: Columbia University Press, 2000.

Marriott, David. "On Racial Fetishism." *Qui Parle* 18, no. 2 (2010): 215–48.

Marriott, David. *Whither Fanon? Studies in the Blackness of Being*. Stanford, CA: Stanford University Press, 2018.

Marx, Karl. *Capital*, vol. 1. London: Penguin, 1990.

Marx, Karl. *Capital*, vol. 3. London, Penguin, 1991.

Marx, Karl. *Grundrisse: Foundations of the Critique of Political Economy*. New York:
Penguin, 1993.

Marx, Karl. *The Poverty of Philosophy: A Reply to M. Proudhon's Philosophy of Poverty*.
New York: International, 1992.

Marx, Karl, and Friedrich Engels. "The Holy Family." In *Collected Works*, vol. 4:
78–143. New York: International, 1975.

Mbembe, Achille. "The Age of Humanism Is Ending." *Mail and Guardian*, December 22, 2016. https://mg.co.za/article/2016-12-22-00-the-age-of-humanism-is
-ending.

Mbembe, Achille. "Necropolitics." *Public Culture* 15, no. 1 (2003): 11–40.

Mbembe, Achille. *On the Postcolony*. Berkeley: University of California Press, 2001.

McRuer, Robert. "Capitalism and Disabled Identity: Sharon Kowalski, Interdependency, and Queer Domesticity." In *Crip Theory: Cultural Signs of Queerness and Disability*, 77–102. New York: NYU Press, 2006.

Meillassoux, Claude. *The Anthropology of Slavery: The Womb of Iron and Gold*. Chicago: University of Chicago Press, 1991.

Melamed, Jodi. "Racial Capitalism." *Critical Ethnic Studies* 1, no. 1 (2015): 76–85.

Mercer, Kobena. "Looking for Trouble." *Transition* 51 (1991): 184–97.

Meronek, Toshio. *Miss Major Speaks*. London: Verso, forthcoming.

Metz, Christian. *The Imaginary Signifier: Psychoanalysis and the Cinema*. Bloomington: Indiana University Press, 1986.

Metz, Christian. "Photography and Fetish." *October* 34 (1985): 87–88.

Mogul, Joey L., Andrea J. Ritchie, and Kay Whitlock. *Queer (In)Justice: The Criminalization of LGBT People in the United States*. Boston: Beacon, 2011.

Morgan, Jennifer L. *Laboring Women: Reproduction and Gender in New World Slavery*. Philadelphia: University of Pennsylvania Press, 2004.

Moten, Fred. "Democracy." In *Keywords for American Cultural Studies*, 2nd ed. Edited by Bruce Burgett and Glenn Hendler, 73–75. New York: NYU Press, 2014.

Moten, Fred. *In the Break: The Aesthetics of the Black Radical Tradition*. Minneapolis: University of Minnesota Press, 2003.

Moten, Fred. "The Subprime and the Beautiful." *African Identities* 11, no. 2 (2013): 237–45.

Mulvey, Laura. "Visual Pleasure and Narrative Cinema." In *Film Theory and Criticism: Introductory Readings*, edited by Leo Braudy and Marshall Cohen, 833–44. New York: Oxford University Press, 1999.

Muñoz, José Esteban. *Cruising Utopia: The Then and There of Queer Futurity*. New York: NYU Press, 2009.

Musser, Amber Jamilla. *Sensual Excess: Queer Femininity and Brown Jouissance*. New York: NYU Press. 2018.

Nair, Yasmin. "The New Yorker Sheds More Light on the Clementi-Ravi Story." February 7, 2012. https://yasminnair.com/the-new-yorker-sheds-more-light-on -the-clementi-ravi-story/.

National Coalition of Anti-Violence Programs. "Reports," AVP.org. https://avp.org/ resources/reports/.

Negri, Antonio. "Value and Affect." *boundary 2* 26, no. 2 (1999): 77–88.

Newton, Huey P. *Revolutionary Suicide*. New York: Harcourt Brace Jovanovich, 1973.

NIH AIDS Reagent Program. "Home." http://hivreagentprogram.org.

Nye, Coleman. "The Commons as Accumulation Strategy: Postgenomic Mutations in Biological Property." *Social Text 1* 37, no. 2 (2019): 1–28.

Olsson, Göran Hugo, Annika Rogell, Joslyn Barnes, Danny Glover, Axel Arnö, Questlove, Om'Mas Keith, et al. *The Black Power Mixtape 1967–1975: A Documentary in 9 Chapters*. New York: MPI Media Group, 2011.

Ophelian, Annalise, dir. *Major!* San Francisco: Floating Ophelia Productions, 2016.

Paris, William M. "Humanism's Secret Shadow: The Construction of Black Gender/Sexuality in Frantz Fanon and Hortense Spillers." *philoSOPHIA* 8, no. 1 (2018): 81–99.

Patterson, Orlando. *Slavery and Social Death: A Comparative Study*. Cambridge, MA: Harvard University Press, 1985.

Pépin, Jacques. *The Origins of AIDS*. Cambridge: Cambridge University Press, 2011.

Petryna, Adriana, Andrew Lakoff, and Arthur Kleinman, eds. *Global Pharmaceuticals: Ethics, Markets, Practices*. Durham, NC: Duke University Press, 2006.

Plato. *The Republic*. New York: Basic Books, 1968.

Prosser, Jay. *Second Skins: The Body Narratives of Transsexuality*. New York: Columbia University Press, 1998.

Puar, Jasbir K. *The Right to Maim: Debility, Capacity, Disability*. Durham, NC: Duke University Press, 2017.

Quest, Matthew. "Direct Democracy and the Search for Identity for Colonized People: The Contemporary Meanings of C. L. R. James's Classical Athens." *Classical Receptions Journal* 9, no. 2 (2017): 237–67.

Raha, Nat. "Queer Capital: Marxism in Queer Theory and Post-1950 Poetics." PhD diss., University of Sussex, 2018.

"Rapping with a Street Transvestite Revolutionary: An Interview with Marcia Johnson." In *Out of the Closets: Voices of Gay Liberation*, edited by Karla Jay and Allen Young, 112–21. New York: NYU Press, 1992.

Reddy, Chandan. *Freedom with Violence: Race, Sexuality, and the US State*. Durham, NC: Duke University Press, 2011.

Richardson, Matt. *The Queer Limit of Black Memory: Black Lesbian Literature and Irresolution*. Columbus: Ohio State University Press, 2013.

Robinson, Cedric J. *An Anthropology of Marxism*. Chapel Hill: University of North Carolina Press, 2001.

Robinson, Cedric J. *Black Marxism: The Making of the Black Radical Tradition*. Chapel Hill: University of North Carolina Press, 2000.

Rodney, Walter. *How Europe Underdeveloped Africa*. London: Bogle-l'Ouverture, 1972.

Rodríguez, Dylan. *Forced Passages: Imprisoned Radical Intellectuals and the U.S. Prison Regime*. Minneapolis: University of Minnesota Press, 2006.

Rose, Nikolas. *The Politics of Life Itself: Biomedicine, Power, and Subjectivity in the Twenty-First Century*. Princeton, NJ: Princeton University Press, 2009.

Rosenberg, Jordy. "The Molecularization of Sexuality: On Some Primitivisms of the Present." *Theory and Event* 17, no. 2 (2014). https://muse.jhu.edu/article/546470.

Rosenthal, Caitlin. *Accounting for Slavery: Masters and Management*. Cambridge, MA: Harvard University Press, 2018.

Salamon, Gayle. *The Life and Death of Latisha King: A Critical Phenomenology of Transphobia*. New York: NYU Press, 2018.

Santana, Dora Silva. "*Mais Viva!* Reassembling Transness, Blackness, and Feminism." *Transgender Studies Quarterly* 6, no. 2 (2019): 210–22.

Santana, Dora Silva. "Transitionings and Returnings: Experiments with the Poetics of Transatlantic Water." *Transgender Studies Quarterly* 4, no. 2 (2017): 181–90.

Sartre, Jean-Paul. *Being and Nothingness*. Translated by Hazel E. Barnes. London: Routledge, [1943] 1995.

Scott, Darieck. *Extravagant Abjection: Blackness, Power, and Sexuality in the African American Literary Imagination*. New York: NYU Press, 2010.

Sedgwick, Eve Kosofsky. "How to Bring Your Kids Up Gay." *Social Text* 29 (1991): 18–27.

Sedgwick, Eve Kosofsky. *Tendencies*. Durham, NC: Duke University Press, 1993.

Sekyi-otu, Ato. *Fanon's Dialectic of Experience*. Cambridge, MA: Harvard University Press, 1996.

Shahani, Nishant. "How to Survive the Whitewashing of AIDS: Global Pasts, Transnational Futures." *QED: A Journal in GLBTQ Worldmaking* 3, no. 1 (2016): 1–33.

Sharpe, Christina. *In the Wake: On Blackness and Being*. Durham, NC: Duke University Press, 2016.

Sharpe, Christina. *Monstrous Intimacies: Making Post-Slavery Subjects*. Durham, NC: Duke University Press, 2010.

Sharpley-Whiting, T. Denean. *Frantz Fanon: Conflicts and Feminisms*. Lanham, MD: Rowman and Littlefield, 1997.

Shepard, Benjamin. "Sylvia and Sylvia's Children: The Battle for a Queer Public Space." In *That's Revolting! Queer Strategies for Resisting Assimilation*, edited by Mattilda Bernstein Sycamore, 123–40. Brooklyn, NY: Soft Skull, 2008.

Silverman, Kaja. *The Subject of Semiotics*. New York: Oxford University Press, 1983.

Singh, Nikhil Pal. "On Race, Violence, and So-Called Primitive Accumulation." *Social Text 128* 34, no. 3 (2016): 27–50.

Sitrin, Marina. *Horizontalism: Voices of Popular Power in Argentina*. Oakland, CA: AK Press, 2006.

Skloot, Rebecca. *The Immortal Life of Henrietta Lacks*. New York: Crown, 2010.

Snorton, C. Riley. *Black on Both Sides: A Racial History of Trans Identity*. Minneapolis: University of Minnesota Press, 2017.

Snorton, C. Riley, and Jin Haritaworn. "Trans Necropolitics: A Transnational Reflection on Violence, Death, and the Trans of Color Afterlife." In *Transgender Studies Reader 2*, edited by Susan Stryker and Aren Z. Aizura, 66–76. New York: Routledge, 2013.

Snorton, C. Riley, and Hentyle Yapp, eds. *Saturation: Race, Art, and the Circulation of Value*. Cambridge, MA: MIT Press, 2020.

Solanas, Fernando, and Octavio Getino. "Toward a Third Cinema." *Cinéaste* 4, no. 3 (1970): 1–10.

Spade, Dean. *Normal Life: Administrative Violence, Critical Trans Politics, and the Limits of Law*. Durham, NC: Duke University Press, 2015.

Spade, Dean, and Rori Rohlfs. "Legal Equality, Gay Numbers and the (After?) Math of Eugenics." *Scholar and Feminist Online*, spring 2016. http://sfonline.barnard.edu/navigating-neoliberalism-in-the-academy-nonprofits-and-beyond/dean-spade-rori-rohlfs-legal-equality-gay-numbers-and-the-aftermath-of-eugenics/0/.

Spillers, Hortense. *Black, White, and in Color: Essays on American Literature and Culture*. Chicago: University of Chicago Press, 2003.

Spillers, Hortense. "Mama's Baby, Papa's Maybe: An American Grammar Book." *Diacritics* 17, no. 2 (1987): 64–81.

Spivak, Gayatri Chakravorty. *A Critique of Postcolonial Reason: Toward a History of the Vanishing Present*. Cambridge, MA: Harvard University Press, 1999.

Spivak, Gayatri Chakravorty. "Scattered Speculations on the Question of Value." *Diacritics* 15, no. 4 (1985): 73–93.

Stanley, Eric A. "The Affective Commons: Gay Shame, Queer Hate, and Other Collective Feelings." GLQ: *A Journal of Lesbian and Gay Studies* 24, no. 4 (2018): 489–508.

Stanley, Eric A. "Gender Self-Determination." *Transgender Studies Quarterly* 1, no. 1 (2014): 89–91.

Stanley, Eric A., and Nat Smith, eds. *Captive Genders: Trans Embodiment and the Prison Industrial Complex*. Oakland, CA: AK Press, 2015.

Starr, Douglas P. *Blood: An Epic History of Medicine and Commerce*. New York: Alfred A. Knopf, 1998.

Stoler, Ann L. *Race and the Education of Desire: Foucault's History of Sexuality and the Colonial Order of Things*. Durham, NC: Duke University Press, 1995.

Stryker, Susan. "Transgender Studies: Queer Theory's Evil Twin." GLQ: *A Journal of Lesbian and Gay Studies* 10, no. 2 (2004): 212–15.

Stryker, Susan, and Victor Silverman, dirs. *Screaming Queens: The Riot at Compton's Cafeteria*. San Francisco: Frameline, 2010.

Sturken, Marita. *Tangled Memories: The Vietnam War, the AIDS Epidemic, and the Politics of Remembering*. Berkeley: University of California Press, 1997.

Tadiar, Neferti X. M. "Life-Times of Disposability within Global Neoliberalism." *Social Text* 115 31, no. 2 (2013): 19–48.

Tadiar, Neferti X. M. *Things Fall Away: Philippine Historical Experience and the Makings of Globalization*. Durham, NC: Duke University Press, 2009.

Táíwò, Olúfémi O. "Being-in-the-Room Privilege: Elite Capture and Epistemic Deference." *The Philosopher* 108, no. 4 (2020).

Taylor, Keeanga-Yamahtta, ed. *How We Get Free: Black Feminism and the Combahee River Collective*. Chicago: Haymarket, 2017.

Terrefe, Selamawit D. "Speaking the Hieroglyph." *Theory and Event* 21, no. 1 (2018): 124–47.

Third World Gay Revolution (New York City). "What We Want, What We Believe." In *Out of the Closets: Voices of Gay Liberation*, edited by Karla Jay and Allen Young, 363–67. New York: NYU Press, 1992.

Tourmaline, dir. *The Personal Things*. 2016. https://www.youtube.com/watch?v=vzafzVv2G2E.

Tourmaline, Eric A. Stanley, and Johanna Burton, eds. *Trap Door: Trans Cultural Production and the Politics of Visibility*. Cambridge, MA: MIT Press, 2017.

Tourmaline and Sasha Wortzel, dirs. *Happy Birthday, Marsha!* New York, 2017.

Treichler, Paula A. "AIDS, Homophobia, and Biomedical Discourse: An Epidemic of Signification." *October* 43 (1987): 31–70.

U.S. Food and Drug Administration. "Revised Recommendations for Reducing the Risk of Human Immunodeficiency Virus Transmission by Blood and Blood Products—Questions and Answers." February 2, 2018. https://www.fda.gov

/vaccines-blood-biologics/blood-blood-products/revised-recommendations
-reducing-risk-human-immunodeficiency-virus-transmission-blood-and-blood.

"USA: Stonewalled: Police Abuse and Misconduct against Lesbian, Gay, Bisexual and Transgender People in the U.S." Amnesty International, September 21, 2005. https://www.amnesty.org/en/documents/AMR51/122/2005/en/.

Valencia, Sayak. *Gore Capitalism*. South Pasadena, CA: Semiotext(e), 2018.

Vergès, Françoise. "Creole Skin, Black Mask: Fanon and Disavowal." *Critical Inquiry* 23, no. 3 (1997): 578–95.

"Victims—Hate Crime Statistics, 2017." Federal Bureau of Investigation, n.d. https://ucr.fbi.gov/hate-crime/2017/tables/table-1.xls.

Viego, Antonio. *Dead Subjects: Toward a Politics of Loss in Latino Studies*. Durham, NC: Duke University Press, 2007.

Vora, Kalindi. *Life Support: Biocapital and the New History of Outsourced Labor*. Minneapolis: University of Minnesota Press, 2015.

Walcott, Rinaldo. "Freedom Now Suite: Black Feminist Turns of Voice." *Small Axe* 22, no. 3 (2018): 151–59.

Waldby, Catherine. *AIDS and the Body Politic: Biomedicine and Sexual Difference*. London: Routledge, 1996.

Waldby, Catherine, and Robert Mitchell. *Tissue Economies: Blood, Organs, and Cell Lines in Late Capitalism*. Durham, NC: Duke University Press, 2006.

Warren, Calvin. "Onticide: Afro-Pessimism, Gay Nigger #1, and Surplus Violence." *GLQ: A Journal of Lesbian and Gay Studies* 23, no. 3 (2017): 391–418.

Washington, Harriet. *Medical Apartheid: The Dark History of Medical Experimentation in Black Americans from Colonial Times to the Present*. Norwell, MA: Anchor, 2008.

Weheliye, Alexander G. *Habeas Viscus: Racializing Assemblages, Biopolitics, and Black Feminist Theories of the Human*. Durham, NC: Duke University Press, 2014.

Weinbaum, Alys Eve. *The Afterlife of Reproductive Slavery: Biocapitalism and Black Feminism's Philosophy of History*. Durham, NC: Duke University Press, 2019.

Weiss, Margot D. "Gay Shame and BDSM Pride: Neoliberalism, Privacy, and Sexual Politics." *Radical History Review* 2008, no. 100 (2008): 87–101.

Wilderson, Frank B. *Red, White and Black: Cinema and the Structure of U.S. Antagonisms*. Durham, NC: Duke University Press, 2010.

Williams, Eric E. *Capitalism and Slavery*. Chapel Hill: University of North Carolina Press, 1994.

Willse, Craig. *The Value of Homelessness: Managing Surplus Life in the United States*. Minneapolis: University of Minnesota Press, 2015.

Wojnarowicz, David. *Close to the Knives: A Memoir of Disintegration*. New York: Vintage, 1991.

Wolfe, Patrick. "Settler Colonialism and the Elimination of the Native." *Journal of Genocide Research* 8, no. 4 (2006): 387–409.

Woubshet, Dagmawi. *The Calendar of Loss: Race, Sexuality, and Mourning in the Early Era of AIDS*. Baltimore: Johns Hopkins University Press, 2015.

Wynter, Sylvia. "No Humans Involved: An Open Letter to My Colleagues." *Forum NHI: Knowledge for the 21st Century* 1, no. 1 (fall 1994): 42–103.

Wynter, Sylvia. "Towards the Sociogenic Principle: Fanon, Identity, the Puzzle of Conscious Experience, and What It Is Like to Be 'Black.'" In *National Identities and Sociopolitical Changes in Latin America*, edited by Mercedes F. Dúran-Cogan and Antonio Gómez-Moriana, 30–66. New York: Routledge, 2001.

Wynter, Sylvia. "Unsettling the Coloniality of Being/Power/Truth/Freedom: Towards the Human, after Man, Its Overrepresentation—An Argument." *CR: The New Centennial Review* 3, no. 3 (2003): 257–337.

Yingling, Thomas E. *AIDS and the National Body*. Edited by Robyn Wiegman. Durham, NC: Duke University Press, 1997.

Zeilig, Leo. *Frantz Fanon: The Militant Philosopher of Third World Revolution*. London: I. B. Tauris, 2014.

INDEX

Page numbers followed by f indicate figures.

157n12; liberal, 10, 16, 40, 47, 56, 78, 96; violence in, 6, 10–11, 16, 40, 109–10, 114–23

Democratic Republic of the Congo, 53; Kinshasa, 52

Derrida, Jacques, 9–10, 117, 138n49, 156n38

Diamond, Ashley, 18, 92, 112–13, 154n23, 155n28; *Memoirs of a Chain Gang Sissy*, 101–9

direct action, 5, 63–64, 87, 120

disability, 30, 45, 78, 94, 107

disability justice, 94, 144n48, 152nn3–4

disciplinary power, 3, 48, 85, 107, 110, 123, 132n39; blood and, 49, 56–57; colonialism and, 12–13; incoherence of, 5; racialized, 78, 82; as state power, 6, 103

dispossession, 45, 55–56, 64

Dixie, 31–32

Douglass, Patrice, 81

drag, 13, 32, 34–35, 110

Du Bois, W. E. B., 47, 140n14

Dupree, Tandi Iman, 110–13

Eighth Amendment, 105, 107

Enlightenment, 14, 18, 24, 37–38, 94, 100, 108, 110; as attitude, 156n37

Enstice, Kathleen, 35

epidemiology, 53, 55, 62, 143n42

epidermalization, 25, 38, 47–48

equality, 25, 34, 39–40, 60, 109, 118, 122; engineered inequalities, 159n23; formal, 6–7, 37, 56; representation and, 85–88; violence and, 16, 23, 43, 69, 82. *See also* Against Equality

Ervin, Lorenzo Kom'boa, 117

ethics, 15, 48, 69

eugenics, 96, 127n6

Fanon, Frantz, 86, 88, 92, 100, 110, 112, 130n26, 148nn20–21; on colonialism, 8, 16, 38, 106, 153n9; on gender/sexuality, 12–13; on Hegel, 17, 38; on the new man, 18, 100–101, 108; on non-

existence, 21, 24, 39; on race, 24–26, 134n14, 140n16; on suicide, 95–98; on violence, 1, 11, 14, 87, 109; on visuality, 72–74, 76–77

Fanon, Josie, 100

Federal Bureau of Investigation (FBI), 43; Criminal Justice Information Services (CJIS), 30–31

Felix-Zambrana, Joelle, 22

feminism, 56, 75, 102, 154n20; anticolonial, 10, 13, 46; Black, 14, 46, 81; carceral, 107, 154n21, 156n34; Native, 132n34, 139n13; socialist, 45, 139n13; trans, 81, 107; trans-exclusionary radical feminists (TERFs), 118, 127n6, 154n27

Fenrich, Steen Keith, 28

fetishism, 73–76, 80. *See also* commodity fetishism

fictive justice, 6, 128n12

FIERCE!, 125n1

Florida, 42; Orlando, 41, 44

Floyd, George, 150n48

Food and Drug Administration (FDA), 42, 50, 52, 55

forced gender transition, 18, 103–5, 154n27

Foucault, Michel, 8, 57–58, 119, 129n16, 130n17, 130n19, 136n37, 156n37

Fourth Amendment, 78

France, 39, 53, 96, 153n9; Lyon, 12

Free France army, 100

Freud, Sigmund, 11, 73

Front de libération nationale (FLN), 11, 101

Fuerzas Armadas de Liberación Nacional, 129n14

fugitivity, 10, 18, 81, 86, 121

Fuller, Lauryn Paige, 31–33, 38–40, 99

Gaines, Christopher, 34–36

Gay Activist Alliance (GAA), 2, 118

Gay Freedom Day, 118

Gay Liberation Front (GLF), 2, 118

New York Life, 46
no-bodies, 67, 72, 87, 90–91
nonage, 94
nonexistence, 6, 20–21, 24, 37–39, 100
the nothing, 34, 39
nothingness, 33–34, 36, 40

Oedipus complex, 12–13
OneBlood, 42, 51
ontological capture, 21, 39–40, 96
opacity, 87–88, 90
organized abandonment, 8
"outside agitators," 22, 134n6
overdetermination, 14, 26, 29, 73, 88, 93, 98
overkill, 17, 32–36

Palestine, 42, 44
para-colonialism, 16
Paris Commune, 129n16
Parton, Dolly, 34
phallus, 73–76
phenomenology, 3, 6, 8, 24, 38, 87, 93
Plato, 117, 157n12
Pneumocystis carinii pneumonia (PCP),
   54
police, 2, 5, 27–28, 44, 64, 86, 122, 130n26,
   140n17, 156n34; police reports, 30,
   67–83; police violence, 10, 15, 17–18,
   22–23, 31, 67–71, 95, 146n6, 147n11,
   150n48; resistance to, 88, 90. See also
   Memphis Police Department; Minneapolis Police Department; San Francisco Police Department (SFPD)
Porter, Robert, 34–36
post-traumatic stress disorder (PTSD),
   106. See also SHU syndrome
praxis of care, 15
pre-exposure prophylaxis (PrEP),
   61–62. See also Truvada
primitive accumulation, 42, 45–46, 59
Prison Rape Elimination Act (PREA),
   108
prisons, 7, 26, 33, 114, 116, 119, 139n11;
   anti-Blackness of, 9–10, 47–48;

carceral feminism, 107, 154n21,
   156n34; gender-responsive/trans
   pods, 154n21, 155n31; ICE detention
   centers, 26, 107, 121, 154n26; prison
   abolition, 70, 103, 146n6, 154n22;
   prison industrial complex, 31, 103,
   135n25, 136n36; secured housing units
   (SHUs), 105–9, 112, 155n31; surveillance in, 149n32; violence of, 18, 101–8,
   154n23, 154nn26–27. See also Attica
   prison uprising; Dannemora prison;
   incarceration
privatization of violence, 6–7, 34, 63, 127
psychiatry, 20, 94, 106–7
psychoanalysis, 11, 73–76, 148n20
Puerto Ricans, 1
Pulse shooting, 17, 41–45, 47, 49–50, 52,
   66, 140n17

racial capitalism, 8, 17, 46, 50–52, 56,
   62–63, 66, 82
racial paranoia, 48
racism, 11, 14, 25, 49, 63, 74, 95, 140n16,
   155n31; of police, 31; state, 57, 136n37;
   visuality and, 71–72, 80. See also anti-
   Blackness; white supremacy
radical trans visual regime, 18, 88
Reagan, Ronald, 54, 145n64
recognition, 18, 24–26, 29, 38, 123;
   facial recognition, 78, 122, 149n32;
   limits of, 6, 82–83, 86–87. See also
   misrecognition
The Red Nation, 139n13
representation, 10, 30, 33, 51, 55, 121,
   151n65; double bind of, 146n3; opacity
   and, 87–91; political, 11, 116, 150n50;
   positive, 18, 85, 87–88, 150n50; of violence, 5, 15, 29, 67–83, 86–87
respectability, 2, 74, 85
revolutionary violence, 14, 87, 101, 109
Riggs, Marlon: Tongue's Untied, 22
Rivera, Sylvia, 1–5, 7, 10, 16, 100, 118, 123,
   126n5, 132n40
River Jordan (Hudson River), 2, 20, 123

Robles, J., 33
Russo, Vito, 2
Rutgers University, 152n2

sadism, 101
Salman, Noor, 43
San Francisco Police Department
(SFPD), 22–23
Santana, Dora, 81, 126n5
Santos, Frank, 31–32
Sartre, Jean-Paul, 38
Savage, Dan: It Gets Better campaign,
128n11, 152n4
scarcity, 55–56
Sedgwick, Eve, 93
self-negation, 18, 98, 107–8, 113
sexual violence, 21, 82–83, 92, 102, 104,
108, 134n7, 154n20
sex work, 2, 20, 26, 32, 53, 85, 86, 149n32
Sharpe, Christina, 132n40
Shelby County Jail, 67
Shepard, Matthew, 128n12
SHU syndrome, 106. See also post-
traumatic stress disorder (PTSD)
simian immunodeficiency virus (SIV),
52–53, 60
slavery, 8, 15, 39, 53, 56, 58, 78, 96; afterlives of, 10, 17, 47, 49; biocapital and,
45–49, 62, 66; democracy and, 115–16;
gendered, 80–83; Hegel on, 38
slow death, 69, 106
Smith, Frank "Big Black," 121, 159n21
Snorton, C. Riley, 15, 81, 86
sociogeny, 11, 92
sovereignty, 10, 38, 48, 58, 77–78, 87, 103,
115–16, 130n19
Spade, Dean, 122, 128n12, 135n16, 156n1
Speakes, Larry, 54
Spillers, Hortense, 80–82, 87
statistics, 29–31, 135n25
status offenses, 118–19
Stonewall uprising, 2–3, 16, 88–89
Street Transvestite Action Revolutionaries
(STAR), 118; STAR House, 2, 126n3

suicide, 1, 5, 18, 34, 92–108, 152nn2–3
sumptuary laws, 103, 119
Superman, 110, 112
surveillance, 18, 59, 67–91, 121, 149nn32–33
Swain, James, 68
Syria, 43

Tadiar, Neferti X. M., 141n18
temporality of violence, 33
Tenderloin AIDS Resource Center
(TARC), 120
Texas: Austin, 31, 39
Third Cinema, 151n65
time-image, 77
Time magazine: "Transgender Tipping
Point" cover, 18, 85
Tocqueville, Alexis de, 116
Tokyo Electron Corporation, 39
Tourmaline, 114, 120, 125n epigraph;
Happy Birthday, Marsha!, 18, 88–90,
151n63; *The Personal Things*, 122
trans-exclusionary radical feminists
(TERFs), 118, 127n6, 154n27
transmisogyny, 23, 54–55, 70. See also
trans-exclusionary radical feminists
(TERFs); transphobia
trans-panic defenses, 33, 95
transphobia, 13, 21, 32, 62, 71, 119, 127n6.
See also trans-exclusionary radical
feminists (TERFs); transmisogyny
trans/queer, definition, 26–27
Trapp, Frank, 69
trauma, 6, 16, 28–29, 68, 99, 106, 108,
135n28
Trump, Donald, 55, 115
Truvada, 61–62
Tunisia: Tunis, 12
Tyler, Bonnie: "Holding Out for a
Hero," 110

ungendering, 81–83
universalism, 18, 38, 100–101, 109–10,
113, 116
Univision, 43

Printed and bound by CPI Group (UK) Ltd, Croydon, CR0 4YY

25/03/2025

14647324-0004